LONGITUDES

and

LATITUDES

Throughout the World

by

Eugene Dernay

First Printing 1948
ISBN Number: 0-86690-068-3

Published by:
American Federation of Astrologers, Inc.
P.O. Box 22040, 6535 South Rural Road
Tempe, Arizona 85282

Printed in the United States of America

P R E F A C E

The kind reception accorded to the previous volume LONGITUDES AND LATITUDES IN THE UNITED STATES, published by the National Astrological Library in 1945, as well as the encouragement received from several friends, among whom Dr. George C. O. Haas, an eminent student of the starry lore, was the first to suggest the compilation of the present volume, induced me to undertake the task in 1946. The result is herewith published, again through the kindness of the National Astrological Library.

The many difficulties encountered in connection with the previous volume were insignificant, so to speak, when compared to those successfully overcome in the preparation of this work. To mention a few: it was found several countries use standard time meridians not based on longitude measured from Greenwich. In other instances it was most difficult to obtain reliable maps and, most important of all, conditions bordering on the chaotic hold sway as regards standard time zones. Through the hearty cooperation given by several United States and foreign government authorities and interested individuals, even these seeming insurmountable problems have been overcome. It should be noted, however, that Washington representatives of two great foreign powers could furnish no adequate information on this important matter concerning their own countries.

The present publication is based on the political subdivisions obtaining throughout the world in 1939, before World War II engulfed the world in flame. Exception has been made in the cases of Albania, Austria, Cezechloslavakia, Ethiopia and Korea, which regained their freedom in 1945, as well as with China and Greece, which countries recovered territories previously lost. No precise frontiers have been established in Eastern Europe as yet. It is therefore suggested that when ascertaining coordinates for cities situated in "doubtful sectors", the list of cities of the countries affected whould be consulted. Cross-references have been made in such cases where reliable information was obtainable.

I wish to apologize to experts of the Arabic, Chinese, and other Eastern, as well as Slav languages, in the event that the translations used herein do not comply with their high standards. This is a compilation of coordinates in the first instance, in which linguistic questions of an academic nature cannot be given the importance they might otherwise deserve. However, the greatest care has been exercised in transcribing foreign names not written in Latin characters in their native tongues, and, whenever possible, the method of transliteration used by the United States Board on Geographic Names was followed. All entries - with the exception of China - figure under their present official names, with references made to known variants; so, for instance, the ancient city of Bratislava in Czechoslovakia is also known as Pressburg in German and Pozsony in Hungarian. These two variants have been properly listed, referring to Bratislava. It is somewhat different in the case of Chinese cities. In listing them I preferred to use accepted and known city names instead of official designations unknown to the West. Who in the West would suspect that Chung Wan is the official designation for Victoria, Hong Kong, or K'Ou-Lun for Ulan Bator Hoto, or Kwang-chowfe for Canton? However, proper cross references have been entered for the benefit of competent sinologists into whose hands this work may come.

This compilation could not have been completed without the generous assistance and cooperation of Dr. Meredith F. Burrill, Director, Board on Geographic Names, United States Department of Interior; or, the Hydrographic Office, United States Navy Department, and Dr. Walter W. Ristow, Chief, Division of Maps, Library of Congress. Those gentlemen and their efficient staffs gave me untiring assistance and support, contributing in no small measure to the successful completion of my task. Every user of this book is indebted to them.

In addition, excellent cooperation was given by United States diplomatic representatives abroad and representatives of foreign nations in Washington; from Charles E. O. Carter, editor of ASTROLOGY, London, England; from Paul L. Edouard-Rayet, editor of PREVISIONS, Paris, France, and from Claudio Necci of Rome. The Information Bureaus of Australia, Brazil, Great Britain and the Netherlands, likewise cooperated to the fullest extent; Captain Arthur S. Page, Topographer of the Post Office Department; the Hawaiian Sugar Planters' Association headquarters officials in Washington, several Chambers of Commerce, astronomical observatories and railroad companies, all gave untiring assistance in the more difficult phases of compilation. Ed. Koppenstaetter's splendid little, yet incomparably valuable book, ZONEN UND SOMMERZEITEN, published in 1937, was a source of much inspiration.

I earnestly request all users of this volume that they kindly advise me of any errors in spelling, in listing administrative subdivisions or coordinates. Let me assure them that much midnight oil was burned in my effort to make the task of fellow-astrologers and others to whom this work can be of value, less strenuous; it is for the users of this compilation to judge to what extent I may have succeeded.

In closing, I wish to express my profound gratitude to Ernest A. Grant, Executive Secretary of the American Federation of Astrologers, whose unremitting efforts, understanding and perseverance in the face of my own shortcomings, has made the publication of this work possible.

                                        ----Eugene Dernay.

July, 1948.

STANDARD TIMES AND CROSS INDEX OF COUNTRIES

Alphabetical list of countries, etc., with Standard Time Meridians, based on the Admiralty List of Radio Signals, Vol. II, for 1940, corrected to December 31, 1939; published by the Hydrographic Department, Admiralty, by His Majesty's Stationery Office, London, England, with cross reference index of known changes up to 1962 with previous names of countries then colonies, etc., but now independent, as supplied by the Board of Geographic Names, Department of the Interior, and Congressioual Library, Washington, D.C.

ABBREVIATIONS USED IN THIS TABLE.

A.....Atlantic	Eu....European	So....South
B.....Baghdad	J.....Japanese	Su....Sumatra
C.....Central	M.....Mountain	T.....Time
E.....Eastern	N.....North	W.....Western
	S.....Standard	

- Minus   / or + Plus

COUNTRY	STANDARD TIME	MERIDIAN	G. M. T. VARIATION FROM S.T. h. m. s.
Aaen (Protectorate)	Aden Time	44°58'30'E	- 2 59 54
(Calculated herein for meridian 45° East			3 00 00)
Afghanistan	No Standard Time used		
Alaska	Pacific S. T.	120°00'W	+ 8 00 00
	Yukon S. T.	135 00 W	+ 9 00 00
	C. Alaskan T.	150 00 W	+10 00 00
	Nome S. T.	165 00 W	+11 00 00
Albania (Communist State)	C. Eu. T.	15 00 E	- 1 00 00
Algeria	W. Eu. T.	0 00	0 00 00
American Samoa	Nome S. T.	165.00 W	+11 00 00
Andamen Islands (India)	N. Su. T.	97 30 E	- 6 30 00
Andorra (Principality)	W. Eu. T	0 00	0 00 00
Anglo-Egyptian Soudan (now Soudan--Sudan--)	E. Eu. T.	30 00 E	- 2 00 00
Argentina	A. S. T.	60 00 W	+ 4 00 00
Ascension Island	W. Africa T.	15 00 W	+ 1 00 00
Australia:			
Canberra, Capital Terr.	Guam S. T.	150 00 E	-10 00 00
New South Wales	Guam S. T.	150 00 E	-10 00 00
Northern Territory	So. Australia T.	142 30 E	- 9 30 00
Queensland	Guam S. T.	150 00 E	-10 00 00
South Australia	So. Australia T.	142 30 E	- 9 30 00
Tasmania	Guam S. T.	150 00 E	-10 00 00
Victoria	Guam S. T.	150 00 E	-10 00 00
Western Australia	China Coast T.	120 00 E	- 8 00 00

COUNTRY	STANDARD TIME	MERIDIAN	G. M. T. VARIATION FROM S.T. h. m. s.
Bahamas (See British West Indies. Strictly speaking the Bahamas are not in the B. W. I. but North Atlantic.)			
Belgian Congo:			
Western Provinces	C. Eu. T.	15 00'E	- 1 00 00
Eastern Provinces	E. Eu. T.	30 00 E	- 2 00 00
Belgium	C. Eu. T.	15 00 E	- 1 00 00
(Formerly W. Eu. T. was S. T. but in 1953 it is known as C. Eu. T. was in use.)			
Bermuda	A. S. T.	60 00 W	+ 4 00 00
Bolivia	A. S. T.	60 00 W	+ 4 00 00
(Prior to March 21, 1932, 68°15' West was S.T. Meridian.)			
Brazil	Azores S. T.	30 00 W	+ 2 00 00
		45 00 W	+ 3 00 00
	A. S. T	60 00 W	+ 4 00 00
	E. S. T	75 00 W	+ 5 00 00
British Cameroons see Nigeria			
British Guaiana		56 15 W	+ 3 45 00
British Honduras	C. S. T.	90 00 W	+ 6 00 00
British North Borneo	China Coast Time	120 00 E	- 8 00 00
British Solomon Islands	U.S.S.R. Zone 10 S.T.	165 00 E	-11 00 00
British Somaliland	Aden Time	44 58'30"E	- 2 59 54
(Calculated herein for meridian 45° E			- 3 00 00
British West Indies	A. S. T.	60 00 W	+ 4 00 00
	E. S. T.	75 00 W	+ 5 00 00
Brunei	China Coast Time	120 00 E	- 8 00 00
Bulgaria (Communist State)	E. Eu. T.	30 00 E	- 2 00 00
Burma (Republic)	N. Su. T.	97 30 E	- 6 30 00
Cambodia see French Indo China. Now independent			
Cameroons:			
French see French West Africa			
British see Nigeria			
Canada:			
Alberta	M. S. T.	105 00 W	+ 7 00 00
British Columbia	P. S. T.	120 00 W	+ 8 00 00
Labrador	Newfoundland S.T.	52 30 W	+ 3 30 00
Manitoba	O. S. T.	90 00 W	+ 6 00 00
New Brunswick	A. S. T.	60 00 W	+ 4 00 00
Newfoundland	Newfoundland S.T.	52 30 W	+ 3 30 00
Northwest Territories	Various. See Canada		
Nova Scotia	A. S. T.	60 00 W	+ 4 00 00
Ontario:			
East of 90° West	E.S.T.	75 00 W	+ 5 00 00
West of 90° West	C.S.T.	90 00 W	+ 6 00 00
Quebec:			
East of 68° West	A. S. T.	60 00 W	+ 4 00 00
West of 68° West	E. S. T.	75 00 W	+ 5 00 00
Prince Edward Island	A. S. T.	60 00 W	+ 4 00 00
Saskatchewan	M. S. T.	105 00 W	+ 7 00 00
Yukon Territory	Yukon S. T.	135 00 W	+ 9 00 00

COUNTRY	STANDARD TIME	MERIDIAN	G. M. T. VARIATION FROM S.T. h. m. s.
Canary Islands	W. Africa T.	15 00 W	+ 1 00 00
Cape Verde Islands	Azores Time	30 00 W	+ 2 00 00
Central African Republic. See French Equatorial Africa			
Ceylon	Indian S. T.	82 30 E	- 5 50 00
Chad. See French Equatorial Africa			
Chatham Island		180 00 E	-12 00 00
Chile	A. S. T.	60 00 W	+ 4 00 00
China (Communist State)	Indian S. T.	82 30 E	- 5 30 00
	U. S. S. R. Zone 5	90 00 E	- 6 00 00
	So. Su. T.	105 00 E	- 7 00 00
	China Coast T.	120 00 E	- 8 00 00
China, Republic of, See Taiwan.			
Cochin China see French Indo China (now Viet Nam)			
Colombia	E. S. T.	75 00 W	+ 5 00 00
Cook Islands		159 30 W	+10 39 00
Costa Rica	C. S. T.	90 00 W	+ 6 00 00
Cuba	E. S. T.	75 00 W	+ 5 00 00
Cyprus	E. Eu. T.	30 00 E	- 2 00 00
Congo See Belgian Congo			
Czechoslovakia (Communist)	C. Eu. T.	15 00 E	- 1 00 00
Dahomey See French Equatorial Africa			
Danzig (now in Poland)	C. Eu. T.	15 00 E	- 1 00 00
Denmark	C. Eu. T.	15 00 E	--1 00 00
Dominican Republic	E. S. T.	75 00 W	+ 5 00 00
Equador	E. S. T.	75 00 W	+ 5 00 00
Egypt (now a Republic)	E. Eu. T.	30 00 E	- 2 00 00
Eire (now a Republic)	E. Eu. T.	0 00	0 00 00
El Salvador	C. S. T.	90 00 W	+ 6 00 00
Eritrea see Italian East Africa.			
Estonia (Communist State)	E. Eu. T.	30 00 E	- 2 00 00
Ethiopia	Baghdad T.	45 00 E	- 3 00 00
Faeroe Islands	W. Eu. T.	0 00	0 00 00
Falkland Islands	A. S. T.	60 00 W	+ 4 00 00
Fiji		180 00 E	-12 00 00
Finland	E. Eu. T.	30 00 E	- 2 00 00
Formosa see Taiwan (Now Republic of China)			
France	W. Eu. T.	0 00	0 00 00
French Cameroons see French West Africa			
French Equatorial Africa	C. Eu. T.	15 00 E	- 1 00 00
French Establishments in India	Indian S. T.	82 30 E	- 5 30 00
French Establishments in Oceania	C. Alaska T.	150 00 W	-10 00 00
French Guiana	A. S. T.	60 00 W	+ 4 00 00
French Indo China (now Viet Nam)	S. Sumatra T.	105 00 E	- 7 00 00
French Morocco see Morocco			
French Somaliland	Baghdad T.	45 00 E	- 3 00 00
French West Africa	W. Africa T.	15 00 W	+ 1 00 00

COUNTRY	STANDARD TIME	MERIDIAN	G. M. T. VARIATION FROM S. T.
			h. m. s.
French West Africa	W. Africa T.	15 00 W	+ 1 00 00
	W. Eu. T.	0 00	0 00 00
	C. Eu. T.	15 00 E	- 1 00 00
Gabon See French Equatorial Africa			
Galapagos Islands	C. S. T.	90 00 W	+ 6 00 00
Gambia	W. Africa T.	15 00 W	+ 1 00 00
Germany	C. Eu. T.	15 00 E	- 1 00 00
(Now divided into Republic of West Germany and Communist East Germany.)			
Ghana See French West Africa			
Gibralter	E. Eu. T.	0 00	0 00 00
Gilbert & Ellice Islands	Nome S. T.	165 00	+11 00 00
Gilbert & Ellice Islands	Nome S. T.	180 00 W	-12 00 00
Great Britain	W. Eu. T.	0 00	0 00 00
Greece	E. Eu. T.	30 00 E	- 2 00 00
Greenland	Azores S. T.	30 00 W	+ 2 00 00
		45 00 W	+ 3 00 00
	Atlantic S. T.	60 00 W	+ 4 00 00
	E. S. T.	75 00 W	+ 5 00 00
Guadeloupe (now a French Administrative Division)	A. S. T.	60 00 W	+ 4 00 00
Guam	Guam S. T.	150 00 E	-10 00 00
Guatemala	C. S. T.	90 00 W	+ 6 00 00
Guinea see French Guiena			
Haiti	E. S. T.	75 00 W	+ 5 00 00
Hawaii	Hawaiian S. T.	157 30 W	+10 30 00
(C. Alaska T. used since 2:00 a.m. June 8, 1947, 150° West			
Hindustan see India			
Honduras	C. S. T.	90 00 W	+ 6 00 00
Hong kong	China Coast T.	120 00 E	- 8 00 00
Hungary (Communist State)	C. Eu. T.	15 00 E	- 1 00 00
Iceland	W. Africa T.	15 00 W	+ 1 00 00
Ifni	W. Eu. T.	0 00	0 00 00
India (except Bengal and Calcutta)	Indian S. T.	82 30 E	- 5 30 00
Bengal	N. Su. T.	97 30 E	- 6 30 00
Calcutta	Local Time	88 20 E	- 5 53 20
(The exact time difference is 5ʰ53ᵐ20.8ˢ)			
Indonesia see Netherlands East Indies			
Iran		53 30 E	- 3 30 00
Iraq	Baghdad T.	45 00 E	- 3 00 00
Israel see Palestineinc			
Italian East Africa (now Ethiopia and Somalia)			
Italy	C. Eu. T.	15 00 E	- 1 00 00
Ivory Coast See French West Africa			
Japan	J. S. T.	135 00 E	- 9 00 00
Jarvis Island		165 00 W	+11 00 00
Johnston Island	Hawaiian S. T.	157 30 W	+10 30 00
Jordan see Trans-Jordan			

	STANDARD TIME	MERIDIAN	G. M. T. VARIATION FROM S.T.
			h. m. s.
Y		41°15'E	- 2 45 00
	U.S.S.R. Zone 4	75 00 E	- 5 00 00
	New Zealand T.	172 30 E	-11 30 00
)45 meridian changed to 180° E. -12h00m)			
	J. S. T.	135 00 E	- 9 00 00
ude 38° is Communist)			
do China			
State)	E. Eu. T.	30 00 E	- 2 00 00
States			
	E. Eu. T.	30 00 E	- 2 00 00
	Liberia S. T.	11 00 W	+ 0 44 00
	C. Eu. T.	15 00 E	- 1 00 00
	C. Eu. T.	15 00 E	- 1 00 00
...st State)	C. Eu. T.	15 00 E	- 1 00 00
Luxembourg	C. Eu. T.	15 00 E	- 1 00 00
Madagascar	Baghdad T.	45 00 E	- 3 00 00
Madeira Islands	W. African T.	15 00 W	+ 1 00 00
Malagasy see Madagascar			
Malaya (except Labaun)		110 00 E	- 7 20 00
Labaun	China Coast T.	120 00 E	- 8 00 00
(Now Federation of States in British Commonwealth)			
Maldive Islands	Local Time	73 30 E	- 4 54 00
Malir see French Sudan			
Malta	C. Eu. T.	15 00 E	- 1 00 00
Marcus Island	Guam S. T.	150 00 E	-10 00 00
Martinique (Martinious)	A. S. T.	60 00 W	+ 4 00 00
(Now a French Department)			
Mauritius	U.S.S.R. Zone 3	60 00 E	- 4 00 00
Mexico	C. S. T.	90 00 W	+ 6 00 00
	M. S. T.	105 00 W	+ 7 00 00
	Pacific S. T.	120 00 W	+ 8 00 00
Midway Islands	Hawaiian S. T.	157 30 W	+10 30 00
(Nome S. T., 165° W. in use in 1948 and subsequently, +11h00m)			
Monaco	W. Eu. T.	0 00	0 00 00
Morocco	W. Eu. T.	0 00	0 00 00
Muscat and Oman see Saudi Arabia			
Nauru Island		172 30 E	-11 30 00
Netherlands	C. Eu. T.	15 00 E	- 1 00 00
(W. Eu.T. Meridian 0° was in use in 1948 but sometime between then and 1953 change was apparently made to C. Eu. T.)			
Netherlands Antilles see Netherlands West Indies.			
Netherlands East Indies now Indonesia.			
Netherlands Guiana see Surinam			
Netherlands New Guinea	J. S. T.	135 00 E	- 9 00 00
Netherlands West Indies	A. S. T.	60 00 W	+ 4 00 00
New Caledonia and Dependencies		165 00 E	-11 00 00
Newfoundland (Canada)	Newfoundland S. T.	52 30 W	+ 3 30 00
New Guinea (except Solomon, which see)		150 00 E	-10 00 00

COUNTY	STANDARD TIME	MERIDIAN	B. M. T. VARIATION FROM S.T. h. m. s.
New Hebrides		165°00'E	-11 00 00
New Zealand	New Zealand S. T.	180 00 E	-12 00 00
(Prior to November 24, 1945 S.T. Meridian was 172°30'			
Nicaragua	C. S. T.	90 00 W	+ 6 00 00
Nicobar Islands	N. Su. S. T.	97 30 E	- 6 30 00
Niger See French West Africa			
Nigeria	C. Eu. T.	15 00 E	- 1 00 00
(Includes British Trust Territory of Cameroons)			
Norfolk Island		168 00 E	-11 12 00
Norway	C. Eu. T.	15 00 E	- 1 00 00
Nyasaland	E. Eu. T.	30 00 E	- 2 00 00
Pacific Islands Trust Territory see South Sea Mandated Territories			
Pakistan see India, although a separate Republic.			
Palestine (Now Israel)	E. Eu. T.	30 00 E	- 2 00 00
Panama	E. S. T.	75 00 W	+ 5 00 00
Panama Canal Zone	E. S. T.	75 00 W	+ 5 00 00
Papua	Guam S. T.	150 00 E	-10 00 00
Paraguay	A. S. T.	60 00 W	+ 4 00 00
Peru	E. S. T	75 00 W	+ 5 00 00
Philippines	China Coast T.	120 00 E	- 8 00 00
Pitcairn Island	C. Alaska T.	150 00 W	+10 00 00
Poland (Communist State)	C. Eu. T.	15 00 W	- 1 00 00
Portugal	W. Eu. T.	0 00	0 00 00
Portuguese East Africa	E. Eu. T.	30 00 E	- 2 00 00
Portuguese India	Indian S. T.	82 30 E	- 5 30 00
	China Coast T.	120 00 E	- 8 00 00
Portuguese Timor	China Coast T.	120 00 E	- 8 00 00
Portuguese West Africa:			
Angola	C. Eu. T.	15 00 E	- 1 00 00
Guinea	W. Africa T.	15 00 W	+ 1 00 00
Principe and Sao Tome	W. Eu. T.	0 00	0 00 00
Puerto Rico (Commonwealth)	A. S. T.	60 00 W	+ 4 00 00
Reunion Island	U.S.S.R. Zone 3	60 00 E	- 4 00 00
Rhodesia	E. Eu. T.	30 00 E	- 2 00 00
Rio de Oro	W. Africa T.	15 00 E	+ 1 00 00
Rodriquez Island	U.S.S.R. Zone 3	60 00 E	- 4 00 00
Rumania (Communist State)	E. Eu. T.	30 00 E	- 2 00 00
Saba see Netherlands West Indies			
St. Eustatius see Netherlands West Indies			
Saint Helena		5 45 W	+ 0 23 00
Saint Maarten see Netherlands West Indies			
Saint Martin see Guadeloupe			
St. Pierre & Miquelon	A. S. T.	60 00 W	+ 4 00 00
San Marino	C. Eu. T.	15 00 E	- 1 00 00
Sarawak (British Colony)	Java Time	112 50 E	- 7 30 00
Saudi Arabia	Local Time		
Savage Island		170 00 W	+11 20 00
Somalia see British Somaliland			
Seychelles	U.S.S.R. Zone 3	60 00 E	- 4 00 00
Siam (Thailand)	S. Su. T.	105 00 E	- 7 00 00
Sierra Leone	W. Africa T.	15 00 W	+ 1 00 00

COUNTRY	STANDARD TIME	MERIDIAN	G. M. T. VARIATION FROM S.T. h. m. s.
Solomon Islands		165 00 E	-11 00 00
Somalia, See British Somaliland			
South Sea Mandated Terr.	J. S. T.	135 00 E	- 9 00 00
	Guam S. T.	150 00 E	-10 00 00
Southwest Africa see Union of South Africa			
Spain	W. Eu. T.	0 00	0 00 00
Spanish Guinea	W. Eu. T.	0 00	0 00 00
Spanish Morocco see Morocco			
Spanish Sahara see Rio de Oro			
Sudan see Anglo-Egyptian Sudan			
Surinam		52 30 W	+ 3 30 00
Swaziland see Union of South Africa			
Sweden	C. Eu. T.	15 00 E	- 1 00 00
Switzerland	C. Eu. T.	15 00 E	- 1 00 00
Syria see Levant States			
Taiwan (now Republic of China; Taipeh 121E 44, 25N08			
	J. S. T.	135 00 E	- 9 00 00
Tanganyika (formerly German East Africa)		41 15 E	- 2 45 00
Tangier see Morocco			
Thailand see Siam			
Tibet see China			
Togo or Togoland see French West Africa or Gold Cost			
Tonga Islands		175 00 W	+11 40 00
Trans-Jordan (Jordan)	Baghdad T.	45 00 E	- 3 00 00
Trieste now Free Territory; see Italy			
Trinidad and Tobago see British West Indies			
Tristan de Cunha	W. Africa T.	15 00 W	+ 1 00 00
Tunisia	C. Eu. T.	15 00 E	- 1 00 00
Turkey	E. Eu. T.	30 00 E	- 2 00 00
Uganda		41 15 E	- 2 45 00
Union of South Africa	E. Eu. T.	30 00 E	- 2 00 00
Union of Soviet Socialist Republics: There are 11 time zones as given on page 129.			
United Kingdom of Great Britain and Northern Ireland.	W. Eu. T.	0 00	0 00 00
Upper Volta see French West Africa			
Uruguay		52 30 W	+ 3 30 00
Vatican City State	C. Eu. T.	15 00 E	- 1 00 00
Venezuala		67 30 W	+ 4 30 00
Viet Nam see French Indo China			
Virgin Islands (U. S. A.)	A. S. T.	60 00 W	+ 4 00 00
Wake Island	Int. Date Line, East	180 00 E	+12 00 00
Wallis Island	Int. Date Line, West	180 00 W	+12 00 00
Western Samoa	Nome S. T.	165 00 W	+11 00 00
Windward Islands see British West Indies and Dutch West Indies			
Yugoslavia (Communist State)	E. Eu. T.	15 00 E	- 1 00 00
Zanzibar		41 15 E	- 2 45 00

x

FURTHER EMENDATION.

Ghana, now independent in British Commonwealth of Nations, see Gold Coast.
Laos, Formerly French Indo China
Somaliland, Trust Territory of. See Italian East Africa
The West Indies. Composed of all British Colonies in the Caribean area.
      except the British Virgin Islands.
United Arab Republic, Formerly Egypt and Syria.

ABYSSINIA see Ethiopia.
ACORES see Azores.
ADEN. British Colony and Protectorate situated   :
    on Arabian Peninsula. City of Aden and en-   :
    vironments time based on meridian 44°58'30"   :
    EAST of Greenwich, G.M.T. being 2^{h}59^{m}54^s :
    minus. Other calculations made for 45° EAST   :
    of Greenwich, Baghdad Time, with Time Differ-: L. M. T.   G. M. T.
    ence of Minus 3^h, with exception of Makalla, : VARIATION VARIATION
    which, though located 49°07' EAST, uses the   : FROM   FROM
    Longitude 33°45' EAST as Standard Time Mer-   : STANDARD   L. M. T.
    idian, G.M.T. being Minus 2^{h}15^m.   : TIME

			L.M.T. m. s.	G.M.T. h. m. s.
Aden, Aden	45E02	12N47	+ 0 08	- 3 00 08
Habida see Tamrida				
Laheg, Abdali	44E43	13N03	- 1 08	- 2 58 52
Makalla, Hadhramaut	49E07	14N31	see above	- 3 16 28
Makalla, see Makalla				
Perim, Perim.............	43E25 ...	12N38	- 6 20 ..	- 2 53 40
Saiwun see Sayoun				
Seyoun, Hadhramaut	48E47	15N57	No S.T.used	- 3 15 08
Sheik Othman, Abdali	44E59	12N52	- 0 04	- 2 59 56
Tamrida, Sokotra	54E03	12N40	+36 12	- 3 36 12

ADMIRALTY ISLANDS see New Guinea.
AEGEAN ISLANDS see Greece.
AFGHANISTAN   Capital: Kabul. Kingdom situated
        in Western Asia. No standard time used.

Herat	62E11	34N21	- 4 08 44
Kabul	69E13	34N30	- 4 36 52
Kandahar	65E42 ...	31N36	- 4 22 48
Mazar-i-Sharif	67E06	36N43	- 4 28 24
Shindand	62E08	33N18	- 4 08 32

AFRIQUE ANGLAISE DU SUD see Union of South Africa
AFRIQUE DU SUD see Union of South Africa.
AFRIQUE EQUATORIALE FRANCAISE see French Equatorial Africa
AFRIQUE OCCIDENTALE FRANCAISE See French West Africa.
AFRIQUE OCCIDENTALE PORTUGAISE see Portuguese West Africa.
AFRIQUE ORIENTALE ALLEMANDE see 1, Belgian Congo.
                            2. Tanganyika
AFRIQUE ORIENTALE ANGLAISE see Kenya, Uganda & Zanzibar.
AFRIQUE ORIENTALE ITALIENNE see Italian East Africa.
AFRIQUE ORIENTALE PORTUGAISE see Portuguese East Africa.
AGNES ISLAND see Johnston Island.
ALBANIA .. Capital: Tirane
        Kingdom situated in southeastern Europe.
        Central European Time used.

Alessio see Lesh				
Argirocastro see Gjinokaster				
Berat	19E57	40N43	+ 19 48	- 1 19 48
Durazzo see Durres				
Durres	19E26	41N19	+ 17 44	- 1 17 44
Elbasan	20E04	41N06	+ 20 16 ..	- 1 20 16
Gjinokaster	20E08	40N04	+ 20 32	- 1 20 32

			L. M. T. VARIATION FROM S.T. m.s.	G. M. T. VARIATION FROM LMT h. m. s.

ALBANIA (Continued)

Korce	20E47	40N37	+ 23 08	- 1 23 08
Koritsa see Korce				
Lesh	19E40	41N48	+ 18 40	- 1 18 40
Scutari see Shkoder				
Shkoder	19E31	42N03	+ 18 04	- 1 18 04
Vlone (Valone)	19E30	40N28	+ 18 00	- 1 18 00

ALEUTIAN ISLANDS see Alaska

ALGERIA. Capital: Alger / Algiers/.

French Colony, situated in North Africa.
Western European (G.M.T.) used.

Alger (Algiers), Algiers	3E04	36N47	+ 12 16	- 0 12 16
Batna, Constantine	6E11	35N33	+ 24 44	- 0 24 44
Biskra, Constantine	5E44	34N52	+ 22 56	- 0 22 56
Bone (Bona), Constantine	7E46	36N54	+ 31 04	- 0 31 04
Bougie, Constantine	5E05	36N46	+ 20 20	- 0 20 20
Colomb-Bechar, Oran	2W13	31N37	- 8 52	+ 0 08 52
Constantine, Constantine	6E37	36N22	+ 26 28	- 0 26 28
Fort Laperrine see Tamenresset				
Geryville, Oran	1E01	33N41	+ 4 04	- 0 04 04
Ghardaia, Alger	3E41	32N29	+ 14 44	- 0 14 44
Guelma	7E26	36N28	+ 29 44	- 0 29 44
Laghouat, Alger	2E53	33N49	+ 11 32	- 0 11 32
Maison Carree, Alger	3E09	36N43	+ 12 36	- 0 12 36
Mascara, Oran	0E08	35N24	+ 0 32	- 0 00 32
Medea, Alger	2E45	36N16	+ 11 00	- 0 11 00
Miliana, Alger	2E14	36N19	+ 8 56	- 0 08 56
Mostaganem, Oran	0E05	35N56	+ 0 20	- 0 00 20
Oran, Oran	0W38	35N42	- 2 32	+ 0 02 32
Orleansville, Alger	1E18	36N10	+ 5 12	- 0 05 12
Ouargla, Constantine	5E20	31N59	+21 20	- 0 21 20
Phillippeville, Constantine	6E55	36N52	+27 40	- 0 27 40
Setif, Constantine	5E25	36N12	+21 40	- 0 21 40
Sidi-el-Abbes, Oran	0W38	35N12	- 2 32	+ 0 02 32
Tamanrasse, Oasis Territory	5E32	22N48	+22 08	- 0 22 08
Tabessa, Constantine	8E08	35N24	+32 32	- 0 32 32
Tizi Ouzou, Alger	4E03	36N43	+16 12	- 0 16 12
Tlemcen, Oran	1W19	34N53	- 5 16	+ 0 05 16
Touggourt, Constantine	6E04	33N06	+24 16	- 0 24 16

ALLEMAGNE see Germany.

ALOFI ISLANDS see New Caledonia.

ALSACE-LORRAIN see France

AMATONGALAND see Union of South Africa.

AMBOINE see Netherlands East Indies

AMERICAN SAMOA. Capital: Pago Pago.

Possession of the U.S.A., situated in the
South Pacific. S.T. Meridian 165° West.

Aloafao, Ofu	169W43	14S10	- 18 52	+ 11 18 52
Leone, Leone	170W47	14S20	- 23 08	+ 11 23 08
Pago Pago, Tutuila	170W42	14S16	- 22 48	+ 11 22 48
U. S. Naval Station, Tutuila	170W41	14S17	- 22 44	+ 11 22 44

			L. M. T. VARIATION FROM S.T. m. s.	G. M. T. VARIATION FROM LMT h. m. s.
AMIRAUTE, ILES DE L' see New Guinea				
AMIS, Iles Des see Tonga				

ANDAMAN ISLANDS. Capital: Port Blair. The
    Andaman Islands, situated in the Indian
    Ocean, together with the Nicobar Islands
    form a Province of India. North Sumatra
    Time used, meridian 97°30' East.

Herbertabad	92E37	11N43	- 19 32	- 6 10 26
Port Blair	92E46.....	11N42	- 18 56..	- 6 11 04
Port Cornwallis	93E05	13N18	- 17 40	- 6 12 20

ANDORRA Capital: Andorra. Principality situated
    in Europe, Between France and Spain.
    Western European Time (G.M.T.) used.

Andorra	1E30	42N31	+ 6 00	- 0 06 00
Ordino	1E31	42N34	+ 6 04	- 0 06 04

ANDREANOF ISLANDS see Alaska

ANGLETERRE see Great Britain

ANGLO-EGYPTIAN SUDAN, Capital: Khartoum.
    Independency situated in East Africa. Eastern
    European Time used, meridian 30° East.

Abu Hamed	34E40	19N33	+ 18 40	- 2 18 40
Atbara	34E01	17N43	+ 16 04	- 2 16 04
Ed Damer	33E02.....	17N35......	+ 8 08..	- 2 08 08
Ed Dueim	32E19	13N59	+ 9 16	- 2 09 16
El Fasher	25E21	13N58	- 18 36	- 1 41 24
El Obeid	30E14	13N10	+ 0 56	- 2 00 56
En Nahud	28E26	12N42	- 6 16	- 1 53 44
Kassala	36E24.....	15N27......	+ 25 36..	- 2 25 36
Khartoum	32E32	15N36	- 10 08	- 2 10 08
Khartoum North	32E33	15N37	- 10 12	- 2 10 12
Kosti	32E40	13N10	+ 10 40	- 2 10 40
Musmar	36E22	18N13	+ 25 28	- 2 25 28
Omdurman	32E29......	15N38.....	+ 9 56..	- 2 09 56
Malakal	31E38	9N32	+ 6 32	- 2 06 32
Port Sudan	37E14	19N37	+ 30 56	- 2 30 56
Singa	33E55	13N09	+ 15 40	- 2 15 40
Suskin	37E20	19N06	+ 29 20	- 2 29 20
Wadi Halfa.................	31E19.....	21N56......	+ 5 16..	- 2 05 06
Wad Medani	33E31	14N24	+ 14 04	- 2 14 04

ANGOLA see Portuguese East Africa

ANGUILLA see British West Indies (Leeward Islands)

ANJOUAN ISLANDS see Madagascar.

ANNAM see French Indo-China.

ANTIGUA see British West Indies.

ARABIA see Saudi Arabia

ARABIE SAOUDITE see Saudi Arabie.

ARGENTINE Capital: Buenos Aires. Republic
    situated in South America. Atlantic
    Standard Time used, meridian 60° West.

Almirante Brown, Buenos Aires	58W24	34S48	+ 6 24	+ 3 53 36
Azul, Buenos Aires	59W50	36S48	+ 0 40	+ 3 59 20
Bahia Blanca, Buenos Aires	62W17	38S43	- 9 08	+ 4 09 08
Balcarce, Buenos Aires	58W15	37S50	+ 7 00	+ 3 53 00
Baradero, Buenos Aires	59W32	33S48	+ 1 52	+ 3 58 08

ARGENTINE (Continued)

Bolivar, Buenos Aires	61W06	36S15		−	4 24	+	4	04	24
Bragado, Buenos Aires	60W29	35S07		−	1 56	+	4	01	56
Buenos Aires, La Plata	58W27	34S36		+	6 12	+	3	53	48
Campana, Buenos Aires	58W57	34S10		+	4 12	+	3	55	48
Canada de Gomez, Santa Fe	61W41	32S49		−	6 44	+	4	06	44
Carlos Casares, Buenos Aires	61W22	35S38		−	5 24	+	4	05	24
Catamarca, Catamarca	65W47	28S28		−	23 08	+	4	23	08
Chacabuco, Buenos Aires	60W29	34S37		−	1 56	+	4	01	56
Chascomus, Buenos Aires	58W01	35S35		+	7 56	+	3	52	04
Chivilcoy, Buenos Aires	60W02	34S57		−	0 08	+	4	00	08
Chuchimba, Catamarca	66W09	28S45		−	24 36	+	4	24	36
Colonia Las Heras, Santa Cruz	68W57	46S33		−	35 48	+	4	35	48
Concepcion del Uruguay, Entre Rios	58W14	32S29		+	7 04	+	3	52	56
Concordia, Entre Rios	58W02	31S23		+	7 52	+	3	52	08
Cordoba, Cordobu	64W11	31S24		−	16 44	+	4	15	44
Corrientes, Corrientes	58W50	27S28		+	4 40	+	3	55	20
Diamante, Entre Rios	60W39	32S04		−	2 36	+	4	02	36
Dolores, Buenos Aires	57W42	36S19		+	9 12	+	3	50	48
Embarcacion, Embarcacion	64W05	23S33		−	16 20	+	4	16	20
Formosa, Formosa	58W11	26S10		+	7 16	+	3	52	44
General Alvear, Mendoza	67W40	34S59		−	30 40	+	4	30	40
General Lavalle, Buenos A.	56W58	36S24		+	12 08	+	3	47	52
General Sarmiento, Buenos A.	58W43	34S33		+	5 08	+	3	54	52
Goya, Corrientos	59W18	29S09		+	2 48	+	3	57	12
Gualeguay, Entre Rios	59W20	33S08		+	2 40	+	3	57	20
Gualeguaychu, Entre Rios	58W31	33S00		+	5 56	+	3	54	04
Ituzaringo, Corrientes	56W42	27S31		+	13 12	+	3	46	48
Jujuy, Jujuy	65W18	24S11		−	21 12	+	4	21	12
Junin, Mendoza	60W56	34S35		−	3 44	+	4	03	44
La Plata, Buenos Aires	57W57	34S55		+	8 12	+	3	51	48
Las Flores, Buenos Aires	59W07	36S00		+	3 32	+	3	56	28
Lincoln, Buenos Aires	61W31	34S50		+	5 04	+	4	05	04
Lobos (Salvador de) B. A.	59W06	35S11		+	3 36	+	3	56	24
Lujan, Buenos Aires	59W06	34S34		+	3 36	+	3	56	24
Mar del Plata, Buenos Aires	57W33	38S00		+	9 48	+	3	50	12
Mendoza, Mendoza	68W49	33S53		−	35 16	+	4	35	16
Mercedes, Buenos Aires	59W26	34S40		+	2 16	+	3	57	44
Monte Caseros, Corrientes	57W38	30S44		+	9 28	+	3	50	32
Necochea, Buenos Aires	58W45	38S33		+	5 00	+	3	55	00
Neuquen, Nouquen	68W04	38S57		−	32 16	+	4	32	16
Nuere de Julio, Buenos Aires	60W52	35S28		−	3 28	+	4	03	28
Obera, Misiones	55W05	27S30		+	19 40	+	3	40	20
Olavarria, Buenos Aires	60W17	36S54		−	1 08	+	4	01	08
Parana, Entre Rios	60W32	31S41		−	2 08	+	4	02	08
Pergamino, Buenos Aires	60W34	33S54		−	2 16	+	4	02	16
Pilar, Buenos Aires	58W55	34S28		+	4 20	+	3	55	40
Posadas, Mendoza	55W54	27S23		+	16 24	+	3	43	36
Pringles, Buenos Aires	61W23	38S00		−	5 32	+	4	05	32
Rafaela, Santa Fe	61W28	31S15		−	5 32	+	4	05	52

			L. M. T. VARIATION FROM S.T.	G. M. T. VARIATION FROM LMT
			m. s.	h. m. s.

ARGENTINA (Continued)

Rauch, Buenos Aires	59W05	36S47	+ 3 40	+ 3 56 20
Rawson, Chubut	65W06	43S18	-20 24	+ 4 20 24
Resistencia, Chaco	58W59	27S18	+ 4 04	+ 3 55 56
Rio Gallagos, Santa Cruz	69W13	51S38	-36 52	+ 4 36 52
Rosario, Santa Fe............	60W40	...32S57	...... - 2 40	+ 4 02 40
Saladillo, Buenos Aires	59W46	35S38	+ 0 56	+ 3 59 04
Salta, Salta	65W25	24S47	-21 40	+ 4 21 40
San Fernando, Buenos Aires	58W34	34S27	+ 5 44	+ 3 54 16
San Francisco, Cordova	62W05	31S26	- 8 20	+ 4 08 20
San Isidro, Buenos Aires	58W30	...34S28	...... + 6 00	+ 3 54 00
San Juan, San Juan	68W33	31S32	-34 12	+ 4 34 12
San Luis, San Luis	66W20	33S18	-25 20	+ 4 25 20
San Martin, Buenos Aires	58W32	34S34	+ 5 52	+ 3 54 08
San Nicolas, Entre Rios	60W14	33S20	- 0 56	+ 4 05 56
San Pedro, Buenos Aires	59W42	...33S41	...... + 1 12	+ 3 58 48
San Rafael, Mendoza	68W20	34S37	-33 20	+ 4 33 20
Santa Cruz, Santa Cruz	68W31	50S01	-34 04	+ 4 34 04
Santa Fe, Santa Fe	60W42	31S39	- 2 48	+ 4 02 48
Santa Rosa de Toay, Pampa	64W16	36S37	-17 04	+ 4 17 04
Santiago del Estero, S. de E.	64W16	...27S47	...... -17 04	+ 4 17 04
Santo Toma, Corrientes	56W04	28S33	+15 44	+ 3 44 16
Tandil, Buenos Aires	59W08	37S19	+ 3 28	+ 3 56 32
Tres Arroyos, Buenos Aires	60W17	38S23	- 1 08	+ 4 01 08
Tucuman, Tucuman	65W13	26S49	-20 52	+ 4 20 52
Ushuaia, Tierra del Fuego ...	68W20	...54S48	.... -33 20	+ 4 33 20
Viedma, Rio Negros	63W00	40S48	-12 00	+ 4 12 00
Villa Maria, Cordoba	63W15	32S26	-13 00	+ 4 13 00

ARMENIAN S.S.R. See U. S. S. R.

ARRECIFES ISLANDS see South Sea Mandated Territories

ARUBA see Netherlands West Indies

ASCENSION ISLAND. Capital: Georgetown.
   British possession, situated in South Atlantic
West Africa Time used prior to 1946, based on
   15° West. Standard Meridian since 1946 14°15'
   West, G.M.T. + 0^{h}57^{m}00^s.

Georgetown	14W25	7S56	+ 2 20	+ 0 57 40

ASHANTI see Gold Coast.

ASIA MINOR see Turkey.

AUSTRAL ISLANDS see French Establishments in Oceania

AUSTRALIA. Capital: Canberra. Capital Territory.
   Continent and British Commonwealth situated
   in the South Pacific. Canberra, New South Wales, Tasmania,
   Queensland base Standard Time on 150° EAST;
   Northern Territory and South Australia, 142° 30' EAST;
   Western Australia, 120°00' EAST.

Canberra	149E08	35S19	- 3 28	- 9 56 32

NEW SOUTH WALES. Capital: Sydney.

Albury, Goulburn	146E55	36S05	-12 20	- 9 47 40
Bathurst, Bathurst	149E35	....33S25	.... - 1 40	- 9 58 20
Bourke, Cooper	145E59	30S01	-16 04	- 9 43 56

AUSTRALIA (Continued)			L. M. T. VARIATION FROM S.T.		G. M. T. VARIATION FROM LMT h. m. s.		

NEW SOUTH WALES. Capital: Sydney

Broken Hill, Yancowinnia	141E28	31S58	– 34	08	– 9	25	52
Coonamble, Leichhordt	148E24	30S57	– 6	24	– 9	55	36
Dubbo, Lincoln	148E36	32S16	– 5	36	– 9	54	24
Goulburn, Argyle	149E43	34S45	– 1	08	– 9	58	52
Grafton, Clarence	152E55	29S37	+ 11	40	–10	11	40
Lismore, Rous	153E16	28S48	+ 13	04	–10	13	04
Lithgow, Cook	150E09	33S29	+ 0	36	–10	00	36
Maitland, Northumberland	151E35	32S46	– 6	20	–10	06	20
Narrandera, Cooper	146E52	34S45	– 13	52	– 9	46	08
Newcastle, Northumberland	151E45	32S55	+ 7	00	–10	07	00
Sydney, Cumberland	151E10	33S55	+ 4	40	–10	04	40
Tamworth, Parry.............	150E54	31S06	+ 3	36	–10	03	36
Wagga Wagga, Wynward	147E22	35S07	– 10	32	– 9	49	28
Willyama see Broken Hill							
Wollongong. Camden	150E53	34S26	+ 3	32	–10	03	32

NORTHERN TERRITORY Capital: Darwin.

Alice Springs.................	133E54	23S40	– 34	24	– 8	55	36
Adelaide River	131E06	13S14	– 45	36	– 8	44	24
Darwin	130E49	12S28	– 46	44	– 8	43	16
Fort Dundas, Melville Is.	130E29	11S24	– 48	04	– 8	41	56
Fort Hurd, Bathurst Island,..	130E18	11S39	– 48	48	– 8	41	12
Katherine	132E16	14S28	– 40	56	– 8	49	04
Oodnadatta	135E27	27S33	– 28	12	– 9	01	48
Palmerston see Darwin							
Port Darwin	130E50	12S30	– 46	40	– 8	43	20
Ross	133E17	15S41	– 36	52	– 8	53	08
Stuart see Alice Springs							

QUEENSLAND. Capital: Brisbane.

Ayr, North Kennedy	147E21	19S35	– 10	36	– 9	49	24
Brisbane, Moreton	153E02	27S28	+ 12	08	–10	12	08
Bundaberg, Wide Bay	152E21	24S52	+ 9	24	–10	09	24
Burketown, Burke	139E32	17S45	– 41	52	– 9	18	08
Cairns, Cook	145E47	16S56	– 16	52	– 9	43	08
Charleville, Warrego	146E14	26S25	– 15	04	– 9	44	56
Charters Towers, N. Kennedy	146E16	20S05	– 14	56	– 9	45	04
Cloncurry, Burke	140E31	20S43	– 37	56	– 9	22	04
Cooktown, Cook	145E15	15S28	– 19	00	– 9	41	00
Emerald, Leichhardt	148E10	23S31	– 7	20	– 9	52	40
Gladstone, Port Curtis	151E16	23S51	+ 6	56	–10	06	56
Gympie, Wide Bay	152E41	26S13	+ 10	44	–10	10	44
Hughenden, Burke	144E12	20S52	– 23	12	– 9	36	48
Ingham, North Kennedy	146E10	18S39	– 15	20	– 9	44	40
Ipswich, Moreton............	152E46	27S38	+ 11	04	–10	11	04
Longreach, Mitchell	144E15	23S27	– 23	00	– 9	37	00
Mackay, South Kennedy	149E11	21S08	– 2	36	– 9	56	44
Maryborough, Wide Bay	152E42	25S32	+ 10	48	–10	10	48
Rockhampton, Port Curtis	150E31	23S23	+ 2	04	–10	02	04
Roma, Maranoa	148E47	26S35	– 4	52	– 9	55	08
Southport, Martin	153E25	27S58	+ 9	40	–10	09	40

AUSTRALIA (Continued)			L. M. T. VARIATION FROM S.T.	G. M. T. VARIATION FROM LMT
QUEENSLAND (Continued)			m. s.	h. m. s.
Stanthorpe, Darling Downs	151E59	28S58	+ 7 56	- 10 07 56
Toowoomba "	151E58	27S34	+ 7 52	- 10 07 52
Townsville, N. Kennedy	146E49	19S16	-12 44	- 9 47 16
Warwick, Dar. Downs........	152E02	28S13	+ 8 08	- 10 08 08
Windorah, Gregory South	142E40	25S25	-29 20	- 9 30 40
Winton, Gregory North	143E03	22S24	-27 48	- 9 32 12
SOUTH AUSTRALIA. Capital: Adelaide.				
Adelaide, Adelaide	138E35	34S55	-15 40	- 9 14 20
Cummins, Lincoln	135E44	34S15	-27 04	- 9 02 56
Gawler, Port Gawler	138E45	34S36	-15 00	- 9 15 00
Mount Gambier, Grey	140E47	37S50	- 6 52	- 9 23 08
Naracoorte, Rose...........	140E44	36S58	- 7 04	- 9 22 56
Peterborough, Dalhousie	138E50	32S58	-14 10	- 9 15 20
Port Adelaide, Adeleide	138E35	34S51	-15 40	- 9 14 20
Port Augusta, Woolundunca	137E46	32S29	-18 56	- 9 11 04
Port Lincoln, Flinders......	135E53	34S44	-26 28	- 9 03 32
Port Pirie, Pirie	138E01	33S11	-17 56	- 9 12 04
Wallaroo, Kadiha	137E38	33S56	-19 28	- 9 10 32
TASMANIA. Capital: Hobart.				
Burnie	145E54	41S05	-16 24	- 9 43 36
Davenport	146E19	41S11	-14 44	- 9 45 16
Hobart....................	147E22	42S54	-10 32	- 9 49 28
Huonville	147E06	43S03	-11 36	- 9 48 24
Launcestown	147E09	41S26	-11 24	- 9 48 36
Oatsland	147E24	42S18	-10 24	- 9 49 36
Queenstown	145E32	42S07	-17 52	- 9 42 08
VICTORIA. Capital: Melbourne.				
Ararat, Ararat.............142E57		37S17	-22 12	- 9 31 48
Ballarat, Ballarat	143E53	37S33	-24 28	- 9 35 32
Bendigo, Bendigo	144E17	36S46	-22 52	- 9 37 08
Castalmaine, Metcalfe	144E13	37S03	-23 08	- 9 36 52
Colac, Colac	143E36	38S20	-25 36	- 9 34 24
Dandenona, Berwick	145E13	38S00	-19 08	- 9 40 52
Echuca, Deakin	144E45	36S08	-21 00	- 0 39 00
Geelong, Grant	144E21	38S10	-22 36	- 9 37 24
Hamilton, Dundas	142E01	37S45	-31 56	- 9 28 04
Horsham, Borung	142E10	36S43	-31 20	- 9 28 40
Maryborough, Tullaroop	143E44	37S03	-25 04	- 9 34 56
Melbourne, Melbourne	145E00	37S50	-16 00	- 9 44 00
Mildura, Mildura	142E10	34S12	-31 20	- 9 28 40
Shepparton, Shepparton,	145E25	36S23	-18 20	- 9 41 40
Wangaratta, Wangaratta	146E19	36S21	-14 44	- 9 45 16
Warrnambool, Warrnambool....	142E29	38S23	-30 04	- 9 29 56
Wonthaggi, Wonthaggi	145E36	38S37	-17 36	- 9 42 24

			L. M. T. VARIATION FROM S. T.		G. M. T. VARIATION FROM LMT		
			m.	s.	h.	m.	s.

AUSTRALIA (Continued)

WESTERN AUSTRALIA. Capital: Perth.

Albany, Plantagenet	117E53	35S02	- 8	28	-7	51	32
Broome, Broome	122E12	17S58	+ 8	48	-8	08	48
Bunbury, Wellington	115E38	33S19	-17	28	-7	42	32
Carnarven, Cas.-Min.	113E38	24S47	-25	28	-7	34	32
Collie, Collie...............	116E09	33S21	-15	24	-7	44	36
Derby, West Kimberley	123E38	17S18	+14	32	-8	14	32
Esperance, Esperance	121E53	33S51	+ 7	32	-8	07	32
Fremantle, Melville	115E45	32S03	-17	00	-7	43	00
Geraldton, Victoria	114E37	28S46	-21	32	-7	38	28
Hopetoun, Phillips River....	120E08	33S57	+ 0	32	-8	00	32
Kalgoorlie, Kalgoorlie	121E29	30S45	+ 5	56	-8	05	56
Meekatharra, Meekatharra	118E29	26S35	- 6	04	-7	53	56
Narrogin, Williams	117E11	32S55	-11	16	-7	48	44
Northam, Northam	116E39	31S40	-13	24	-7	46	36
Perth, Perth...............	115E50	31S57	-16	40	-7	43	20
Port Headland, Pt. Headland	118E32	20S19	- 5	52	-7	54	08

AUSTRIA. Capital: Wien (Vienna)

Republic, situated in Central Europe. Incorporated into Germany March 13, 1938;
liberated April 28, 1945; independence
recognized October 21, 1945. Central
European Time used, 15° East.

Amstetten	14E51	48N08	- 0	36	- 0	59	24
Bad Aussee, Steierm	13E47	47N37	- 4	52	- 0	55	08
Baden	16E14	48N01	+ 4	56	- 1	04	56
Bad Gastein, Salzburg	13E08	47N08	- 7	28	- 0	52	32
Bad Ischl, Oberosterreich...	13E37	41N43	- 5	32	- 0	54	28
Bludenz	9E48	47N10	-20	48	- 0	39	12
Braunau, Oberosterreich	13E03	48N15	- 7	48	- 0	52	12
Bregenz	9E45	47N30	-21	00	- 0	39	00
Brenner, Tirel	11E30	47N00	-14	00	- 0	46	00
Bruch a. d. Leitha..........	16E47	48N01	+ 7	08	- 1	07	08
Dornbirn	9E45	47N25	-21	00	- 0	39	00
Eisenstadt	16E27	47N51	+ 5	48	- 1	05	48
Feldkirch	9E37	47N15	-21	32	- 0	38	28
Furstenfeld, Steierm.	16E05	47N02	+ 4	20	- 1	04	20
Gmunden, Oberesterreich.....	13E48	47N55	+ 4	48	- 0	55	12
Graz, Steierm	15E26	47N05	+ 1	44	- 1	01	44
Gussing	16E20	47N03	+ 5	20	- 1	05	20
Hainburg	16E57	48N09	+ 7	48	- 1	07	48
Innshruck, Tirol	11E24	47N16	-14	24	- 0	45	36
Ischl see Bad Ischl							
Jennersdorf	16E09	46N56	+ 4	36	- 1	04	36
Judenburg, Steierm	14E39	47N08	- 1	24	- 0	58	36
Klagenfurth, Kaernten	14E19	46N37	- 2	44	- 0	57	16
Klosterneuburg	16E20	48N20	+ 5	20	- 1	05	20
Knittelfeld, Steierm	14E50	47N13	- 0	40	- 0	59	10
Korneuburg..................	16E20	48N20	+ 5	20	- 1	05	20
Krems	15E36	48N25	+ 6	24	- 1	06	24
Kufstein, Tirol	12E11	47N34	-11	16	- 0	48	44
Leoben, Steierm	15E06	47N23	+ 0	24	- 1	00	24

			L. M. T. VARIATION FROM S.T.	G. M. T. VARIATION FROM LMT
			m. s.	h. m. s.
AUSTRIA (Continued)				
Lienz, Osttirol	12E47	46N49	- 8 52	- 0 51 08
Linz, Oberosterreich	14E17	48N18	- 2 52	- 0 57 08
Mariazell, Steierm	15E19	47N47	+ 1 16	- 1 01 16
Melk	15E20	48N14	+ 1 20	- 1 01 20
Modling	16E16	48N05	+ 5 04	- 1 05 04
Neunkirchen	16E05	47N46	+ 4 20	- 1 04 20
Radkersburg, Steierm	16E00	46N42	+ 4 00	+ 1 04 00
Ried, Oberosterreich	13E30	48N13	- 6 00	- 0 54 00
Salzburg, Salzburg	13E03	47N48	- 7 48	- 0 52 12
Sankt Polten	15E30	48N12	+ 2 00	- 1 02 00
Sankt Veit, Kaernten	14E22	46N46	- 2 32	- 0 57 28
Schwechat	16E29	48N09	+ 5 56	- 1 05 56
Steyr, Oberosterreich	14E24	48N03	- 2 24	- 0 57 36
Stockerau	16E12	48N23	+ 4 48	- 1 04 48
Tulln	16E03	48N20	+ 4 12	- 1 04 12
Urfahr see Linz				
Vienna see Wien				
Villach, Kaernten	13E52	46N37	- 4 32	- 0 55 28
Vocklabruck, Oberosterreich	13E40	48N00	- 5 20	- 0 54 40
Wagram	16E35	48N17	+ 6 40	- 1 06 40
Wels, Oberosterreich	14E01	48N10	- 3 56	- 0 56 04
Wien	16E23	48N12	+ 5 32	- 1 05 32
Wiener Neustadt	16E15	47N50	+ 5 00	- 1 05 00
Wolfsberg, Kaernten	14E51	46N50	- 0 36	- 0 59 24
Ybbs	15E05	48N11	+ 0 20	- 1 00 20
Zell am See, Salzburg	12E48	47N19	- 8 48	- 0 51 12

AUTRICHE see Austria
AZERBAIDJAN S.S.R. see U.S.S.R.
AZORES. Capital: Horta. Portuguese Colony
    situated in North Atlantic. Azores
    Standard time based on 30° West.

Angra de Heroismo, Terceira	27W13	38N39	+11 08	+ 1 48 52
Horta, Fayal	28W38	38N31	+ 5 28	+ 1 54 32
Ponta Delgada, San Miguel	25W40	37N42	+17 20	+ 1 42 40
Praia da Victoria, Terceira	27W04	38N43	+11 44	+ 1 48 16
Santa Cruz, Flores	31W08	39N27	- 4 32	+ 2 04 32
Santa Cruz, Graciosa	28W01	39N05	+ 7 56	+ 1 52 04
Santa Luzia, Pico	28W24	38N33	+ 6 24	+ 1 53 36
Vila das Velas, San Jerga	28W13	38N41	+ 7 08	+ 1 52 52
Vila de Porto, San Maria	25W09	36N57	+19 24	+ 1 40 36
Vila de Topo, San Jorge	27W47	38N33	+ 8 52	+ 1 51 08
Vila Franca de Campo, SanMiguel	25W53	37N42	+18 28	+ 1 43 32

BAHAMAS see British West Indies.
BAHREIN ISLAND see Saudi Arabia.
BAKER ISLAND see Gilbert and Ellice Islands.
BALEARIC ISLANDS see Spain
BALI ISLAND see Netherlands East Indies
BALUCHISTAN see India
BANGKA ISLAND see Netherlands East Indies
BANKS ISLANDS see New Hebrides

BARBADOS SEE British West Indies
BARBARY see Libya.
BARBUDA see British West Indies
BASUOTOLAND see Union of South Africa
BAVARIA see Germany. (also BAYERN).
BECHUANALAND see Union of South Africa.
BELGIAN CONGO Capital: Leopoldville.

			L. M. T. VARIATION FROM S.T.		G. M. T. VARIATION FROM LMT		
Belgian Colony, situated in Africa. The Western provinces use Central European Time and Eastern provinces use Eastern European Time, 15° and 30° EAST			m. s.		h. m. s.		
Albertville, Tang.	25E11	5S56	- 3 16		- 1 56 44		
Coquilhatville, Equateur.......	18E16...	0N03.....	+ 13 04..		- 1 13 04		
Boma, B. C.	13E17	5S51	- 7 32		- 0 52 28		
Costermansville, Lowa	28E52	2S29	- 4 32		- 1 55 28		
Elizabethville, Haut Luap	27E28	11S39	- 10 08		- 1 49 52		
Kigali, R. -U.	30E01	1S57	+ 0 04		- 2 00 04		
Kitega, R. -U.	29E57	...3S26.....	- 0 12..		- 1 59 48		
Leopoldville, M. C.	15E18	4S19	+ 1 12		- 1 01 12		
Matadi, B. X.	13E28	5S49	- 6 08		- 0 53 52		
Stanleyville, Stanleyville	25E11	0N30	- 19 16		- 1 40 44		
Thysville, B. C.	14E50	5S14	- 0 40		- 0 59 20		
Usumbura, R. -U.	29E21...	3S24	- 2 36..		- 1 57 24		

BELGIUM Capital: Bruxelles, Kingdom situated
in Western Europe. Central European
Time used 15°East.

			L. M. T. VARIATION		G. M. T. VARIATION		
Aalst see Alost.							
Alost. Flandre Or.	4E02	50N56	- 43 52		- 0 16 08		
Antwerpen see Anvers							
Anvers, Anvers..................	4E25....	51N13....	- 42 20..		- 0 17 40		
Arlon, Lux.	5E49	49N41	- 36 44		- 0 23 16		
Blankenberghe, Flandre Occ	3E08	51N19	- 47 28		- 0 12 32		
Bruges, Flandre Occ	3E13	51N12	- 47 08		- 0 12 52		
Brugge see Bruges							
Brussels see Bruxelles							
Bruxelles, Brabant	4E21	...50N51......	- 42 36..		- 0 17 24		
Charleroi, Hainaut	4E26	50N25	- 42 16		- 0 17 44		
Courtrai, Flandre Occ.	3E16	50N49	- 46 56		- 0 13 04		
Dendermonde, Flandre Or.	4E05	51N02	- 43 40		- 0 16 20		
Eekloo (Eccloo), Flandre Or.	3E34	51N11	- 45 44		- 0 14 16		
Eupen, Liege	6E02...	50N38....	- 35 52....		- 0 24 08		
Gand, Flandre Or.	3E43	51N03	- 45 08		- 0 14 52		
Ghent see Gand							
Gilly, Hainaut	4E30	50N26	- 42 00		- 0 18 00		
Hasselt, Limbourg	5E20	50N56	- 38 40		- 0 21 20		
Hoboken, Anvers	4E21	51N11	- 42 36		- 0 17 24		
Leper, see Ypres							
Jumet, Hainaut..................	4E26...	50N26....	+ 42 16..		- 0 17 44		
Kortrijk see Courtrai							
Laeken, Brabant	4E21	50N53	- 42 36		- 0 17 24		
La Louviere, Hainaut	4E13	50N28	- 43 08		- 0 16 52		
Leuven see Louvain							
Liege, Liege	5E34	50N38	- 37 44		- 0 22 16		

			L. M. T. VARIATION FROM S.T.	G. M. T. VARIATION FROM LMT
			m. s.	h. m. s.
BELGIUM (continued)				
Lierre, Anvers	4E34	51N08	- 41 44	- 0 18 16
Lokeren, Flandre Or.	4E00	51N06	- 44 00	- 0 16 00
Louvain, Louvain	4E42	50N53	- 41 12	- 0 18 48
Luik see Liege				
Maltines, Anvers	4E28	51N02	- 42 08	- 0 17 52
Malmedy, Liege	6E02	50N26	- 35 52	- 0 24 08
Marcinelle, Hainaut	4E24	50N24	- 42 24	- 0 17 36
Menin (Meenen), Flandre Occ	3E08	59N48	- 47 28	- 0 12 32
Merksem (Merxem), Anvers	4E26	51N15	- 42 16	- 0 17 44
Mons, Hainaut	3E56	50N27	- 44 16	- 0 15 44
Mouseron, Flandre Occ.	3E13	50N44	- 47 08	- 0 12 52
Namen see Namur				
Namur, Namur	4E51	50N28	- 40 36	- 0 19 24
Nivelles, Brabant	4E19	50N36	- 42 44	- 0 17 16
Ostende (Oostende), Flandre Occ.	2E55	51N14	- 48 20	- 0 11 40
Renaix, Flandre Or	3E56	50N45	- 44 16	- 0 15 44
Roeselaire see Roulers				
Ronse see Renaix				
Roulers, Flandre Occ	3E07	50N57	- 47 32	- 0 12 28
Saint Nicolas, Flandre Or.	4E08	51N10	- 43 28	- 0 16 32
Saint Troud, Limbourg	5E11	50N49	- 39 16	- 0 20 44
Schaerbeek, Brabant	4E25	50N52	- 42 20	- 0 17 40
Seraing, Liege	5E30	50N36	- 38 00	- 0 22 00
Sint Niklaas see Saint Nicolas				
Sint Truden see Saint Troud				
Termonde see Dendermonde				
Thourout, Flandre Occ.	3E06	51N04	- 47 36	- 0 12 24
Tirlemont, Brabant	4E56	50N48	- 40 16	- 0 19 44
Tournai, Hainaut	3E23	50N37	- 46 28	- 0 13 32
Turnhout, Anvers	4E56	51N20	- 40 16	- 0 19 44
Uccle (obs.) Brabant	4E22	50N48	- 42 32	- 0 17 28
Verviers, Liege	5E51	50N36	- 36 36	- 0 23 24
Waterloo, Brabant	4E24	50N43	- 42 24	- 0 17 36
Ypres, Flandre Occ.	2E53	50N51	- 48 28	- 0 11 32
BELUCHISTAN see India				
BENADIR see Italian East Africa				
BERMUDA Capital: Hamilton, British Colony, Situated in North Atlantic, Atlantic Standard time used, 60° WEST.				
Evans Bay	64W52	32N15	- 19 28	+ 4 19 28
Hamilton	64W47	32N18	- 19 08	+ 4 19 08
Ireland Point	64W50	32N20	- 19 20	+ 4 19 20
Riddles Bay	54W49	32N15	- 19 16	+ 4 19 16
Somerset	64W52	32N18	- 19 28	+ 4 19 28
St. George	64W41	32N23	- 18 44	+ 4 18 44
The Flats Village	64W44	32N19	- 18 56	+ 4 18 56
Tuckers Town	64W42	32N20	- 18 48	+ 4 18 48
BESSARABIA see Rumania				
BHUTAN see India (although technically a separate state).				

BILITON ISLAND   see Netherlands East Indies.
BIRMANIE   see Burma.
BISMARCK ARCHIPELAGO see New Guinea
BOEHMEN   see Czechoslovakia.
BOHEMIA   see Czechoslovakia.
BOLIVIA.   Capital: La Paz. Republic situated
    in South America. Atlantic Standard Time
    used, 60° WEST. The Standard meridian used
    until October 31, 1922; was 68°15'. Day
    light Saving Time was used between October
    1931 and March 1932.

			L. M. T. VARIATION FROM S.T.	G. M. T. VARIATION FROM LMT
			m. s.	h. m. s.
Camargo, Chuquisaca	65W08	20S43	- 20 32	+ 4 20 32
Cochabamba, Cochabamba	65W05	17S24	- 24 20	+ 4 24 20
La Paz, La Paz	68W09	16S30	- 32 36	+ 4 32 36
Oruro, Oruro	67W08	17S59	- 28 32	+ 4 28 32
Potosi, Potosi	65W45	19S35	- 23 00	+ 4 23 00
Riberalta, Colonias	66W06	11S00	- 24 24	+ 4 24 24
Santa Cruz, Santa Cruz	63W10	17S47	- 12 40	+ 4 12 40
Sucre, Chuquisaca	65W17	19S03	- 21 08	+ 4 21 08
Tarija, Tarija	64W45	21S32	- 19 00	+ 4 19 00
Trinidad de Mojos, El Beni	64W39	14S47	- 18 36	+ 4 18 36
Villa Belle, Colonias	65W25	10S24	- 21 40	+ 4 21 40
Villa Montes, Chaco	63W31	21S15	- 14 04	+ 4 14 04

BONAIRE see Netherlands West Indies.
BORNEO   see (1) Netherlands East Indies.
          (2) British North Borneo.
BOSNIA   see Yugoslavia.
BOURBON ISLAND   see Reunion.
BRAZIL.   Capital: Rio de Janeiro. Republic
    situated in South America. An area of 200,000
    square miles forming a belt around Brazil,
    previously parts of States, was taken over by
    the Federal Government on October 1, 1943, and
    were divided into Federal Territories, i.e.,
    Amapa, Río Branco, Guapore, Ponta Pora, Fern-
    ando Noronha and Iguassu. They are marked by
    an *. Iguassu and Ponta Poro were restored
    to the States from which taken in 1946.
    Standard Time meridians are 30°, 45° 60° and 75° WEST

Alagoinhas, Ba.	38W21	12S08	+ 26 36	+ 2 33 24
Amapa, Pa.* (Amapa)	50W32	2N00	- 22 08	+ 3 22 08
Amargosa, Ba.	39W41	13S02	+ 21 16	+ 2 38 44
Amparo, S.P.	46W34	22S42	- 6 16	+ 3 06 16
Aracaju, Ser.	37W05	10S53	+ 31 40	+ 2 28 20
Arassuahi, Min.	41W47	16S55	+ 12 52	+ 2 47 08
Atalai, Al.	36W01	9S30	+ 35 56	+ 2 24 04
Baependi, Min.	44W40	21S59	+ 1 20	+ 2 58 40
Bage, R.G.S.	54W06	31S21	- 36 24	+ 3 36 24
Bahia see Sao Salvador				
Barbacena, Min.	43W35	21S14	+ 5 40	+ 2 54 20
Baturito, Ce.	38W57	4S21	+ 24 12	+ 2 35 48
Belem, Pa.	48W29	1S27	- 13 56	+ 3 13 56

12

			L. M. T. VARIATION FROM S.T. m. s.	G. M. T. VARIATION FROM LMT h. m. s.
BRAZIL (Continued)				
Belmonte, B. A.	38W54	15S52	+ 24 24	+ 2 35 36
Belo Horizonte, Min.	43W56	19S55	+ 4 16	+ 2 55 44
Benjamin Constant, Am..........	70W10...	4S21..	- 40 40...	+ 4 40 40
Bezerros, Per.	35W45	8S15	+ 37 00	+ 2 23 00
Biguassu, S. C.	48W38	27S50	- 14 32	+ 3 14 32
Blumenau, S. C.	49W05	26S55	- 16 20	+ 3 16 20
Boa Vista, Am *(Rio Branco)	60W41	2N50	- 2 44	+ 4 02 44
Bomfim, Ba.....................	40W06...10S21..		+ 19 36...	+ 2 40 24
Bonito, Per.	35W44	8S29	+ 37 04	+ 2 22 56
Braganca, S.P.	4EW18	22S58	- 5 12	+ 3 05 12
Cachoeira, Ba.	39W00	12S33	+ 24 00	+ 2 36 00
Cachoeira,R.G.S.	52W54	30S03	-.31 36	+ 3 31 36
Campinas, S. P................	47W03..	22S54...	.- 8 12...	+ 3 08 12
Carangola, Min.	41W49	20S43	+ 12 44	+ 2 47 16
Ceara see Fortaleza				
Corumba, Go.	43W36	15S55	- 14 24	+ 3 14 24
Coxim, G.	54W44	18S32	+ 21 04	+ 3 38 56
Crato, Ce.....................	39W25...	7S20..	+ 22 20...	+ 2 37 40
Cruzeiro do Sul, Terr.de Acre	72W37	7S38	+ 9 32	+ 4 50 28
Cuiaba, Mt. G.	56W06	15S35	- 15 36	+ 3 44 24
Curitiba, Pna.	49W14	25S26	- 16 56	+ 3 16 56
Curvello, Min.	44W14	18S46	+ 3 04	+ 2 56 56
Diamantina, Min...............	43W33..	18S15..	+ 5 48"..	+ 2 54 12
Dores da Boa Esperanca, Min.	45W21	21S06	- 1 24	+ 3 01 24
Feira da Sant' Anna, Ba.	38W54	12S12	+ 24 24	+ 2 35 36
Fern. de Noronha see Remedios or Villa				
Florianopolis, S.C.	48W34	27S36	- 14 16	+ 3 14 16
Fortaleza, Ce.................	38W31...	3S44..	+ 25 56...	+ 2 34 04
Foz do Iguassu, Pna. *(Iguassu)	54W26	25S33	- 37 44	+ 3 37 44
Goiania, Go.	49W16	16S40	- 17 04	+ 3 17 04
Goianna, Per.	34W57	7S34	+ 40 12	+ 2 19 48
Goiaz, Go.....................	50W08..	15S55...	.- 20 32..	+ 3 20 32
Guaratingueta, S. P.	45W11	22S44	- 0 44	+ 3 00 44
Iguassu, Par.	54W33	25S35	- 38 12	+ 3 38 12
Itaperuna, R.J.	41W53	21S11	+ 12 28	+ 2 47 32
Jaguarao, R.G.S.	53W23	32S33	- 33 32	+ 3 33 32
Joao, Pessoa, Pba:............	34W43...	7S07..	+ 41 08...	+ 2 18 52
Joinville, S.C.	48W52	26S18	- 15 28	+ 3 15 28
Juiz de Fora, Min.	43W09	21S46	+ 7 24	+ 2 52 36
Lageado, R.G.S.	51W58	29S28	- 27 52	+ 3 27 52
Laguna, S.C.	37W24	28S29	+ 30 24	+ 2 29 36
Macae, R.J.	41W47..	22S21..	+ 12 52...	+ 2 46 08
Macapa, Pa.	51W02	00N01	- 24 08	+ 3 24 08
Maceio, Al.	35W44	9S39	+ 37 04	+ 2 22 56
Manaos, Am.	60W01...	3S07..	- 0 04 ...	+ 4 00 04
Maranhao see Sao Luiz				
Mar da Espanha, Min.	42W49	21S52	+ 8 44	+ 2 51 16
Marianna, Min.	43W12	20S22	+ 7 12	+ 2 52 48
Matto Grosso see Cuiaba				
Minas Novas, Min.	43W38	17S18	+ 5 28	+ 2 54 32

			L. M. T. VARIATION From S.T.	G. M. T. VARIATION From LMT
			m. s.	
BRAZIL. (Continued)				
Montes Claros, Min	43W33	16S43	+ 5 48	+ 2 54 12
Natal, R.G.N.	35W09	5S47	+ 39 24	+ 2 20 36
Nazareth, Per	35W14 ... 7S44 ...		+ 39 04	+ 2 20 56
Niteroi (Nichtheroi), R.J.	43W06	22S53	+ 7 36	+ 2 52 24
Noronha see Remedios or Villa				
Nova Cruz, R. G. N.	35W23	6S28	+ 38 28	+ 2 21 32
Olinda, Per.	34W51	6S01	+ 40 36	+ 2 19 24
Ouro Fino, Min.	46W11 .. 22S18		- 4 44	+ 3 04 44
Para see Belom				
Paraiba see Joao Pessoa				
Patrocinio,Min.	46W45	19S00	- 7 00	+ 3 07 00
Pelotas, R. G. S.	52W22	31S48	- 29 28	+ 3 29 28
Pernambuco see Recife				
Petropolis, R. J.	43W10	22S31	+ 7 20	+ 2 52 40
Piracicaba, S. P.	47W38	22S42	- 10 32	+ 3 10 32
Piranga, Min.	43W04	20S39	+ 7 44	+ 2 52 16
Ponta Grossa, Pna.	50W01	25S06	- 20 04	+ 3 20 04
Ponta Pora, Mt. G. *(Ponta Pora)	55W44 .. 22S29		+ 17 04	+ 3 42 56
Porto Alegre, R.G.S.	51W13	30S02	- 24 52	+ 3 24 52
Porto Velho, Am. *(Guapore)	63W52	8S46	- 15 28	+ 4 15 28
Recife, Per	34W50	8S50	+ 40 40	+ 2 19 20
Ribeirao Preto, S.P.	47W49	21S12	- 11 16	+ 3 11 16
Rio de Janeiro, D.F.	43W15 ... 22S54		+ 7 00	+ 2 53 00
Rio Grande, R.G.S.	52W07	32S03	- 28 28	+ 3 28 28
Rio Pardo, Min.	42W06	15S55	+ 11 36	+ 2 48 24
Santa Barbara, Min.	43W10	19S55	+ 7 20	+ 2 52 40
Santa Cruz, D.F.	43W40	22S54	+ 5 20	+ 2 54 40
Santa Cruz, R. G. S.	52W26 ... 29S44		- 29 44	+ 3 29 44
Santa Luzia do Crangola see Carangola				
Santa Maria (da Boca do Monte), R.G.S.	53W48	29S40	- 35 12	+ 3 35 12
Santo Amara, Bc.	38W46	12S31	+ 24 56	+ 2 35 04
Santos, S.P.	46W18 ... 23S56		- 5 12	+ 3 05 12
Remedios, Fern. de Noronha Island, *	32W25	3S20	- 0 40	+ 2 09 40
Santos Dumont, Min.	43W33	21S28	+ 5 48	+ 2 54 12
Senna Madueira, Terr.do Acre	68W39	9S04	+ 25 24	+ 4 34 36
Sao Gabriel, Am.	67W03 ... 0S12		- 28 12	+ 4 28 12
Sao Salvador, Ba.	38W31	12S59	+ 25 56	+ 2 34 04
Sao Luiz, Mar.	44W18	2S32	+ 2 48	+ 2 57 12
Sao Paulo, S.P.	46W35	23S33	- 6 20	+ 3 06 20
Senador Pompeu, Ce.	39W27	5S34	+ 22 12	+ 2 37 49
Serro, Min.	43W08 ... 18S36		+ 7 28	+ 2 52 32
Sorocaba, S. P.	47W28	23S30	+ 9 52	+ 3 09 52
Taubate, S. P.	45W34	23S01	- 2 15	+ 3 02 16
Teresopolis, R. J.	42W56	22S27	+ 8 16	+ 2 51 44
Terezina, Pi.	42W49	5S05	+ 8 44	+ 2 51 16
Timbauba, Per	35W21 .... 7S32 ...		+ 38 36	+ 2 21 24
Touros, R.G.N.	35W28	5S12	+ 38 08	+ 2 21 52
Uberlandia, Min.	48W18	18S56	- 13 12	+ 3 13 12

				L. M. T. VARIATION FROM S.T.	L. M. T. VARIATION FROM LMT
				m. s.	h. m. s.
BRAZIL (Continued)					
Uberlandia, Min.	48W18	18S56		-13 12	+ 3 13 12
Uniao, Al.	36W04	9S11		+35 44	+ 2 24 16
Vicosa, Al	36W14	9S22 ..		+35 04	+ 2 24 56
Vicosa, Min.	42W40	20S44		+ 9 20	+ 2 50 40
Victoria, E. S.	40W20	20S19		+18 40	+ 2 41 20
Victoria, Per.	35W17	8S11		+38 52	+ 2 21 08
Villa, Fern. de Noronha, *	32W26	3S50		- 9 44	+ 2 09 44

BRESIL see Brazil.

British Africa see Union of South Africa.

BRITISH BECHUANALAND see Union of South Africa.

BRITISH CENTRAL AFRICA PROTECTORATE see Nyasaland.

BRITISH COLUMBIA see Canada.

BRITISH EAST AFRICA see 1. Kenya.
                     2. Uganda.
                     3. Zanzibar.

BRITISH GUIANA. Capital: Georgetown, British
    Colony, situated in South America. Standard
    Time meridian 56°15'WEST.

Bartica, Ess.	58W37	6N24		- 9 28	+ 3 54 28
Dadanawa, Ess.	59W30	2N50		-13 00	+ 3 58 00
Georgetown, Demerara	58W10	6N48		- 7 40	+ 3 52 40
Hyde Park, Demarara	58W16	6N30		- 8 04	+ 3 53 04
Marlborough, Ess	58W33 ...	7N29		- 9 32	+ 3 54 32
Morawhanna, Ess.	59W44	8N17		-13 56	+ 3 58 56
New Amsterdam	57W33	6N17		- 5 12	+ 3 50 12
Taruma, Ess.	58W22	2N02		- 8 22	+ 3 53 22

BRITISH INDIA see India.

BRITISH MALAYA see Malaya

BRITISH NEW GUINEA see Papua.

BRITISH NORTH AMERICA see Canada.

BRITISH HONDURAS. Capital: Belize, British
    Crown Colony, situated in Central America.
    Standard Time meridian 90° WEST.

Belize, Belize	88W12	17N30		+ 7 12	+ 5 52 48
Cayo, Cayo	89W04	17N10		+ 3 44	+ 5 56 16
Corozal, Corozal..............	88W24	18N24 ...		+ 6 24	+ 5 53 36
Orange Walk, Northern Dist.	88W33	18N06		+ 5 48	+ 5 54 12
Punta Gorda, Toledo	88W48	16N07		+ 4 48	+ 5 55 12
Stann Creek, Stann Creek	88W13	16N58		+ 7 08	+ 5 52 52

BRITISH NORTH BORNEO. Capital: Sandaken.
    Brithsh Protected State situated in the
    East Indies. Standard Time Meridian 120°
    EAST.

Beaufort, West C.R.	115E45	5N40 ...		-17 00	- 7 43 00
Jesselton, West Coast Res.	116E05	5N59		-15 40	- 7 44 20
Kudat, East Coast Res.	116E50	6N53		-12 40	- 7 47 20
Labuan (see Malaya. Incorporated into British North Borneo in 1946)					
Penom, Interior Res.	115E57	5N27		-16 12	- 7 43 48
Sandaken, East Coast Res. ...	118E07	5N50 ...		- 7 32	- 7 52 28
Tawau, Tawau Res.	117E54	4N15		- 8 24	- 7 51 36

BRITISH SAMOA see Western Samoa.

BRITISH SOLOMON ISLANDS. Capital: Tulagi.
British Protectorate situated in the South
Pacific. Standard Time Meridian 165° EAST:

			L. M. T. VARIATION FROM S.T.		G. M. T. VARIATION FROM LMT		
			m.	s.	h.	m.	s.
Adam Port, Maramasike	161E33	9S34	-13	49	-10	46	12
Aola, Guadalcanal	160E30 ...	9S32 ...	-18	00..	-10	42	00
Auki, Malaita	160E42	8S47	-17	12	-10	42	48
Bagarai, South Cristobal	162E04	10S48	-11	44	-10	43	16
Bambatana, Choiseul	156E48	7S03	-22	48	-10	27	12
Buin, Bougainville	155E45	6S50	-37	00	-10	23	00
Carola Hafen see Queen Carola Harbour.							
Fual (Fula), Malaita	161E06	8S57	-15	36	-10	44	24
Henderson Field, Guadalcanal	160E02	9S26	-19	52	-10	40	08
Kieta, Bougainville	155E40	6S11	-37	20	-10	22	40
Kirakira, South Cristobal	161E55 ..	10S27	-12	20..	-10	47	40
Kolombagia, New Georgia	157E36	8S01	-29	36	-10	30	24
Korrigole Harbour, S. Isabel	158E59	8S03	-24	04	-10	35	56
Lambeti, New Georgia	157E17	8S20	-30	52	-10	29	08
Luti, Choiseul	157E00	7S15	-32	00	-10	28	00
Manano (Manango), Choiseul ...	157E58 ...	6S51 ...	-32	08..	-10	27	52
Maraugoa, South Cristobal	161E27	10S26	-14	12	-10	45	48
Mundi Mundi, Vella Lavella	156E30	7S39	-34	00	-10	26	00
Pukauli, Guadalcanal	160E23	9S50	-18	28	-10	41	32
Queen Carola Harbour, Buka	154E33	5S09	-41	48	-10	18	12
Rendova, Rendova	157E18 ...	8S27 ...	-30	48..	-10	29	12
Rubiana see Lambetti							
Siota, Florida	160E19	9S03	-18	44	-10	41	16
Susubona, South Isabel	159E27	8S19	-22	12	-10	37	48
Suu, Malaita	160E56	9S10	-16	16	-10	43	44
Tanabuli, South Isabel	159E49 ...	8S24 ...	-20	44..	-10	39	16
Tinputs, Bougainville	155E03	5S33	+20	12	-10	20	12
Tomba-tomba, Choiseul	156E37	6S38	-33	32	-10	26	28
Tulagi, Tulagi	160E09	9S05	-19	24	-10	40	36
Tunnibuli see Tanabuli							
Ugali, Rendova	157E25 ...	8S27 ...	-30	20..	-10	29	40
Velaviruru, Choiseul	157E30	7S25	-30	00	-10	30	00
Viru Harbour, New Georgia	157E45	8S30	-29	00	-10	31	00
Visale Mission, Guadalcanal	159E42	8S15	-21	12	-10	38	48

BRITISH SOMALILAND. Capital: Berbera, British
Protectorate, situated in Africa Standard
Time meridian 45° EAST.

Berbera	45E02	10N26	+ 0	08	- 3	00	08
Burao	45E33	9N30	+ 2	12	- 3	02	12
Hargeisa	44E02	9N33	- 3	52	- 2	56	08
Zaila (Zeila)	43E28 ...	11N21	.. - 6	08...	- 2	53	52

BRITISH TOGOLAND see Gold Coast.

BRITISH VIRGIN ISLANDS see British West Indies.

BRITISH WEST INDIES: Colony, Capital, S. T. Meridian.
    1. Colony of Bahamas: Capital, Nassau, 75° WEST.
    2. Colony of Barbados; Capital, Bridgetown, 60° WEST.
    3. Colony of Jamaica, with Cayman, Turks & Caicos Islands;
        Capital, Kingston; 75° WEST.

BRITISH WEST INDIES (continued)

    4. Colony of Leeward Islands (Antigua
        with Barbuda and Redonda; Dominica;
        Montserrat; St. Christopher or St.
        Kitts with Nevis and Anguilla; Vir-
        gin Islands with Sombrero): Capital
        St. Johns; 60° West.

    5. Colony of Trididad and Tobago:
        Capital, Port of Spain, 60° WEST.

    6. Colony of Windward Islands (Grenada
        the Grenadines, St. Lucie, St. Vincent):
        Capital, St. George's, 60° WEST.

			L.M.T. VARIATION FROM S.T. M. S.	G.M.T. VARIATION FROM LMT H. M. S.
BAHAMAS				
Albert Town, Long Cay	74W21	22N36	+ 2 36	+ 4 57 24
Alice, Biminis	79W17	25N44	-17 08	+ 5 17 08
Arthurs Town, Cat Island	75W42	24N38	- 2 48	+ 5 02 48
Bannerman Town, El.	76W10	24N38	- 4 40	+ 5 04 40
Bennets Harbour, Cat Island	75W38	24N35	- 2 32	+ 5 02 32
Blanket Sound, Andros	77W54	24N51	-11 36	+ 5 11 36
Bullock Harbour, Berry Is	77W51	25N47	-11 24	+ 5 11 24
Cherokee Sound, Abaco	77W02	26N17	- 8 08	+ 5 08 08
Clarence Town, Long Is.	74W59	23N06	+ 0 04	+ 4 59 56
Free Town, Gr. Bahama	78W27	26N34	-13 48	+ 5 13 48
George Town, Great Exuma	75W46	23N30	- 3 04	+ 5 03 04
Governor's Harbour, Eleuthern	76W14	25N10	- 4 56	+ 5 04 56
Hope Town, Abaco	76W57	26N33	- 7 48	+ 5 07 48
Mangrove Cay, Andros	77W39	24N15	-10 36	+ 5 10 36
Matthew Town, Great Inagua Island	73W41	21N57	+ 5 16	+ 4 54 44
Nassau, New Providence	77W20	25N05	- 9 20	+ 5 09 20
Nicolls Town, Andros Is.	78W00	25N08	-12 00	+ 5 12 00
Pirate Well. Mayaguana	73W04	22N26	+ 7 44	+ 4 52 16
Port Nelson, Rum Cay	74W50	23N38	+ 0 40	+ 4 59 20
Rolleville, Great Exuma	76W00	23N41	- 4 00	+ 5 04 00
BARBADOS.				
Bridgetown	59W37	13N06	+ 1 32	+ 3 58 28
Speightstown	59W39	13N15	+ 1 24	+ 3 58 36
St. Andrew	59W33	13N15	+ 1 48	+ 3 58 12
JAMAICA.				
Bodden Town, Jamaica	81W16	19N17	-25 04	+ 5 25 04
Four Paths, Clarendon	77W18	17N58	- 9 12	+ 5 09 12
Grand Turk, Turks & Caicos Islands	71W08	21N28	+15 28	+ 4 44 32
Kingston, St. Andrews	76W48	18N00	- 7 12	+ 5 07 12
Mandeville, Manchester	77W31	18N03	-10 04	+ 5 10 04
Montego Bay, St. James	77W55	18N28	-11 40	+ 5 11 40
Old Harbour, St. Catherine	77W07	17N56	- 8 28	+ 5 08 28
Port Morant, St. Thomas	76W19	17N54	- 5 15	+ 5 05 16
Spanish Town, St. Catherine	76W57	18N00	- 7 48	+ 5 07 48
West Bay, Grand Cayman	81W25	19N22	-25 40	+ 5 25 40

			L. M. T. VARIATION FROM S.T.	G. M. T. VARIATION FROM LMT
			m. s.	h. m. s.
BRITISH WEST INDIES				
LEEWARD ISLANDS				
Anguilla	63W04	18N12	- 12 16	+ 4 12 16
Basseterre, St. Christ.	62W43	17N18	- 10 52	+ 4 10 52
Cadrington, Barbuda	61W50	17N38	- 7 20	+ 4 07 20
Charles Fort Leper Asylum				
St. Christopher	62W50	17N21	-11 20	+ 4 11 20
Charlestown, Nevis	62W37	17N08	-10 28	+ 4 10 28
Falmouth, Antigua	61W47 ..	17N00	- 7 08	+ 4 07 08
Fort Byham, Antigua	61W48	17N08	- 7 12	+ 4 07 12
Plymouth, Montserrat	62W13	16N42	- 8 52	+ 4 08 52
Newcastle, Nevis	62W34	17N13	-10 16	- 4 10 16
Portsmouth, Dominica	61W28	15N35	- 5 52	+ 4 05 52
Road Town, British Virgin				
Islands	64W37 ..	18N27	-18 28	+ 4 18 28
Roseau, Dominican	61W24	15N18	- 5 36	+ 4 05 36
Saint Johns, Antigua	61W51	17N06	- 7 28	+ 4 07 28
Sandy Point, St. Christ.	62W50	17N22	-11 20	+ 4 11 20
Salem Montserrat	62W15	16N45	- 8 52	+ 4 08 52
Spanish Town, Brit. Virg.Is	64W26	18N27	-17 44	+ 4 17 44
Tabernacle, St. Christ.	64W46	17N23	-11 04	+ 4 11 04
Vieille Case, Dominica	61W43	15N36	- 6 52	+ 4 06 52
Zion Hill, Nevis	62W32	17N09	-10 08	+ 4 10 08
TRINIDAD AND TOBAGO				
Arima, St. George	61W17...	10N38	- 5 08	+ 4 05 08
Plymouth, Tobago,	60W47	11N13	- 3 08	+ 4 03 08
Port Louis see Scarborough				
Port-of-Spain, Trinidad	61W31	10N39	- 6 04	+ 4 06 04
Princess Town, Victoria	61W23	10N16	- 5 32	+ 4 05 32
Rosborough, Tobago	60W35...	11N15	- 2 20	+ 4 02 20
San Fernando, Victoria	61W28	10N17	- 5 52	+ 4 05 52
Sangre Grande, Trinidad	61W07	10N35	- 4 28	+ 4 04 28
Scarborough, Tobago	60W44	11N11	- 2 56	+ 4 02 56
WINDWARD ISLANDS				
Barrouaille, St. Vincent	61W17	13N14	- 5 08	+ 4 05 08
Castries, St. Lucie	61W00 ..	14N01	- 4 00	+ 4 04 00
Cheltenham, Grenadines	61W11	12N53	- 4 44	+ 4 04 44
Choiseul, St. Lucia	61W03	13N47	- 4 12	+ 4 04 12
Dumfries, Grenadines	61W27	12N28	+ 5 48	+ 4 05 48
Georgetown, St. Vincent	61W08	13N16	- 4 32	+ 4 04 32
Gouyave, Granada	61W44 ..	12N10	- 6 56	+ 4 06 56
Hillsboro, Grenadines	61W28	12N29	- 5 52	+ 4 05 52
Kingstown, St. Vincent	61W14	13N09	- 4 56	+ 4 04 56
Mirabeau, Grenada	61W39	12N08	- 6 36	+ 4 06 36
Soufriere, St. Lucia	61W04	13N52	- 4 16	+ 4 04 16
St. George's, Grenada	61W45	12N03	- 7 00	+ 4 07 00
BRUNEI. Capital: Brunei. A Native State under British				
Protectorate on Borneo. S.T. Meridian 120° EAST				
Bangar	115E04....	4N43	-19 44	- 7 40 16
Brooketown	115E03	5N02	-19 48	- 7 40 12
Brunei	114E57	4N54	-20 12	- 7 39 48
Kuala Belait	114E11	4N35	-23 16	- 7 36 44
Tutong	114E39	4N48	-21 24	- 7 38 36

			: L. M. T. : VARIATION : FROM S.T. : m. s.	G. M. T. VARIATION FROM LMT h. m. s.
BUKOVINA see Rumania.				
BULGARIA. Capital: Sofia. Kingdom situated in southeastern Europe. Standard Time meridian 30° EAST.				
Burgas, Burgas	27E28	42N30	-10 08	- 1 49 52
Eski Zagra see Stara Zagora				
Ferdinand (Ferdinandova) Vratza	23E12	43N25	-27 12	- 1 32 48
Gabrova, Gabrova	25E19	42N52	-18 44	- 1 41 16
Ivailovgrad, Stara Zagora	26E07	41N33	-15 32	- 1 44 28
Jamboli see Yambol				
Kazanlik (Kazanluk) Stara Zagora	25E24	42N37	-18 24	- 1 41 36
Khaskova, Khaskova	25E32	41N55	-17 52	- 1 42 08
Kustendjil, Sofia	22E41	42N17	-29 16	- 1 30 44
Lom (Lom Palanka), Vratsa.....	23E12	43N49	-27 12.....	- 1 32 48
Nikopol, Pleven	24E54	43N42	-20 24	- 1 39 36
Ortakioi see Ivailovgrad				
Pazardjik, Plovdiv	24E19	42N11	-22 44	- 1 37 16
Philippopolis see Plovdiv				
Pleven (Plevna), Pleven.......	24E37	43N25	-21 32.....	- 1 39 28
Plovdiv, Plovdiv	24E44	42N08	-21 04	- 1 38 56
Razgrad, Shumen	26E31	43N32	-13 56	- 1 46 04
Rustchuk (Russe), Shuman	25E57	43N50	-16 12	- 1 43 48
Shipka, Kazanlik	25E20	42N43	-18 40	- 1 41 20
Shumen, Shumen	26E55	43N17	-12 20.....	- 1 47 40
Sistova see Svishtov				
Sliven (Slivno), Burgas	26E19	42N40	-14 44	- 1 45 16
Sofia, Sofia	23E20	42N42	-26 40	- 1 33 20
Stara Zagora, Stara Zagora	25E38	42N25	-17 28	- 1 42 32
Sumla see Shumen				
Svishtov, Svishtov	25E19	43N37	-18 44	- 1 41 16
Tatar Pazardjik see Pazardjik				
Tirnova, Pleven	25E40	43N04	-17 20	- 1 42 40
Trnovo see Tirnovo				
Turnova see Tirnova				
Varna, Shumen	27E55	43N10	- 8 20	- 1 51 40
Vidin(e), Vratza	22E51	44N00	-28 36	- 1 31 24
Yambol, Burgas	26E31	42N28	-13 56	- 1 46 04
Vratsa, Vratsa	23E33	43N12	-25 48	- 1 34 12
BURGENLAND see Austria.				
BURMA. Capital: Rangoon (in hot weather season-Maymyo). Independent June 17, 1947. Standard Time Meridian 97°30' EAST.				
Amarapura, Mandalay	96E04	21N54	- 5 44	- 6 24 16
Akyab, Akyab	92E54	20N09	-18 24	- 6 11 36
Amherst, Amherst	97E35	16N05	+ 0 20	- 6 30 20
Bassein, Bassein	94E44	16N47	-11 04	- 6 18 56
Bhawa, Bhawa.................	97E14	24N15	- 1 04	- 6 28 56
Port White, Chin Hills	93E48	23N14	-14 48	- 6 15 12
Henzada, Henzada	95E28	17N38	- 8 08	- 6 21 52
Kalewa, Upper Chindwin	94E18	23N12	-12 48	- 6 17 12

			L. M. T. VARIATION FROM S. T. m. s.	G. M. T. VARIATION FROM LMT h. m.s.
BURMA (continued)				
Kyaikkama see Amherst				
Lashio, North Shan States	27E45	22N56	+ 1 00	- 6 31 00
Loikaw, Karenni	97E13	19N40	- 1 08	- 6 28 52
Magwe, Magwe	94E55	20N10	-10 20	- 6 19 40
Mandalay, Mandalay.............	96E05....	21N59	- 5 40....	- 6 24 20
Maymyo, Mandalay	96E28	22N02	- 4 08	- 6 25 52
Mergui, Mergui	98E36	12N26	+ 4 24	- 6 34 24
Minbu, Minbu	94E53	20N11	-10 28	- 6 19 32
Moulmein, Amherst	97E38	16N30	+ 0 32	- 6 30 32
Myingyan, Myingyan............	95E23....	21N28	- 8 28....	- 6 21 32
Myitkyna, Myitkyna	97E24	25N23	- 0 24	- 6 29 36
Nattalin, Tharr.	95E33	18N26	- 7 48	- 6 22 12
Pakokku, Pakokku	95E06	21N20	- 9 36	- 6 20 24
Pegu, Pegu	96E29	17N20	- 4 04	- 6 25 56
Prome, Prome	95E13....	18N49	- 9 08....	- 6 20 52
Rangoon, Rangoon	96E09	16N48	- 5 24	- 6 24 36
Sandoway, Sandoway	94E22	18N28	-12 32	- 6 17 28
Shwebo, Shwebo	95E42	22N34	- 7 12	- 6 22 48
Tavoy, Tavoy	98E12	14N04	+ 2 48	- 6 32 48
Tenasserim, Tenasserim.........	99E01....	12N05	+ 6 04....	- 6 36 04
Thazi, Thazi	96E03	20N51	- 5 48	- 6 24 12
Toungoo, Toungoo	96E26	19N57	- 4 16	- 6 25 44
Yanangyaung, Magwe	94E53	20N28	-10 28	- 6 19 32

BYELORUSSIAN S.S.R. see U.S.S.R.

CAICOS ISLANDS see British West Indies.

CAMEROONS See French West Africa. Independent January 1, 1960.

CAMBODIA See French Indo-China. Independent December 29, 1954.

CANADA. Capital: Ottawa. British Dominion,
    situated on North American Continent. Standard Time
    meridians shown by Provinces and Territories.

ALBERTA. Capital: Edmonton, S.T. meridian 105°WEST

Banff	115W34	51N11	-42 16	+ 7 42 15
Calgary	114W04	51N03	-36 16	+ 7 36 16
Camrose	112W50	53N02	-31 20	+ 7 31 20
Cardston	113W29....	49N12	-33 56....	+ 7 33 56
Chipewyan	111W20	58N42	-25 20	+ 7 25 20
Drumheller	112W43	51N28	-31 52	+ 7 31 52
Edmonton	113W20	53N32	-34 00	+ 7 34 00
Fort Vermillion	116W00	58N24	-44 00	+ 7 44 00
Lethbridge	112W50	49N41	-31 20	+ 7 31 20
Lloydminster	110W00	53N17	-20 00	+ 7 20 00
Macleod	113W24	49N44	+33 36	+ 7 33 36
Medicine Hat	110W41	50N02	-22 44	+ 7 22 44
Peace River	117W18	56N14	-49 12	+ 7 49 12
Raymond....................	112W38....	49N30	-30 32....	+ 7 30 32
Red Der	113W48	52N16	-35 12	+ 7 35 12
Metaskiwin	113W22	52N58	-33 28	+ 7 33 28

BRITISH COLUMBIA. Capital: Vancouver, S.T. Meridian 120° West.

Chilliwack, Fraser Valley	121W57	49N10	- 7 48	+ 8 07 48
Cranbrock, Kootenay-East	115W46	49N31	+16 56	+ 7 43 04
Fernie Kootenay-East	115W05	49N30	+19 40	+ 7 40 20
Kamloops, Carlboro	120W20	50N40	- 1 20	+ 8 01 20
Kalowna, Yale	119W30	49N53	+ 2 00	+ 7 58 00

			L. M. T. VARIATION FROM S. T. m. s.	G. M. T. VARIATION FROM LMT h. m. s.

CANADA (continued)

BRITISH COLUMBIA (continued)

			L.M.T.	G.M.T.
Nanaimo, Nanaimo	123W56	49N10	- 15 44	+ 8 15 44
Nelson, Kootenay-West	117W17	49N29	+ 10 52	+ 7 49 08
New Westminster, N.West.	122W55	49N13	- 11 40	+ 8 11 40
North Vancouver, Vancouver North	123W04	49N19	- 12 16	+ 8 12 16
Port Alberni, Comox-Alberni	124W48	49N14	- 19 12	+ 8 19 12
Prince George, Carlboro......	122W46 ...	53N56...	- 11 04...	+ 8 11 04
Queen Charlotte, Skeena	132W04	53N15	- 48 16	+ 8 48 16
Rossland, Kootenay-West	117W49	49N05	+ 8 44	+ 7 51 16
Trail, Kootenay-West	117W44	49N06	+ 9 04	+ 7 50 56
Vancouver, Vancouver	123W07	49N14	-12 28	+ 8 12 28
Vernon, Yale...............	119W16....	50N16....	+ 2 56..	+ 7 57 04
Victoria, Nanaimo	123W21	48N25	- 13 24	+ 8 13 24

LABRADOR (Newfoundland): CAPITAL, St. John's, S.T. meridian 52°30' WEST

Nachvak	63W53	59N03	- 45 32	+ 4 15 32
Nain	61W43	56N33	- 36 52	+ 4 06 52
Okkak.........................61W56.....		57N31...	- 37 44..	+ 4 07 44
Rigolet	56W57	51N11	- 17 48	+ 3 47 48

MANITOBA. Capital: Winnipeg, S.T. meridian 90° WEST

Beausejour	96W31	50N10	- 26 04	+ 6 26 04
Boissevain	100W13	49N14	- 40 52	+ 6 40 52
Brandon.....................	99W57.....	49N51...	- 39 48..	+ 6 39 48
Dauphin	100W04	51N09	- 40 16	+ 6 40 16
Le Pas see The Pas.				
Minnadosa	99W48	50N15	- 39 12	+ 6 39 12
Morden	98W06	49N11	- 32 24	+ 6 32 24
Portage la Prairie..........	98W18.....	49N58...	- 33 12..	+ 6 33 12
Port Nelson	92W50	57N01	- 11 20	+ 6 11 20
St. Boniface	97W08	49N56	- 28 32	+ 6 28 32
Selkirk	96W54	50N08	- 27 36	+ 6 27 36
The Pas	101W15	53N49	- 45 00	+ 6 45 00
Transcona.................,	97W00.....	53N47...	- 28 00..	+ 6 28 00
Winnipeg	97W09	49N53	- 28 36	+ 6 28 36

NEW BRUNSWICK. Capital: Fredericton, S.T. meridian 60° WEST.

Bathurst, Gloucester	65W39	47N37	- 22 36	+ 4 22 36
Campbellton, Restigouche	66W40	48N00	- 26 40	+ 4 26 40
Chatham, Northumberland......	65W28....	47N02...	- 21 52..	+ 4 21 52
Dalhousie, Restigouche	66W22	48N04	- 25 28	+ 4 25 28
Edmunston, Madawaska	68W20	47N22	- 33 20	+ 4 33 20
Frederickton, York	66W39	45N58	- 26 36	+ 4 26 36
Moncton, Westmorland	64W48	46N05	- 19 12	+ 4 19 12
Newcastle, Northunberland....	65W34....	47N00...	- 22 16..	+ 4 22 16
Saint John, Saint John	66W03	45N16	- 24 12	+ 4 24 12
St. Stephen, Charlotte	67W17	45N12	- 29 08	+ 4 29 08
Sackville, Westmorland	64W22	45N54	- 17 38	+ 4 17 28
Sussex, Royal	65W30	45N43	- 22 00	+ 4 22 00
Woodstock, Carleton..........	67W34....	46N09...	- 30 16..	+ 4 30 16

				L. M. T. VARIATION FROM S.T. m. s.	G. M. T. VARIATION FROM LMT h. m. s.

CANADA (Continued)

NORTHWEST TERRITORIES. No Capital. S.T. meridians 60° to 120° WEST.

			L.M.T.	G.M.T.
Albert Harbour, Franklin	77W40	72N47	- 10 40	+ 5 10 40
Elizabeth Harbour, Franklin	92W50	70N35	- 11 20	+ 6 11 20
Fort Franklin, Mackenzie....	123W28.....	65N11...	- 13 52..	+ 8 13 52
Fort McPherson, Mackenzie	134W52	67N26	- 59 28	+ 8 59 28
Fort Smith, Mackenzie	111W53	60N00	+ 32 28	+ 7 27 32
Lake Harbour, Franklin	69W53	62N51	- 39 32	+ 4 39 52
Norman Wells, Mackenzie	126W51	65N17	- 27 24	+ 8 27 24
Pritzler Harbour, Franklin	67W20	62N07	- 29 20	+ 4 29 20

NOVA SCOTIA, Capital: Halifax, S.T. meridian 60° WEST.

Amherst, Cumberland	64W13	45N50	- 16 52	+ 4 16 52
Antigonish, Antigonish	61W58	45N38	- 7 52	+ 4 07 52
Bridgewater, Lunenburg.......	64W33.....	44N22....	- 18 12..	+ 4 18 12
Glace Bay, Cape Breton	59W57	46N12	+ 0 12	+ 3 59 48
Dartmouth, Halifax	63W33	44N40	- 14 12	+ 4 14 12
Guysborough, Guysborough	61W30	45N24	- 6 00	+ 4 06 00
Halifax, Halifax	63W35	44N38	- 14 20	+ 4 14 20
Inverness, Inverness.........	61W18.....	46N14...	- 5 12..	+ 4 05 12
Kentville, Kings	64W30	45N05	- 18 00	+ 4 18 00
Liverpool, Queens	64W43	44N02	- 18 52	+ 4 18 52
Lunenburg, Lunenburg	64W19	44N23	- 17 16	+ 4 17 16
New Glasgow, Pictou	62W39	45N35	- 10 36	+ 4 10 36
New Waterford, Cape Breton...	60W05.....	46N15...	- 0 20..	+ 4 00 20
North Sydney, Cape Breton	60W15	46N13	- 1 00	+ 4 01 00
Pictou, Pictou	62W43	45N41	- 10 52	+ 4 10 52
Port Hawkesbury, Inverness	61W21	45N37	- 5 24	+ 4 05 24
Shelburne, Shelburne	65W19	43N45	- 21 16	+ 4 21 16
Springhill, Cumberland.......	64W04....	45N39...	- 16 16....	+ 4 16 16
Stellarton, Pictou	62W38	45N34	- 10 32	+ 4 10 32
Sydney, Cape Breton	60W12	46N09	- 0 48	+ 4 00 48
Sydney Mines, Cape Breton	60W14	46N15	- 0 56	+ 4 00 56
Trenton, Pictou	62W38	45N37	- 10 32	+ 4 10 32
Truro, Colchester...........	63W17.....	45N22...	- 13 08..	+ 4 13 08
Yarmouth, Yarmouth	66W07	43N50	- 24 28	+ 4 24 28
Westville, Pictou	62W43	45N35	- 10 52	+ 4 10 52
Windsor, Hants.	64W08	45N00	- 16 52	+ 4 16 32

ONTARIO. Capital: Toronto. S.T. Meridians 75° and 90° WEST.

Almonte, Lanark.............	76W12.....	45N14...	- 4 48 ..	+ 5 04 48
Amherstburg, Essex	83W07	42N07	-32 28	+ 5 32 28
Araprior, Renfrew	76W41	45N26	- 6 44	+ 5 06 44
Aurora, York	79W38	44N00	-17 52	+ 5 17 52
Barrie, Simcoe	79W41	44N23	-18 44	+ 5 18 44
Belleville, Hastings........	77W24.....	44N10...	- 9 36 ..	+ 5 09 36
Berlin, Waterloo	80W29	43N27	-21 56	+ 5 21 56
Blind River, Algoma	82W58	46N11	-31 52	+ 5 31 52
Bowmanville, Durham	78W40	43N55	-14 40	+ 5 14 40
Brampton, Peel	79W45	43N41	-19 00	+ 5 19 00
Brantford, Brantford........	80W16.....	43N08...	-21 04 ..	+ 5 21 04
Brockville, Leeds	75W42	44N35	- 2 48	+ 5 02 48
Burlington, Halton	79W49	43N19	-19 16	+ 5 19 16
Campbellford, Northumberland	77W47	44N19	-11 08	+ 5 11 08

CANADA (continued)

			L. M. T. VARIATION FROM S.T.		G. M. T. VARIATION FROM LMT		
ONTARIO (continued)			m. s.		H. M. A.		
Carleton Place, Lanark	76W08	45N09	- 4	32	+ 5	04	32
Chatham, Kent	82W12	42N24	-28	48	+ 5	28	48
Cobalt, Timiskaming..........	79W41.....	47N24...	-18	44...	+ 5	18	44
Cochrane, Cochrane	81W01	49N04	-24	04	+ 5	24	04
Collingwood, Simcoe	80W12	44N30	-20	48	+ 5	20	48
Copper Cliff, Nipissing	81W03	46N28	-24	12	+ 5	24	12
Cornwall, Stormont	74W44	45N01	+ 1	04	+ 4	58	56
Dundas, Wentworth............	79W59....	43N16...	-19	56...	+ 5	19	56
Dunnville, Haldimand	79W37	42N55	-18	28	+ 5	18	28
Eastview see Ottawa							
Fort Erie, Welland	78W56	42N54	-15	44	+ 5	15	44
Fort Frances, Kenora	93W23	48N37	-13	32	+ 6	13	32
Fort William, Algoma.........	89W13.....	48N22...	-56	52...	+ 5	56	52
Galt, Waterloo	80W19	43N22	-21	16	+ 5	21	16
Genanoque, Leeds	76W10	44N20	- 4	40	+ 5	04	40
Georgetown, Halton	79W56	43N39	-19	44	+ 5	19	44
Geraldton, Port Arthur	86W58	49N43	-47	52	+ 5	47	52
Goderich, Huron.............	81W43.....	43N44...	-26	52...	+ 5	26	52
Guelph, Wellington	80W15	43N33	-21	00	+ 5	21	00
Hamilton, Wentworth	79W53	43N16	-19	32	+ 5	19	32
Hanover, Grey	81W01	44N09	-24	04	+ 5	24	04
Hawkesbury, Prescott	74W37	45N37	+ 1	32	+ 4	58	28
Hespeler, Waterloo...........	80W18.....	43N26...	-21	12...	+ 5	21	12
Huntsville, Muskoka	79W14	45N19	-16	56	+ 5	16	56
Ingersoll, Oxford	80W53	43N03	-23	32	+ 5	23	32
Kapuskasing, Cochrane	82W26	49N25	-29	44	+ 5	29	44
Kenora, Kenora	94W26	49N17	-17	44	+ 6	17	44
Kincardine, Bruce............	81W37....	44N11...	-26	88...	+ 5	26	28
Kitchener, Waterloo	80W29	43N27	-21	56	+ 5	21	56
Kingston, Frontenac	76W29	44N14	- 5	56	+ 5	05	56
Listowel, Perth	80W57	43N44	-23	48	+ 5	23	48
Leamington, Essex	82W37	42N03	-30	28	+ 5	30	28
Leaside, York................	79W21....	43N42...	-17	24...	+ 5	17	24
Lindsay, Victoria	78W43	44N21	-14	52	+ 5	14	52
Liskeard, Timiskaning	79W40	47N30	-18	40	+ 5	18	40
London, London	81W15	42N59	-25	00	+ 5	25	00
Meaford, Grey	80W34	44N36	-22	16	+ 5	22	16
Merritton, Lincoln...........	79W13....	43N08...	-16	52...	+ 5	16	52
Midland, Simcoe	79W55	44N05	-19	40	+ 5	19	40
Mimico, York	79W30	43N37	-18	00	+ 5	18	00
Napanee, Lennox & Add.	76W57	44N15	- 7	48	+ 5	07	48
Newmarket, York	79W27	44N03	-17	48	+ 5	17	48
New Toronto, York............	79W31.....	43N36...	-18	04...	+ 5	18	04
Niagara Falls, Welland	79W06	43N04	-16	24	+ 5	16	24
North Bay, Nipissing	79W28	46N18	-17	52	+ 5	17	52
Oakville, Halton	79W40	43N27	-18	40	+ 5	18	40
Orangeville, Dufferin	80W06	43N55	-20	24	+ 5	20	24
Orillia, Simcoe..............	79W25....	44N36...	-17	40..	+ 5	17	40
Oshawa, Ontario	78W51	43N53	-15	24	+ 5	15	24
Ottawa, Carleton	75W42	45N25	- 2	48	+ 5	02	48
Owen Sound, Grey	80W57	44N34	-23	48	+ 5	23	48

CANADA (Continued)
  ONTARIO (Continued)

			L. M. T. VARIATION FROM S.T. m s.	G. M. T. VARIATION FROM LMT h. M. S.
Paris, Brant	80W23	43N12	-21 32	+ 5 21 32
Parry Sound, Parry Sound	80W02	45N21	-20 08	+ 5 20 08
Pembroke, Renfrew...........	77W08.....	45N49...	- 8 32...	+ 5 08 32
Penetanguishone, Simcoe	79W57	44N46	-19 48	+ 5 19 48
Perth, Lanark	76W15	44N54	- 5 00	+ 5 05 00
Peterborough, Peterborough	78W20	44N18	-13 20	+ 5 13 20
Petrolia, Lambton	82W09	42N52	-28 36	+ 5 28 36
Picton, Prince Edward.......	77W08.....	44N00....-	- 8 32.....	+5 08 32
Port Arthur, Algoma	89W13	48N25	-56 52	+ 5 56 52
Port Colborne, Welland	79W15	42N53	-17 00	+ 5 17 00
Port Hope, Durham	78W17	43N57	-13 08	+ 5 13 08
Prescott, Granville	75W31	44N43	- 2 04	+ 5 02 04
Preston, Waterloo...........	80W20.....	43N24...	-21 20...	+ 5 21 20
Renfrew, Renfrew	76W42	45N29	- 6 48	+ 5 06 48
Riverside, Essex	82W58	42N20	-31 52	+ 5 31 52
St. Catharines, Lincoln	79W15	43N10	-17 00	+ 5 17 00
St. Marys, Perth	81W08	43N15	-24 32	+ 5 24 32
St. Thomas, Elgin..........	81W12.....	42N47...	-24 48...	+ 5 24 48
Sernia, Lambton	82W24	42N58	-29 36	+ 5 29 36
Sault Ste. Marie, Algoma	84W21	46N21	-37 24	+ 5 37 24
Simcoe, Norfolk	80W18	42N50	-21 12	+ 5 21 12
Smiths Fall, Lanark	76W01	44N54	- 4 04	+ 5 04 04
Southampton, Bruce.........	81W23.....	44N30.....	-25 32...	+ 5 25 32
Stratford, Perth	80W59	43N22	-23 56	+ 5 23 56
Strathroy, Middlesex	81W37	42N57	-26 28	+ 5 26 28
Sturgeon Falls, Nipissing	79W56	46N22	-17 44	+ 5 17 44
Sudbury, Nipissing	81W00	46N30	-24 00	+ 5 24 00
Thorold, Welland...........	79W12.....	43N07...	-16 48...	+ 5 16 48
Tillsonburg, Oxford	80W44	42N52	-22 56	+ 5 22 56
Timmins, Cochrane	81W20	48N28	-25 20	+ 5 25 20
Toronto, York	79W22	43N39	-17 28	+ 5 17 28
Trenton, Hastings	77W34	44N07	-10 16	+ 5 10 16
Walkerton, Grey............	81W09.....	44N07...	-24 36...	+ 5 24 36
Wallaceburg, Kent	82W23	42N35	-29 32	+ 5 29 32
Waterloo, Waterloo	80W31	43N28	-22 04	+ 5 22 04
Welland, Welland	79W15	43N00	-17 00	+ 5 17 00
Weston, York	79W31	43N42	-18 04	+ 5 18 04
Whitby, Ontario...........	78W55.....	43N52...	-15 40...	+ 5 15 40
Windsor, Essex	83W02	42N19	-32 08	+ 5 32 08
Woodstock, Oxford	80W45	43N07	-23 00	+ 5 23 00

QUEBEC. Capital: Quebec, S.T., meridian 60° and 75° West;
   68° WEST is dividing line.

Amos, Abitibi..............	78W07.....	48N34...	-12 28...	+ 5 12 28
Arvida, Chicoutini	71W11	48N26	+15 16	+ 4 44 44
Asbestos, Richmond	71W57	45N46	+12 12	+ 4 47 48
Aylner East, Hull	75W52	45N23	- 3 28	+ 5 03 28
Bagotville, Chicoutini	70W53	48N21	+16 28	+ 4 43 32
Beauharnois, Beauharnois,....73W53.....		45N19...	+ 4 28...	+ 4 55 32
Beauport, Quebec	71W12	46N52	+15 12	+ 4 44 48
Berthierville, Berthier	73W11	46N05	+ 7 16	+ 4 52 44
Buckingham, Hull	75W25	45N37	- 1 40	+ 5 01 40

CANADA (Continued)			L. M. T. VARIATION FROM S.T.	G. M. T. VARIATION FROM LMT
QUEBEC (Continued)			m. s	h. m. s
Cap de la Madeleine Champlain	72W30	46N22	+10 00	+ 4 50 00
Chicoutimi, Chicoutimi	71W05	48N26	+15 40	+ 4 44 20
Coaticook, Stanstead........	71W49.....	45N08...	+12 44...	+ 4 47 16
Cote St. Michel, Hochelaga	73W36	45N34	+ 5 36	+ 4 54 24
Cowansville, Missisquoi	72W45	45N12	+ 9 00	+ 4 51 00
Dolbeau, Roberval	72W15	48N53	+11 00	+ 4 49 00
Donnacona, Portneuf........	71W42.....	46N40...	+13 12...	+ 4 46 48
Drummondville, Drumond	72W29	46N53	+10 04	+ 4 49 56
East Angus, Compton	71W40	45N29	+13 20	+ 4 46 40
Farnham, Missisquoi	72W59	45N17	+ 8 04	+ 4 51 56
Granby, Shefford	72W44	45N24	+ 9 04	+ 4 50 56
Grand Mere, St. Maurice ...	72W41.....	46N37...	+ 9 16...	+ 4 50 44
Hull, Hull	75W44	45N26	- 2 56	+ 5 02 56
Iberville, Iberville	73W14	45N18	+ 7 04	+ 4 52 56
Joliette, Joliette	73W27	46N01	+ 6 12	+ 4 53 48
Jonquiere, Chicoutimi	71W05	48N26	+15 40	+ 4 44 20
Kenogami, Chicoutimi........	71W14....	48N26...	+15 04...	+ 4 44 56
Lachine, Jacques-Cartier	73W40	45N26	+ 5 20	+ 4 54 40
Dachute, Argenteuil	74W20	45N39	+ 2 40	+ 4 57 20
Laprairie, Laprairie	73W29	45N25	+ 6 04	+ 4 53 56
La-Tuque, St. Maurice	72W47	47N26	+ 8 52	+ 4 51 08
Lauzon, Levis...............	71W10....	46N50...	+15 20...	+ 4 44 40
Laval Rapides, Laval	75W41	45N33	+ 5 16	+ 4 54 44
Levis, Levis	71W12	46N49	+15 12	+ 4 44 48
Longueuil, Chambly	73W31	45N32	+ 5 56	+ 4 54 04
Louiseville, Maskinonga	72W57	46N16	+ 8 12	+ 4 51 48
Magog, Stanstead............	72W10....	45N17...	+11 20...	+ 4 48 40
Malaretic, Pontiac	78W07	48N08	-12 28	+ 5 12 28
Matune, Matane	67W34	48N50	-30 16	+ 4 30 16
Magantic, Frontenac	70W52	45N35	+16 32	+ 4 43 28
Montmagny, Montmagny	70W33	46N59	+17 48	+ 4 42 12
Montreal, Iron....	73W34....	45N32...	+ 5 44...	+ 4 54 16
Nicolet, Nicolet	72W38	46N14	+ 9 28	+ 4 50 32
Noranda, Timiskaming	79W04	48N15	-15 16	+ 5 16 16
Outramont, Hochalaga	73W37	45N31	+ 5 32	+ 4 54 28
Pointe-aux-Trambles, Laval	75W29	45N38	+ 6 04	+ 4 53 56
Point Claira, Jacques-Cartier..................	73W49.....	45N26...	+ 4 44...	+ 4 55 16
Port Alfred, Chicoutimi	70W53	48N20	+16 28	+ 4 43 32
Quebec, Quebec	71W13	46N48	+15 08	+ 4 44 52
Richmond, Richmond	72W09	45N40	+11 24	+ 4 48 36
Rimouski, Rimouski..........	68W32.....	48N27...	+25 52...	+ 4 34 08
Riviere du Loup, R. du Loup	69W32	47N49	+21 52	+ 4 38 08
Robervale, Roberval	72W14	48N31	+11 04	+ 4 48 56
Rouyn, Timiskeming	79W02	48N14	-16 08	+ 5 16 08
Ste. Anne de Bellevue, Jacques Cartier..........	73W55.....	45N39...	+ 4 20...	+ 4 55 40
Ste Hyacinthe, Ste. Hyacinth	72W58	45N38	+ 8 08	+ 4 51 52
St. Jean, St. Joan	73W15	45N19	+ 7 00	+ 4 53 00
St. Jerome, Terrebonne	74W00	45N47	+ 4 00	+ 4 56 00

			L. M. T. VARIATION FROM S.T.	G. M. T. VARIATION FROM LMT
			m. s.	h. m. s.
CANADA (Continued)				
QUEBEC (Continued)				
St. Lambert, Chambly	73W30	45N30	+ 6 00	+ 4 54 00
St. Laurent, Jac. Cartier	73W39	45N31	+5 24	+ 4 54 36
St. Laurent d'Orleans, Montmorency..............	71W01.....	46N32...	+15 56...	+ 4 44 04
St. Pierre, Jac. Cartier	73W39	45N26	+ 5 24	+ 4 54 36
Ste. Agathe des Monts, Torrebonne	74W17	46N03	+ 2 52	+ 4 57 08
Sta. Therese de Blainville, Terrebonne	73W50	45N38	+ 4 40	+ 4 55 20
Shawinigan Falls, St. Maur.	72W45	46N33	+ 9 00	+ 4 51 00
Sherbrooke, Sherbrooke	71W54	45N24	+12 24	+ 4 47 36
Sorel, Richelieu	73W07	46N03	+ 7 32	+ 4 52 28
Thetford Mines, Megantic....	71W18......	46N05...	+14 42...	+ 4 45 12
Trois Rivieres (Three Rivers), Three Rivers	72W34	46N21	+ 9 44	+ 4 50 16
Val d'Or, Pontiac	77W46	48N07	-11 04	+ 5 11 04
Valleyfield (Salaberry-de-) Beauharnois..............	74W03...	45N16...	+ 3 28...	+ 4 56 32
Verdun, Hochelaga	73W34	45N27	+ 5 44	+ 4 54 16
Victoriaville, Arthabaska	71W58	46N04	+12 08	+ 4 47 52
Ville La Salle, Hochelaga	73W38	45N25	+ 5 28	+ 4 54 32
Waterloo, Shefford	72W31	45N21	+ 9 56	+ 4 50 04
Westmount, Hochelaga.........73W36....	45N29...	+ 5 36...	+ 4 54 24	
Windsor, Richmond	72W00	45N34	+12 00	+ 4 48 00
PRINCE EDWARD ISL. Capital: Charlotteville, S.T. meridian 60° WEST.				
Alma, Prince	64W06	45N52	-16 24	+ 4 16 24
Charlottstown, Queens	63W07	46N14	-12 28	+ 4 12 28
Georgetown, Kings............	62W31.....	46N11...	-10 08 ..	+ 4 10 08
Souris, Kings	62W15	46N21	- 9 00	+ 4 09 00
Summerside, Prince	63W47	46N24	-15 08	+ 4 15 08
SASKATCHEWAN. Capital: Saskatoon, S.T. meridian 105° WEST.				
Estevan, Assiniboia	103W00	49N09	+ 8 00	+ 6 52 00
Island Falls..............	102W21.....	55N32...	+10 36...	+ 6 49 24
Kinderlev	109W09	51N27	-16 36	+ 6 16 36
Melfort, Melfort	104W37	52N52	+ 1 32	+ 6 58 28
Melville, Melville	102W47	50N56	+ 8 52	+ 6 51 08
Moose Jaw, Moose Jaw	105W33	50N24	- 2 12	+ 7 02 12
North Battleford, The Battlefords.............	108W18......	52N46...	-13 12...	+ 7 13 12
Prince Albert, P. Albert	105W45	53N13	- 3 00	+ 7 03 00
Regina, Regina	104W36	50N27	+ 1 36	+ 6 58 24
Suskatoon, Saskatoon	106W39	52N08	- 6 36	+ 7 06 36
Shaunavon................	108W25.....	49N37...	-13 40...	+ 7 13 40
Swift Current, S. Current	107W47	50N17	-11 08	+ 7 11 08
Weyburn, Weyburn	103W51	49N39	+ 4 36	+ 6 55 24
Yorktown, Saskatoon	102W28	51N14	+10 08	+ 6 49 52
YUKON TERRITORY. Capital: Dawson, S.T. meridian 135° WEST.				
Black Hills	138W52	63N29	-15 28	+ 9 15 28
Bonanza	139W19	63N55	-17 16	+ 9 17 16
Carcross	134W42	60N10	+ 1 12	+ 8 58 48
Carmacks Post	136W17	62N05	- 5 08	+ 9 05 08

			L. M. T. VARIATION FROM S.T.		G. M. T. VARIATION FROM LMT		
			m.	s.	h.	m.	s.

CANADA (Continued)

YUKON TERRITORY (Continued)

Conrad	134W33	60N04	+ 1	48	+ 8	58	12
Dawson	139W26	64N04	-17	44	+ 9	17	44
Dugdale...................	134W55.....	60N35...	+ 0	20...	+ 8	59	40
Fortymile	140W33	64N26	-22	12	+ 9	22	12
Keno Hill	135W21	63W57	- 1	24	+ 9	01	24
Klondike see Dawson							
Mayo Landing	135W51	63N36	- 3	24	+ 9	03	24
Ogilvie..................	139W45.....	63N34...	-19	00...	+ 9	19	00
Pelly see Selkirk							
Radford	139W07	63N45	-16	28	+ 9	16	28
Selkirk	137W24	62N46	- 9	36	+ 9	09	36
Stewart	139W27	63W19	+17	48	+ 9	17	48
Teslin..................	132W43.....	60N10...	+ 9	08...	+ 8	50	52
Thistle Creek	139W29	63N04	-17	56	+ 9	17	56
Whitehorse	135W03	60N43	- 0	12	+ 9	00	12
Woundedmoose	138W39	63N33	-14	36	+ 9	14	36
Yukon Crossing	136W30	62N21	- 6	00	+ 9	06	00

CAMBODIA see French Indo China.

CAMEROONS see 1. French Equatorial Africa.
2. Nigeria.

CANAL ZONE see Panama Canal Zone.

CANARY ISLANDS. Capital: Santa Cruz de Tenerife.

The Canary Islands, located in the NorthAtlantic, belong to Spain and were divided into the Provinces of Santa Cruz de Tenerife and Las Palmas in 1927. Standard Time Meridian 15° WEST.

Arrecife, Lanzarote	13W32	28N58	+ 5	52	+ 0	54	08
Cabras, Fuert.	13W51	28N28	+ 4	36	+ 0	55	24
Las Palmas, Gran Canaria	15W24	28N07	- 1	36	+ 1	01	36
Orotava, Tenerife	16W32	28N25	- 6	08	+ 1	06	08
San Sebastian, Gomera	17W06	28N05	- 8	24	+ 1	08	24
Santa Cruz, Palma...........	17W46.....	28N40...	-11	04...	+ 1	11	04
Santa Cruz de Tenerife, Ten.	16W15	28N28	- 5	00	+ 1	05	00
Valverde, Hierro	17W55	27N48	-11	40	+ 1	11	40

CAPE VERDE ISLANDS. Capital: Praia.

Portuguese Colony, situated in the North Atlantic. Standard Time Meridian 30° WEST.

Mindelo, St. Vincente	24W57	16N53	+20	04	+ 1	39	56
Nova Sintra, Brava	24W42	14N52	+21	12	+ 1	38	48
Porto Inglez, Mayo	23W13	15N09	+27	08	+ 1	32	52
Praia, St. Tiago	23W31	14N56	+25	56	+ 1	34	04
Ribeira Brava, St. Nicolau..	24W19.....	16N37...	+22	44...	+ 1	37	16
Ribeira Grande, St. Antao	25W04	17N11	+19	44	+ 1	40	16
Sal-Rei, Boa Vista	22W57	16N11	+28	12	+ 1	31	48
Santa Maria, Sal	22W54	16N36	+28	24	+ 1	31	36
Sao Felipe, Fogo	24W30	14N54	+22	00	+ 1	38	00

CAROLINA ISLANDS see South Sea Mandated Territories

CATALANIA see Spain.

CAYMAN ISLANDS see British West Indies.

CELEBES see Netherlands East Indies.

CENTRAL AFRICAN PROTECTORATE see Nyasaland.
CENTRAL AFRICAN REPUBLIC See French Equatorial Africa.

			: L. M. T.	G. M. T.
Independent August 13, 1960			: L. M. T.	G. M. T.
CERAM ISLAND see Netherlands East Indies			: VARIATION	VARIATION
CESKOSLOVENSKO see Czechoslovakia			: FROM S.T.	FROM LMT

CEYLON. Capital: Colombo. Independent February 4, 1948

Standard Time Meridian 82°30' EAST			m. s.	h. m. s.
Anuradhapura, North Central	80E24	8N21	- 8 24	- 5 21 36
Badulla, Uva	81E03	6N59	- 5 48	- 5 24 12
Batticaloa, Eastern	81E42	7N45	- 3 12	- 5 26 48
Colombo, Western	79E53	6N57	-10 28	- 5 19 32
Galle, Southern	80E13	6N02	- 9 08	- 5 20 56
Jaffna, Northern............	80E01......	9N40...	- 9 56...	- 5 20 04
Kandy, Central	80E38	7N18	- 7 28	- 5 22 32
Kurunegale, North-Western	80E22	7N29	- 8 32	- 5 21 28
Ratnapura, Sabar.	80E24	7N41	- 8 24	- 5 21 36
Trincomalea, Eastern	81E15	8N33	- 5 00	- 5 25 00

CHAD see French Equatorial Africa. Independent August 11, 1960
CHANNEL ISLANDS see Great Britain.
CHATHAM ISLANDS. Capital: Waitangi, Dependency of New
     Zealand. A peculiar situation exists here in
     Standard Time meridian. It is based on 183°45'
     EAST (actually 176°15' West) of Greenwich upon
     which calculation is based. However, at present
     time (1948) the meridian being used is 180° EAST.

Waitangi	176E34	43S57	-28 44	-11 46 16

CHILE. Capital: Santiago. Republic situated in South
     America. Standard Time meridian 60° WEST.

Ancud, Chiloe	73W50	41S52	-55 20	+ 4 55 20
Angol, Arauco	72W43	37S48	-50 52	+ 4 50 52
Antofagasta, Antofagasta....	70W24......	23S39...	-41 36...	+ 4 41 36
Arauco, Arauco	73W19	37S46	-53 16	+ 4 53 16
Arica, Tarapaca	70W20	18S29	-41 20	+ 4 41 20
Bulnes, Nuble	72W19	36S45	-49 16	+ 4 49 16
Calama, Antofagasta	68W56	22S28	-35 44	+ 4 35 44
Cauquenes, Maule........	72W19......	35S59..	- 49 16	+ 4 49 16
Chillan, Nuble	72W07	36S36	-48 28	+ 4 48 28
Charanal, Atacama	70W40	26S21	-42 40	+ 4 42 40
Concepcion, Concepcion	73W03	36S49	-52 12	+ 4 52 12
Constitucion, Maule	72W24	35S20	-49 36	+ 4 49 36
Copiapa, Atacama...........	70W21......	27S22..	- 41 24...	+ 4 41 24
Coquimbo, Coquimbo	71W22	29S58	-45 28	+ 4 45 28
Curepto, Talca	72W01	35S08	-48 04	+ 4 48 04
Curicó, Curico	71W15	35S00	-45 00	+ 4 45 00
Illapel, Cocuimbo	71W11	31S37	-44 44	- 4 44 44
Iquique, Tarapaca..........	70W10	20S13..	-40 40....	+ 4 40 40
La Serena, Coquimbo	71W16	29S54	-45 04	+ 4 45 04
La Union, Valdivia	73W02	40S10	-52 08	+ 4 52 08
Ligua, Aconcagua	71W16	32S28	-45 04	+ 4 45 04
Linares, Linares	71W37	35S51	-46 28	+ 4 46 28
Los Angeles, Bio-Bio........	72W22......	37S28..	-49 28...	+ 4 49 28
Magallanes see Punta Arenas				
Molina, Talca	71W16	35S08	-45 04	+ 4 45 04

			L. M. T. VARIATION FROM S.T.		G. M. T. VARIATION FROM LMT		
			M.	S.	h.	m.	s.
CHILE (Continued)							
Nueva Imperial, Cautin	72W57	38S45	-51	48	+ 4	51	48
Osorno, Osorno	73W08	40S35	-52	32	+ 4	52	32
Parral, Linares............	71W50.....	36S08...	-47	20...	+ 4	47	20
Pitrufquen, Cautin	72W39	38S59	-50	36	+ 4	50	36
Puerto Aysen, Aysen	72W51	45S23	-51	24	+ 4	51	24
Puerto Montt, Llanquihue	72W56	41S28	-51	44	+ 4	51	44
Puerto Natales, Mag.	72W30	51S43	-50	00	+ 4	50	00
Punta Arenas, Mag...........	70E53.....	53S10....	-43	32...	+ 4	43	32
Quillota, Valparaiso	71W16	32S53	-45	04	+ 4	45	04
Rancagua, O'Higgins	70W45	34S10	-43	00	+ 4	43	00
Rango, O'Higgins	70W53	34S24	-43	32	+ 4	43	32
San Antonio, Santiago	71W39	33S35	-46	36	+ 4	46	36
San Bernardo, Santiago......	70W44.....	33S36....	-42	56...	+ 4	42	56
San Carlos, Nuble	71W57	36S26	-47	48	+ 4	47	48
San Felipe, Acpncagua	70W45	32S45	-43	00	+ 4	43	00
San Fernando, Colchagua	71W00	34S35	-44	00	+ 4	44	00
Santa Cruz, Curico	71W22	34S38	-45	28	+ 4	45	28
Santiago, Santiago..........	70W40.....	33S27....	-42	40...	+ 4	42	40
Talca, Talca	71W40	35S26	-46	40	+ 4	46	40
Talcahuano, Concepcion	73W06	36S45	-52	24	+ 4	52	24
Tamuco, Cautin	72W36	38S45	-50	24	+ 4	50	24
Tocopilla, Antogagasta	70W13	22S06	-40	52	+ 4	40	52
Tome, Concepcion............	72W53.....	36S38...	-51	32...	+ 4	51	32
Traiguen, Cautin	72W40	38S15	-50	40	+ 4	50	40
Valdivia, Valdivia	73W17	39S49	-53	08	+ 4	53	08
Valparaiso, Valparaiso	71W39	33S03	-46	36	+ 4	46	36
Victoria, Cautin	72W19	38S13	-49	16	+ 4	49	16
Vicuna, Coquimbo............	70W43.....	30S01....	-42	52...	+ 4	42	52
Vina del Mar, Aconcaqua	71W35	33S01	-46	20	+ 4	46	20

CHINA, Peoples Republic, September 21, 1949

Capital: Peiping (Peking). Standard Time Meridians are 82°30', 90°, 105° and 120° EAST. Cities
belonging to Manchukuo between 1932 and 1945
are marked "M". Chinese city names ending in -fu
denote cities of first rank; those ending in -ting,
cities of second rank; -chou or -chow, cities of third
rank; and in -hsien, cities of fourth rank. Those end-
ings are frequently omitted. Coordinates based on Index
to V. K. Ting's Atlas of China.

Amoy, Fu.	118E05	24N27	- 7	40	- 7	52	20
Antung, Ku. M...............	119E18.....	33N46...	- 2	40...	- 7	57	12
Bielotsarsk see Kysyl Khoto							
Buluni-Tokhoi, Mo.	87E19	47N02	-10	44	- 5	49	16
Canton, Kwg.	113E16	23N07	-26	56	- 7	33	04
Changan, She.	108E34	34N16	+14	16	- 7	14	16
Changchun, Kir. M..........	125E20.....	43N54...	+21	20...	- 8	21	20
Changsha, Hun.	112E59	28N12	-28	04	- 7	31	56
Changteh, Hun.	111E32	29N02	-33	52	- 7	26	08
Chaoyang, Kwg.	116E35	23N17	+46	20	- 7	46	20

CHINA (Continued)

Charbin see Harbin					
Chefoo, Shg.	121E24	37N32	+ 5 36	- 8 05 36	
Chengtu, Sz.	104E04	30N40	- 3 44	- 6 56 16	
Chiangtzu see Gyantse.					
Chilin see Kirin.					
Chi-Lung see Girang Dzong.					
Chinan see Licheng.					
Chincow see Chinhsien					
Chinguan, Hop...............	115E29.....	38N32...	-18 04...	- 7 41 56	
Chinhsien, L.	121E07	41N07	+ 4 28	- 8 04 28	
Chungking see Pahsien					
Chung Wan see Victoria, Hongkong.					
Darien, M.	121E39	38N56	+ 6 36	- 8 06 36	
Fangcheng, L.................	124E05.....	40N28...	+16 20...	- 8 16 20	
Fort Bayard (French), Kwg.	110E24	21N11	+21 36	- 7 21 36	
Fuchow see Minhow					
Girang Kzong, Tib.	85E16	28N28	+11 04	- 5 41 04	
Gyantse, Tib.	89E36	28N57	+28 24	- 5 59 24	
Haicheng, L................122E45......40N51....+11 00...				- 8 11 00	
Haimen (ting), Ku.	121E11	31N56	+ 4 44	- 8 04 44	
Hangchow, Che.	120E10	30N17	+ 0 40	- 8 00 40	
Hankow, Hup.	114E17	30N33	-22 52	- 7 37 08	
Harbin, Kir.	126E39	45N47	-33 24	- 8 26 36	
Hofei, see Luchow					
Hong Kong (See British Colony)114E12		22N16	-23 24	- 7 36 40	
Hoppo, Kwg.	109E10	21N38	-16 40	- 7 16 40	
Hopu see Hoppo.					
Hsian see Changan.					
Hsiang-Chiang see Hongkong.					
Hsiangsiang see Siangsiang					
Hsinking see Changehun.					
Huangyen, Che................121E15......28N41...			+ 5 00...	- 8 05 00	
Hwaian, Ku.	119E12	33N31	- 3 12	- 7 56 48	
Hwaining, An.	117E02	30N31	-11 52	- 7 48 08	
Iyang see Yiyang.					
Jibhalanta, Mo.	96E49	47N45	+27 16	- 6 27 16	
Jikotse see Zikatse.					
Jirgalanta, Mo.	91E38	48N01	+ 6 32	- 6 06 32	
Jukao, Ku.	120E33	32N24	+ 2 12	- 8 02 12	
Kaifeng, Hon.................	114E21.....	34N48...	-22 36...	- 7 37 24	
Kalgan see Wanchuan.					
Kanting see Tatsienlu.					
Kaoyu, Ku.	119E28	32N46	- 2 08	- 7 57 52	
Kashgar. Sin.	75E59	39N27	-26 04	- 5 03 56	
Khem-Belder see Kysyl Khoto.					
Kiangpeih, Sz.	106E35	29N36	+ 6 20	- 7 06 20	
Kiangtu, Ku.	119E27	32N24	- 2 12	- 7 57 48	
Kiangyin, Ku.	120E16	31N55	+ 1 04	- 8 01 04	
Kienli, Hup.	112E56	29N49	-28 16	- 7 31 44	
Kirin, Kir..M.................	126E32.....	43N51	+26 08...	- 8 26 08	
Kobdo see Jirgalanta.					
Kongmoon City see Sunwui.					
Koputo see Jirgalanta					
k'Ou-Lun see Ulan Bater Hotl.					

			L. M. T. VARIATION FROM S.T.	G. M. T. VARIATION FROM LMT
			m. s.	h. m. s.

CHINA (continued)

Place	Long.	Lat.	L.M.T. Variation from S.T. (m. s.)	G.M.T. Variation from LMT (h. m. s.)
Kulan, see Ulan Bator Hotc.				
Kunming, Yun.	102E41	25N04	- 9 16	- 6 50 44
Kwangchou, Kwg.	113E16	23N07	+33 04	- 7 33 04
Kwangchentzu see Changchun.				
Kwangchowfu see Canton.				
Kweisui, Sui.	111E37	40N17	-33 32	- 7 26 28
Kweiyer, Kwei.	106E13	26N35	+ 4 52	- 7 04 52

(This is based on 105°, but there is still some question whether Kweiyang S.T. is not based on 120° EAST.)

Place	Long.	Lat.	L.M.T. Variation from S.T. (m. s.)	G.M.T. Variation from LMT (h. m. s.)
Kysyl Khorai see Kysyl Khoto.				
Krysl Khoto, see Tannu Tuva	94E02	51N41	+16 08	- 6 18 08
Lasa (Lhassa), Tibet	91E11	29N43	+34 44	- 6 04 44
Laiyang, Hun	112E30.....	26N26..	-30 00..	- 7 30 00
Liaoyang, L.	123E12	41N16	+12 48	- 8 12 48
Licheng, Shg.	117E00	36N41	-12 00	- 7 48 00
Lienshui see Antung.				
Liling, Hung.	113E30	27N41	-25 00	- 7 34 00
Linchou (Linchow) see Hoppo.				
Lingling, Hun.	111E32	26N15	-33 52	- 7 26 00
Luchow, An. M.	117E18	31N54	-10 48	- 7 49 12
Lungchiang see Taitsihar.				
Lushur see Port Arthur.				
Lwanhsien, Hop.	118E44.....	38N45..	- 5 04.	- 7 54 56
Maoming, Kwg. M	110E53	21N45	+23 32	- 7 23 32
Minhow, Fu.	119E19	26N05	- 2 44	- 7 57 16
Mukden, L. M.	113E26	41N48	-26 16	- 7 33 44
Namling Dzong, Tibet	89E03	29N40	+26 12	- 5 56 12
Namulingshun see Namling Dzong.				
Nanchang, Ki.	115E53	28N40	-16 28	- 7 43 32
Nanching see Nanking				
Nankang, Ki................	116E04.....	29N24..	-15 44..	- 7 44 16
Nanking, Ku.	118E48	32N03	- 4 48	- 7 55 12
Nanning see Yungning.				
Nengluang see Ngamring.				
Newchwang see Yingkow.				
Ngamring, Tibet	87E36	30N25	+20 24	- 5 50 24
Ninghsia, Ni.	106E19	38N28	+ 5 16	- 7 05 16
Ninghsian, Che..............	121E32.....	29N54..	+ 6 08..	- 8 06 08
Ningpo see Ninghsien.				
Ocheng see Wuchang.				
Pahsien, Sz.	103E40	30N38	- 5 20	- 6 54 40
Pakhoi see Peihai.				
Poaking see Shaoyang.				
Paoting see Chingyuan				
Peihai, Kwg.	109E05	21N24	+16 20	- 7 16 20
Peiping, Hop.	116E24	39N36	-14 24	- 7 45 36
Peking see Peiping.				
Penglai, Shg...............	117E14.....	35N08..	- 11 04..	- 7 48 56
Pinchiang see Harbin.				
Port Arthur, Kwg.	121E16	38N48	+ 5 04	- 8 05 04
Ryojunko see Port Arthur.				

			L. M. T. VARIATION FROM S.T.	G. M. T. VARIATION FROM LMT
			m. s.	h. m. s.
CHINA (Continued)				
Shanghai, Ku.	121E30	31N14	+ 6 00	- 8 86 00
Shaosing, Che.	120E34	30N00	+ 2 16	- 8 02 16
Shaoyang, Hun.	111E23	27N15	-34 28	- 7 25 32
Shenyang(shih) see Mukden.				
Sian see Changan.				
Siangsiang, Hun.	112E28	27N48	-30 08	- 7 29 52
Siackan, Hup	113E55	30N56	-24 20	- 7 35 40
Sining, Ts.	101E49	36N37	-12 44	- 6 47 16
Sinmin, L.	122E48	41N59	+ 7 12	- 8 07 12
Soochow see Wuhsien.				
Suchou (Suchow) see Tungshan.				
Sufu see Kashgar.				
Sunwui, Kwg.	113E03	22N31	-27 48	- 7 32 12
Taian, Shg.	117E09	36N14	-11 24	- 7 48 36
Talien see Darien.				
Tatsienlu, Si.	102E02	30N03	-11 52	- 6 48 08
Tengchow see Penglai.				
Tientsin, Hop.	117E12	39N08	-11 12	- 7 48 48
Tihua (Tihwafu) see Urumchi.				
Tsitsihar, Hei. M	123E57	47N22	+15 48	- 8 15 48
Tungshau, Ku.	117E16	34N18	-10 56	- 7 49 04
Ulaan Goom, Mo.	92E02	49N58	+ 8 08	- 6 08 08
Ulan Bater Hoto, Mo.	106E45	47N56	+ 7 00	- 7 07 00
Uliossutai see Jibhalanta.				
Urga see Ulan Bator Hoto.				
Urumchi, Sin.	87E36	43N48	+20 24	- 5 50 24
Wanchuan, Cha.	114E55	40N50	-20 20	- 7 39 40
Weihaiwei, Shg.	122E06	37N31	+ 8 24	- 8 08 24
Wuchang, Hup	114E53	30N23	-20 28	- 7 39 32
Wuhsien. Ku.	120E18	31N35	+ 1 12	- 8 01 12
Wuhu, An	118E23	31N2J	- 6 28	- 7 53 32
Yangchow see Kiangtu.				
Yangchuan, Sha.	112E35	37N32	-29 40	- 7 30 20
Yatung, Tibet	89E53	27N26	- 0 28	- 5 59 32
Yentai see Chefco.				
Yingkow, L.	122E13	40N10	+ 8 52	- 8 08 52
Yiyang, Hun.	112E20	28N43	-30 40	- 7 29 20
Yungchou (Yungchow) see Lingling:				
Yungki see Kirin.				
Yunnan see Kunming.				
Yungning, Kwi	108E18	28N48	+13 12	- 7 13 12

(This is based on 105°, but there is still
some question whether Yungning S.T. is not
based on 120° EAST.)

| Zikatse, Tibet | 88E53 | 29N15 | - 4 28 | - 5 55 32 |

CHINESE TURKESTAN see China.

CHOSEN see Korea.

COCHIN-CHINA see French Indo-China.

CHUNG-HUA MIN-KUO see China.

CHUVASHIAN REPUBLIC see U.S.S.R.

CHYPRE see Cyprus.

COLOMBIA. Capital: Bogota. Republic, situated in South America. Standard Time meridian 75° WEST.			L. M. T. VARIATION FROM S.T. m. s.	G. M. T. VARIATION FROM LMT h. m. s.
Aipe, Huila	75W15	3N13	- 1 00	+ 5 01 00
Antioquia, Antioquia	75W50	6N36	- 3 20	+ 5 03 20
Arauca, Arauca	70W45	7N05	+17 00	+ 4 43 00
Barranquilla, Atlantico	74W47	10N58	+ 0 52	+ 4 59 08
Bogota, Cund.	74W05	4N40	+ 3 40	+ 4 56 20
Bolivar, Santander..........	73W46	5N59	+ 4 58	+ 4 55 04
Bucaramanga, Santander	73W09	7N10	+ 7 24	+ 4 52 36
Buenaventura, Valle	77W05	3N54	- 8 20	+ 5 08 20
Cali, Valle	76W30	3N25	- 6 00	+ 5 06 00
Caqueza, Cund.	73W55	4N25	+ 4 20	+ 4 55 40
Cartagena, Bolivar..........	75W32	10N26	- 2 08	+ 5 02 08
Chiquinquira, Boyaca	73W50	5N37	+ 4 40	+ 4 55 20
Cucuta, Norte de Santander	72W31	7N54	+ 9 55	+ 4 50 04
Guapi, Cauca	77W53	2N36	-11 32	+ 5 11 32
Ibague, Tolima	75W13	4N27	- 0 52	+ 5 00 52
La Union, Antiequia..........	75W22	5N58	- 1 28	+ 5 01 28
Manizales, Caldas	75W32	5N05	- 2 08	+ 5 02 08
Medellin, Antiequia	75W35	6N15	- 2 20	+ 5 02 20
Mitu Airport, Vaupes	70W03	1N08	+19 48	+ 4 40 12
Mocoa, Putumayo	76W39	1N09	- 6 36	+ 5 06 36
Neiva, Huila..........	75W17	2N56	- 1 08	+ 5 01 08
Pasto, Narino	77W17	1N13	- 9 08	+ 5 09 08
Payan, Narino	78E08	1N49	-12 32	+ 5 12 32
Popoyan, Cauca	76W36	2N26	- 6 24	+ 5 06 24
Puerto Asis, Atlantico	76W32	0N30	- 6 08	+ 5 06 08
Puerto Carreno, Vicha da.....	67W29	6N11	+29 56	+ 4 30 04
Puerto Colombia, Atlantico	74W55	10N58	+ 0 20	+ 4 59 40
Quibdo, Choco	76W40	5N42	- 5 20	- 5 05 20
Rio Hacha, Magdalena	72W54	11N34	+ 8 24	+ 4 51 36
Santa Marta, Magdalena	74W14	11N15	+ 3 04	+ 4 56 56
Santander, Cauca..........	76W28	3N01	- 5 52	+ 5 05 52
Tumaco, Narino	78 46	1N49	-15 04	+ 5 15 04
Tunja, Bocaya	73W22	5N32	+ 6 32	+ 4 53 28
Valle, Santander	73W07	6N29	+ 7 32	+ 4 52 28
Villavicencio, Meta	73W37	4N09	+ 5 32	+ 4 54 28

COLON ARCHIPELAGO see Galapagos Islands.

COMMONWEALTH OF AUSTRALIA see Australia.

COMMONWEALTH OF PHILIPPINES see Philippines.

COMORO ISLANDS see Madagascar.

CONFEDERATION SUISSE see Switzerland.

CONGO See 1. Belgian Congo. Independent June 30, 1960
          2. French Equatorial Africa. Independent August 15, 1960.

CONGO MOYEN see French Equatorial Africa.

COOK ISLAND see Gilbert and Ellice Islands.

COOK ISLANDS. Capital: Avarua. Dependency of New Zealand,
    situated in the South Pacific. S.T. Meridian 159°30' WEST.

Arutunga, Aitutaki	159W46	18S53	- 1 04	+10 39 04
Avarua, Rarotonga	159W46	21S12	- 1 04	+10 39 04
Nukuoa, Mauke Island	157W23	20S08	+ 8 28	+10 29 32

			L. M. T. VARIATION FROM S.T. m. s.	G. M. T. VARIATION FROM LMT h. m. s.

COOK ISLANDS (continued)

Oneroa, Mangaia Island	157W58	21S54	+ 6 08	+10 31 52
Penhryn Island	158W03	9S00	+ 7 48	+10 32 12
Taunganui, Atiu	158W09	20S01	+ 5 24	+10 32 36

Tongareva Island see Penrhyn Island.

COREE see Korea.

CORNWALLIS ISLAND see Johnston Island.

CORSICA see France.

COSTA RICA. Capital: San Josa. Republic situated in Central America. Standard Time Meridian 90° WEST.

Alajuela, Alajuela	84W13	10N02	+23 08	+ 5 36 52
Cartago, Cartago	83W56	9N51	+24 16	+ 5 35 44
Esparta, Puntarenas	84W40	9N59	+21 20	+ 5 38 40
Grecia, Alajuela	84W18	10N05	+22 48	+ 5 37 12
Heredia, Heredia	84W07	10N01	+23 32	+ 5 36 28
Liberia, Guanacaste	85W27	10N38	+18 12	+ 5 41 48
Limon, Limon	83W02	10N01	+27 52	+ 5 32 08
Nicoya, Guanacaste	85W29	10N07	+18 04	+ 5 41 56
Paraiso, Cartago	83W53	9N51	+24 28	+ 5 35 32
Puntarenas, Puntarenas	84W51	9N58	+20 36	+ 5 39 24
San José, San Jose	84W05	9N56	+23 40	+ 5 36 20
San Pablo, Guanacaste	84W26	9N54	+22 16	+ 5 37 44
Santo Domingo, Heredia	84W05	9N59	+23 40	+ 5 36 20
Turrialba, Cartago	83W42	9N56	+25 12	+ 5 34 48

COTE D'IVOIRE see French West Africa.

COTE D'OR see Gold Coast.

COTE FRANCAISE DES SOMALIS see French Somaliland.

CRETE see Greece.

CROATIA see Yugoslavia.

CUBA. Capital Habana (Havana). Republic, situated in the Great Antilles. Standard Time Meridian 75° WEST.

Aguada de Pasajeros, Las Villas	80W50	22N24	-23 20	+ 5 23 20
Alacranes, Matanzas	81W34	22N46	-26 16	+ 5 26 15
Alfonso XII See Alacranes.				
Alquizar, Habana	82W36	22N48	-30 24	+ 5 30 24
Artemisia, Pinar del Rio	81W06	22N48	-24 24	+ 5 24 24
Baracoa, Oriente	74W30	20N21	+ 2 00	+ 4 58 00
Batabano, Habana	82W17	22N44	-29 08	+ 5 29 08
Bayamo, Oriente	76W40	20N23	- 6 40	+ 5 06 40
Caibarion, Las Villas	79W28	22N32	-17 52	+ 5 17 52
Camaguey, Camaguey	77W55	21N23	-11 40	+ 5 11 40
Candelaria, Pinar del Rio	82W57	22N44	-31 48	+ 5 31 48
Cardenas, Matanzas	81W13	23N02	-24 52	+ 5 24 52
Cidra, Matanzas	81W32	22N56	-26 08	+ 5 26 08
Ciego de Avila, Camaguey	78W47	21N51	-15 08	+ 5 15 08
Cienfuegos, Las Villas	82W27	22N09	-21 48	+ 5 21 48
Colon, Matanzas	80W54	22N44	-23 36	+ 5 23 36
Cruces, Las Villas	80W16	22N20	-21 04	+ 5 21 04
Esmeralda, Camaguey	78W08	21N52	-12 32	+ 5 12 32
Florida, Camaguey	78W14	21N32	-12 56	+ 5 12 56

			L. M. T. VARIATION FROM S.T.		G. M. T. VARIATION FROM LMT		
			m.	s.	h.	m.	s.

CUBA   (Continued)

			m.	s.	h.	m.	s.
Fomento, Las Villas	79W44	22N06	-18	56	+ 5	18	56
Guainmare, Camaguey	77W23	21N03	- 9	32	+ 5	09	32
Guanabacoa, Habana	82W18	23N08	-29	12	+ 5	29	12
Gibara, Orienta...............	76W09...	21N07.....	- 4	36....	+ 5	04	36
Guanajay, Pinar del Rio	82W42	22N55	-30	48	+ 5	30	48
Guantanamo, Oriente	75W12	20N08	- 0	48	+ 5	00	48
Guines, Habana	82W02	22N51	-28	08	+ 5	28	08
Habana, Habana	82W24	23N08	-29	36	+ 5	29	36
Holguin, Oriente.............	76W16...	20N53.....	- 5	04....	+ 5	05	04
Jatibonico, Camaguey	79W12	21N56	-16	48	+ 5	16	48
Jovellanos, Matanzas	81W12	22N48	-24	48	+ 5	24	48
La Coloma, Pinar del Rio	83W34	22N15	-34	16	+ 5	34	16
Manacas, Las Villas	80W19	22N36	-21	16	+ 5	21	16
Mantua, Pinar del Rio.........	84W17...	22N15......	-37	08....	+ 5	37	08
Manzanillo, Oriente	77W08	20N20	- 8	32	- 5	08	32
Marianao, Habana	82W26	23N05	-29	44	+ 5	29	44
Matanzas, Matanzas	81W35	23N03	-26	20	+ 5	26	20
Maximo Gomez, Matanzas	81W02	22N55	-24	08	+ 5	24	08
Moron,Camaguey................	78W38...	22N07......	-14	32....	+ 5	14	32
Niquero, Oriente	77W35	20N03	-10	20	+ 5	10	20
Nueva Gerona, Isla de Pinos, Habana	82W48	21N50	-31	12	+ 5	31	12
Palma Soriano, Oriente	76W00	20N13	- 4	00	+ 5	04	00
Pinar del Rio, Pinar del Rio..	83W42...	22N25...	-34	48....	+ 5	34	48
Placetas, Las Villas	79W40	22N19	-18	40	+ 5	18	40
Puerto Padre, Oriente	76W36	21N12	-6	24	+ 5	06	24
Remedios, Las Villas	79W35	22N29	-18	20	+ 5	18	20
Sagua de Tanamo, Oriente	75W15	20N37	- 1	00	+ 5	01	00
Sagua La Grande, Las Villas....80W05...		22N49.....	-20	20....	+ 5	20	20
San Antonio de los Banos,Habana 82W31.		22N54	-30	04	+ 5	30	04
Sancti Spiritus, Las Villas	79W27	21N55	-17	48	+ 5	17	48
Santa Clara, Las Villas	79W57	22N25	-19	48	+ 5	19	48
Santiago de Cuba, Oriente.....	75W50...	20N01.....	- 3	20....	+ 5	03	20
Sierra Morena, Las Villas	80W32	22N57	-22	08	+ 5	22	08

CURACAO   See Netherlands West Indies.

CYCLADES See Greece.

CYPRUS.   Capital: Nicosia. Independent August 11, 1960
       Standard Time meridian 30° EAST.

			m.	s.	h.	m.	s.
Famagusta	33E57	35N07	+15	48	- 2	15	48
Larnaca (Skala)	33E38	34N54	+14	32	- 2	14	32
Limassol	33E03	34N41	+12	12	- 2	12	12
Nicosia	33E22	35N10	+13	28	- 2	13	28
Paphos	32E25	34N45	+ 9	40	- 2	09	40
Yialousa	34E12	35N32	+16	48	- 2	16	48

CYRENAICA see Libya.

CZECHOSLOVAKIA. Capital: Praha (Prague).
       Republic situated in Central Europe.
       Standard Time Meridian 15° EAST.

Altschl see Zvolen.

				L. M. T. VARIATION FROM S.T. m. s.	G. M. T. VARIATION FROM LMT h. m. s.
CZECHOSLOVAKIA (Continued)					
As (Asch)	12E10	50N10		- 11 20	- 0 48 40
Aussig a. d. Elbe, see Usti n. Lab.					
Austerlitz see Slavkov.					
Benska Bystrica	19E08	48N45		+16 32	- 1 16 32
Banska Stiavnica	18E54	48N28		+15 36	- 1 15 36
Berehova, see Beregszasz, Hungary					
Beroun (Beraun)	14E04	49N57		- 3 44	- 0 56 16
Besztercebanya see Banska Bystrica.					
Bodenbach see Podmolky.					
Bratialava	17E06	48N08		+ 8 24	- 1 08 24
Brno	16E37	49N12		+ 6 28	- 1 06 28
Bruex see Most.					
Bruenn see Brno.					
Budweis see Ceske Budejovice.					
Ceske Budejovice	14E29	48N59		- 2 04	- 0 57 56
Cheb	12E23	50N04		-10 28	- 0 49 32
Chomutov	13E25	50N28		- 6 20	- 0 53 40
Chrudim	15E48	49N57		+ 3 12	- 1 03 12
Duchov (Dux)	13E45	50N36		- 5 00	- 0 55 00
Eger see Cheb.					
Eperjes see Presov.					
Gablonz see Jablonec.					
Galanta see Galanta, Hungary.					
Graslitz see Kraslice.					
Hradec Kralove	15E32	50N13		+ 3 28	- 1 03 28
Igleu see Jihlava.					
Jablonec	15E11	50N43		+ 0 44	- 1 00 44
Jachymov	12E56	50N22		- 8 16	- 0 51 54
Jaegerndorf see Krnov.					
Jihlava	15E36	49N23		+ 2 24	- 1 02 24
Jindr. Hradec	15E01	49N09		+ 0 04	- 1 00 04
Jungbunzlau see Mlada Boleslav.					
Karlovy Vary	12E54	50N13		- 8 24	- 0 51 36
Karlsbad see Karlovy Vary.					
Koeniggraetz see Hradec Kralove.					
Komarno see Komarom, Hungary.					
Komotau see Chomutov.					
Kormoobanya see Kremnica.					
Kosice see Kassa, Hungary.					
Kladno	14E05	50N08		- 3 40	- 0 56 20
Kreslice	12E31	50N19		- 9 56	- 0 50 04
Kremnica (Kremnitz)	18E55	48N42		+15 40	- 1 15 40
Krnov	17E43	50N06		+10 52	- 1 10 52
Kutna Hora (Kuttenberg)	15E16	49N57		+ 1 04	- 1 01 04
Leitmeritz see Litomerice.					
Liderec	15E04	50N46		+ 0 16	- 1 00 16
Litomerice	14E08	50N32		- 3 28	- 0 56 32
Lusenec see Losonc, Hungary.					
Moehr. Ostrau see Mor. Ostrava.					
Marianske Lazne	12E43	49N59		- 9 08	- 0 50 52
Marienbod see Marianske Lazne.					

			L. M. T. VARIATION FROM S.T m.s.	G. M. T. VARIATION FROM LMT h. m. s.
CZECHOSLOVAKIA (Continued)				
Melnik	14E30	50N21	- 2 00	- 0 58 00
Mikulov	13E38	50N48	- 5 28	- 0 54 32
Mlada Boleslav	14E55	50N21	- 0 20	- 0 59 40
Mor. Ostrava	18E18	49N50	+13 12	- 1 13 12
Most	13E38	50N32	- 5 28	- 0 54 32
Mukacevo see Munkacs, Hungary.				
Nagyszollos see Velki Sevljus.				
Nagyszombat see Trnava				
Neuhaus see Jundr. Hradec.				
Neuhaeusel see Ersekujvar, Hungary.				
Neuschl see Banska Bystrica.				
Neutra see Nitra.				
Nikolsburg see Mikulov.				
Nitra (Nyitra)	18E06	48N19	+12 24	- 1 12 24
Nove Zamky see Ersekujwar, Hungary.				
Cloumuc (Olmuetz)	17N15	49N36	+ 9 00	- 1 09 00
Opava	17E54	49N57	+11 36	- 1 11 36
Pardubice (Pardubitz)	15E46	50N03	+ 3 04	- 1 03 04
Piestany (Postyan)	17E50	48N37	+11 20	- 1 11 20
Pilsen see Plzen				
Pisek	14E09	49N19	- 3 24	- 0 56 36
Plzen	13E23	49N45	- 6 28	- 0 53 32
Podmokly	14E13	50N46	- 3 08	- 0 52 52
Postyen see Piestany				
Pozsony see Bratislava.				
Praha (Prag. Prague)	14E26	50N05	- 2 16	- 0 57 44
Prerov (Prerau)	17E27	49N27	+ 0 48	- 1 09 48
Presov	21E14	49N00	+24 56	- 1 24 56
Pressburg see Bratislava.				
Pribram	14E00	49N42	- 4 00	- 0 56 00
Projestov	17E06	49N28	+ 8 24	- 1 08 24
Prossnitz see Projestov.				
Reichenberg see Liderec.				
Rimovska Sobota see Rimaszombat, Hungary.				
Rosenberg see Ruzemberck.				
Roudnice (Raudnitz)	14E16	50N26	- 2 56	- 0 57 04
Rozsahegy see Ruzomberok.				
Ruzomberok	19E18	49N05	+18 48	- 1 18 48
Saaz see Zatec.				
Sankt Joachimsthal see Jachymov.				
Schemnitz see Banska Stiavnica.				
Selmecbanya see Banska Stiavnica.				
Sillein see Zilina.				
Slavkov	16E52	49N09	+ 7 28	- 1 07 28
Svitavy	16E27	49N46	+ 5 48	- 1 05 48
Tabor	14E41	49N26	- 1 16	- 0 58 44
Tachov (Tachau)	12E39	49N48	- 9 24	- 0 50 36
Teplice-Sanov	13E49	50N39	- 4 44	- 0 55 16
Tencin (Trencsen)	18E02	48N53	+12 08	- 1 12 08
Trnava	17E35	48N23	+10 20	- 1 10 20
Troppau see Opava				
Trutnov (Trautenau)	15E55	50N34	+ 3 40	- 1 03 04

			L. M. T. VARIATION FROM S.T. m. s.	G. M. T. VARIATION FROM LMT h. m. s.

CZECHOSLOVAKIA (Continued)

Turc-Sv.OMartin	18E56	49N04	+15 44	- 1 15 44
Tyrnau see Trnava.				
Usti n. Iab.....................	14E03...	50N40...	- 3 48.....	- 0 56 12
Uzhorod see Ungvar, Hungary.				
Varnsdorf	14E37	50N55	- 1 32	- 0 58 28
Velki Sevljus	23E02	49N09	+32 08	- 1 32 08
Warnsdorf see Varnsdorf.				
Zatec....................	13E33...	50N19...	- 5 48....	- 0 54 12
Zilina	18E45	49N13	+15 00	- 1 15 00
Zlin	17E40	49N14	+10 40	- 1 10 40
Znojmo (Znaim)	16E02	48N52	+ 4 08	- 1 04 08
Zolyom see Zvolen.				
Zsolna see Zilina.				
Zvolen.......................	19E07...	48N35...	+16 28.....	- 1 16 28
Zwittau see Svitavy.				

DAHOMEY see French West Africa. Independent Aug. 1, 1960.

DAKAR and DEPENDENCIES see French West Africa.

DALMATIA See Yugoslavia.

DAMARALAND see Union of South Africa.

DANEMARK see Denmark.

DANGER ISLANDS. Capital: Pukapuka. Dependency of
   New Zealand, situated in the South Pacific.
      Standard Time meridian 165 WEST.

Pukapuka	165W49	10S53	- 3 16	-11 03 16

DANZIG. Free City, formerly belonging to Germany
      Standard Time Meridian 15° EAST.

Danzig	18E39	54N21	+14 36	- 1 14 36
Zoppot	18E29	54N26	+13 56	- 1 13 56

DARDANELLES see Turkey.

DENMARK. Capital: Kjobenhavn (Copenhagen).
      Kingdom, situated in Northern Europe.
      Standard Time Meridian 15° EAST.

Aalborg, Aalborg	9E55	57N03	-20 20	- 0 39 40
Aarhus, Aarhus	10E12	57N09	-19 12	- 0 40 48
Copenhagen see Kjobenhavn.				
Elsinore, see Helsingor.				
Esbjaerg, Ribe..............	8E26...	55N28...	-26 16.....	- 0 33 44
Fredericia, Vejle	9E45	55N34	-21 00	- 0 39 00
Frederiksborg, Frederiksborg	12E23	55N58	-10 28	- 0 49 32
Frederikshavn, Hjorring	10E32	57N26	-17 52	- 0 42 08
Haderslev, Haderslev	9E30	55N15	-22 00	- 0 38 00
Helsinger, Frederiksborg.......12E36...		56N02...	- 9 36.....	- 0 50 24
Hjorring, Hjorring	9E39	57N27	-20 04	- 0 39 56
Holbaek, Holbaek	11E44	55N43	-13 04	- 0 46 56
Kalundborg, Holbaek	11E06	55N41	-15 36	- 0 44 24
Kjobenhavn, Kjobenhavn	12E35	55N41	- 9 40	- 0 50 20
Maribo, Maribo...............	11E30....	54N47...	-14 00.....	- 0 46 00
Nakskov, Praesto	11E08	54N50	-15 28	- 0 44 32
Nykjobing, Sjaelleland	11E42	55N56	-13 12	- 0 46 48
Odense, Odense	10E23	55N23	-18 28	- 0 41 32
Praesto, Praesto	12E02	55N08	-11 52	- 0 48 08

			L. M. T. VARIATION FROM S.T.	G. M. T. VARIATION FROM LMT
			m. s.	h. m. s.
DENMARK (Continued)				
Randers, Renders	10E02	56N28	-19 52	-0 40 08
Ribe, Ribe	8E46	55N20	-24 56	-0 35 04
Ringkjobing, Ringkjobing......	8E15...	56N05...	-27 00....	-0 33 00
Ronne, Bornholm	14E43	55N05	- 1 08	-0 58 52
Roskilde, Kjobenhavn	12E06	55N38	-11 36	-0 48 24
Sonderborg, Sonderborg	9E48	54N55	-20 48	-0 39 12
Soro, Soro	11E36	55N26	-13 36	-0 48 24
Svendborg, Svendborg..........	10E36...	55N03	...-17 36....	-0 42 24
Thisted, Thisted	8E41	56N57	-25 16	- 0 34 44
Tonder, Tonder	8E53	54N56	-24 28	-0 35 32
Vejle, Vejle	9E32	55N43	-21 52	-0 38 08
Viborg, Viborg	9E24	56N27	-22 24	-0 37 36

DOBRUDJA see Rumania.

DODECANESE ISLANDS see Greece.

DOMINICA see British West Indies.

DOMINICAN REPUBLIC. Capital: Ciudad Trujillo (Santo Domingo).
    Republic situated in the Greater Antilles. Standard
    Time Meridian 75 WEST. Prior to April 1, 1933 S.T. Merid-
    ian was 70° WEST.

Azua, Azua	70W44	18N27	+17 04	+4 42 56
Bani, Tr. Waldez	70W20	18N16	+18 40	+4 41 20
Banica, San Rafael	71W41	19N06	+13 16	+4 46 44
Barahona, Barahona............	71W06...	18N12...	+15 36....	+4 44 24
Ciudad Trujillo, D.S.D.	69W53	18N29	+20 28	+4 39 32
Dabajon, Libertador	71W42	19N33	+13 12	+4 46 48
Duarte, Duarte	69W52	18N29	+20 32	+4 39 28
Hato Mayor, El Seybo	69W15	18N46	+23 00	+4 37 00
La Romana, Alta Gracia........	68W58...	18N26...	+24 08...	+4 35 52
La Vega, La Vega	70W31	19N14	+17 56	+4 42 04
Moca, Espaillat	70W30	19N25	+18 00	+4 42 00
Monte Cristi, Monte Cristi	71W39	19N51	+13 24	+4 46 36
Neiba, Bahuroco	71W23	18N28	+14 28	+4 45 32
Puerta Plata, Puerto Plata....	70W41...	19N48...	+17 16...	+4 42 44
Samana, Samana	69W19	19N13	+22 44	+4 37 16
Sanchez, Samana	69W36	19N14	+21 36	+4 38 24
San Cristobal, Trujillo	70W07	18N24	+19 32	+4 40 28
San Francisco de Macoris,Duarte	70W15...	19N18...	+19 00....	+4 41 00
San Juan, Benefactor	71W13	18N48	+15 08	+4 44 52
San Pedro de Macoris, San				
Pedro de Macoris	69W18	18N27	+22 48	+4 37 12
Santiago (de los Caballeros),				
Santiago..................	70W42...	19N28...	+17 12....	+4 42 48
Santo Domingo see Ciudad Trujillo.				
Seibo, El Seibo	69W02	18N45	+23 52	+4 36 08

DUTCH GUIANA see Surinam.

DUTCHLAND see the Netherlands.

DUTCH EAST INDIES see Netherlands East Indies.

DUTCH WEST INDIES see Netherlands West Indies.

			L. M. T. VARIATION FROM S.T. m. s.	G. M. T. VARIATION FROM LMT h. m. s.

EAST AFRICAN PROTECTORATE see Kenya.

EASTER ISLAND. Capital: Hanga Roa. Island in the South Atlantic belongint to Chile: Standard Time Meridian 105° WEST.

Cook Bay see Hanga Roa.

Hanga Roa	109W26	27S09	-17 44	+ 7 17 44
Vaihu Ho	109W22	27S10	-17 28	+ 7 17 28

EAST PRUSSIA see Germany.

ECOSSE see Great Britain.

ECUADOR. Capital: Quito. Republic, situated in South America. Standard Time Meridian 75° EAST.

Alausi, Chimborazo	78W50	2S12	-15 20	+ 5 15 20
Ambato, Tungurahua	78W36	1S14	-14 24	+ 5 14 24
Azogues, Canar	78W50	2S44	-15 20	+ 5 15 20
Babahoyo, Los Rios	79W27	1S46	-17 48	+ 5 17 48
Catarama, Los Rios	79W23	1S31	-17 32	+ 5 17 32
Chone, Manabi	80W05	0S36	-20 20	+ 5 20 20
Corazon, Cotopaxi	79W06	1S12	-16 24	+ 5 16 24
Guayaquil, Guayas	79W50	2S10	-19 20	+ 5 19 20
Cuenca, Azuay	78W59	2S53	-15 56	+ 5 15 56
Esmeraldas, Esmeraldas	79W42	0N59	-18 48	+ 5 18 48
Guaranda, Bolivar	79W00	1S23	-16 00	+ 5 16 00
Ibarra, Imbabura	78W09	1N21	-12 36	+5 12 36
Latacunga, Leon	78W35	0S56	-14 20	+ 5 14 20
Loja, Loja	79W11	4S 02	-16 44	+ 5 16 44
Machala, El Oro	79W58	3S16	-19 52	+ 5 19 52
Manta, Manabi	80W44	0S57	-22 56	+ 5 22 56
Palmira, Chimborazo	78W43	2S05	-14 52	+ 5 14 52
Portoviejo, Manabi	80W24	1S03	-21 36	+5 21 36
Quito, Pichincha	78W30	0S13	-14 00	+ 5 14 00
Riobamba, Chimborazo	78W38	1S40	-14 32	+ 5 14 32
Santa Elena, Guayas	80W51	2S14	-23 24	+ 5 23 24
Tulcan, Carchi	77W42	0N48	-10 48	+ 5 10 48

EGYPT. Capital: Cairo. Kingdom, situated in Africa. Standard Time Meridian 30° EAST.

Alexandria, Alexandria	29E54	31N11	- 0 24	- 1 59 36
Aswan, Aswan	32E54	24N05	+11 36	- 2 11 36
Asyut, Asyut	31E11	27N11	+ 4 44	- 2 04 44
Benha, Qalybiya	31E11	30N27	+ 4 44	- 2 04 44
Beni Suef, Beni Suef	31N06	29N04	+ 4 24	- 2 04 24
Cairo, Cairo	31E15	30N03	+ 5 00	- 2 05 00
Damanhur, Behera	30E28	31N02	+ 1 52	- 2 01 52
Damiette, Dumiat	31E49	31N26	+ 6 16	- 2 06 16
Dumiat see Damiette				
El Alamein, W. D. G.	28E58	30N49	- 4 08	- 1 55 52
El Arish, Sinai	33E48	31N08	+15 12	- 2 15 12
El Ashmouneyn, Asyut	30E48	27N46	+ 3 12	- 2 03 12
El Fayum, El Fayum	30E51	29N19	+ 3 24	- 2 03 24
El Minya, El Minya	30E45	29N13	+ 3 00	- 2 03 00
El Qahira see Cairo				
Girga, Girga	31E54	26N20	+ 7 36	- 2 07 36
Eshmouneyn see El Ashmouneyn.				

			L. M. T. VARIATION FROM S.T.	G. M. T. VARIATION FROM LMT
			m. s.	h. m. s.

EGYPT (Continued)

Giza, Giza	31E13	30N01	+ 4 52	- 2 04 52
Heliopolis, Cairo	31E19	30N06	+ 5 16	- 2 05 16
Hermopolis Magna see El Ashmouneyn.				
Ismaila, Suez Canal	32E17	30N35	+ 9 08	- 2 09 08
Juba, Sudan	31E26	4N51	+ 5 44	- 2 05 44
Luxor, Qena	32E39	25N42	+10 36	- 2 10 36
Maballa el Kubra, Gharbia	31E10	30N58	+ 4 40	- 2 04 40
Mansura, Daqabiya...............	31E23	31N03	+ 5 32	- 2 05 32
Matruh, W. D. G.	27E15	31N21	-11 00	- 1 49 00
Qena, Qona	32E43	26N10	+10 52	- 2 10 52
Port Said, Suez Canal	32E18	31N15	+ 9 12	- 2 09 12
Rashid see Rosetta				
Rosetta, Behera.................	30E25	31N24	+ 1 40	- 2 01 40
Salum, W. D. G.	25E09	31N33	-19 24	- 1 40 36
Shibin el Kem, Linufiya	31E01	30N34	+ 4 04	- 2 04 04
Sidi Barrani, W. D. G.	25E55	31N36	-16 20	- 1 43 40
Suez, Suez Gov.	32E33	29N59	+10 12	- 2 10 12
Suhag, Guirga..................	31E42	26N33	+ 6 48	- 2 06 48
Tanta, Gherbiya	31E00	30N48	+ 4 00	- 2 04 00
Thebes, see Luxor				
Zagazig, Sharqiya	31E30	30N35	+ 6 00	- 2 06 00

EGYPTIAN SUDAN see Anglo-Egyptian Sudan.

EIRE (IRELAND). Capital: Dublin. Free State within the British Commonwealth, situated in Atlantic Ocean west of England. Standard Time Meridian 0°.

Abbeyfeale, Limerick	9W18	52N23	-37 12	+ 0 37 12
An Uaimh, Meath	6W40	53N39	-26 40	+ 0 26 40
Athlone, Roscommon	7W56	53N25	-31 44	+ 0 31 44
Ath Luain see Athlone.				
Baile Atha Chinth see Dublin				
Ballinaloe, Galway	8W14	53N20	-32 56	+ 0 32 56
Bantry, Cork	9W27	51N41	-37 48	+ 0 37 48
Beal Atha na Sluagh see Ballinaloe.				
Beanntraighe see Bantry.				
Blackrock, Dublin	6W10	53N18	-24 40	+ 0 24 40
Blarna see Blarney				
Blarney, Cork	8W34	51N56	-34 16	+ 0 34 16
Bray, Wicklow	6W05	53N12	-24 20	+ 0 24 20
Bri Chualam see Bray				
Cabhan see Cavan				
Carlow, Carlew	6W56	52N51	-27 44	+ 0 27 44
Carraig Dhubh see Black Rock				
Cathair na Mart See Westport				
Cavan, Cavan	6W22	54W00	-25 28	+ 0 25 28
Coatharlach see Carlow				
Cill Airne see Killarney				
Cill Choinnigh see Kilkenney				
Clonmel, Tipperary	7W42	52N21	-30 48	+ 0 30 48
Cluain Meala see Clonmel				
Cobh see Queenstown				

EIRE

			L. M. T. VARIATION FROM S.T. m. s.	G. M. T. VARIATION FROM LMT h. m. s.
Corcaigh see Cork.				
Cork, Cork	8W29	51N54	-33 56	+ 0 33 56
Dalkey, Dublin	6W06	53N16	-24 24	+ 0 24 24
Deilginis see Dalkey				
Donegal, Donegal	8W06	54N39	-32 24	+ 0 32 24
Droichead Atha see Drogheda				
Dublin, Dublin	6W15	53N20	-25 00	+ 0 25 00
Drogheda, Louth	6W21	53N42	-25 24	+ 0 25 24
Dundalk, Louth	6W25	54N01	-25 40	+ 0 25 40
Dun Dealgan see Dundalk				
Dun Laoghaire, Dublin	6W08	53N18	-24 32	+ 0 24 32
Dun na Gail see Donegal				
Eochali see Youghal				
Ennis, Claire	8W59	52N51	-35 56	+ 0 35 56
Gaillimh see Galway				
Galway, Galway	9W04	53N17	-36 16	+ 0 36 16
Inis see Ennis				
Kilkenny, Kilkenny	7W15	52N39	-29 00	+ 0 29 00
Killarney, Kerry	7W30	52N04	-30 00	+ 0 30 00
Kingstown see Dun Laoghaire				
Limerick, Limerick	8W38	52N40	-34 32	+ 0 34 32
Lios Tuathail see Listowel				
Listowel, Kerry	9W29	52N26	-37 56	+ 0 37 56
Loch Garman see Wexford				
Longford, Longford	7W48	53N44	-31 12	+ 0 31 12
Longphort see Longford				
Luimneach see Limerick				
Mainistir na Feile see Abbyfeale				
Monaghan, Monaghan	6W58	54N15	-27 52	+ 0 27 52
Muileann Cearr see Mullingar				
Muineachan see Monaghan				
Mullingar, Westmeath	7W20	53N31	-29 20	+ 0 29 20
Navan see An Uaimh				
New Ross, Wexford	6W57	52N24	-27 48	+ 0 27 48
Pembroke, Dublin	6W12	53N19	-24 48	+ 0 24 48
Port Lairge see Waterford				
Queenstown, Cork	8W19	51N51	-33 16	+ 0 33 16
Rathgar, Dublin	6W18	53N18	-25 04	+ 0 25 04
Rath Garbh see Rathgar				
Rathimines, Dublin	6 W15	53N19	-25 00	+ 0 25 00
Rath Meana's see Rathmines				
Rineanna see Shannon				
Ros Comain see Roscommon				
Roscommon, Roscommon	8W11	53N37	-32 44	+ 0 32 44
Ros hic Treoin see New Ross				
Ross see New Ross				
Schull (Skull), Cork	9W33	51N32	-38 12	+ 0 38 12
Sligeach see Sligo				
Sligo, Sligo	5W29	54N16	-21 56	+ 0 21 56
Tiobraid Arann see Tipperary				
Tipperary, Tipperary	7W10	52N28	-28 40	+ 0 28 40
Traighli see Tralee				
Tralee, Kerry	7W43	52N16	-30 52	+ 0 30 52

			L. M. T. VARIATION FROM S.T.	G. M. T. VARIATION FROM LMT
			m. s.	h. m. s.

EIRE (Continued)

Tulach Mhor see Tullamore				
Tullamore, Offaly	7W30	53N16	-30 00	+ 0 30 00
Waterford, Waterford	7W07	52N16	-28 28	+ 0 28 28
Westport, Mayo	9W31	53N48	-38 04	+ 0 38 04
Wexford, Wexford	6W28	52N20	-25 52	+ 0 25 52
Youghal, Cork	7W52	51N57	-31 28	+ 0 31 28

EL SALVADOR. Capital: San Salvador. Republic situated in Central America. Standard Time Meridian 90° WEST.

Ahuachapan, Ahuachapan	84W51	13N55	+ 0 36	+ 5 59 24
Chalatenango, Chalatenago	88W54	14N02	+ 4 24	+ 5 55 36
Cajutepoque, Cuscutlan	88W56	13N43	+ 4 16	+ 5 55 44
La Libertad	89W19	13N29	+ 2 44	+ 5 57 16
La Union, La Union............	87W51...	13N20...	+ 8 36...	+ 5 51 24
Nueva San Salvador, La Lib.	89W18	13N40	+ 2 48	+ 5 57 12
San Miguel, San Miguel	88W11	13N28	+ 7 16	+ 5 52 44
San Salvador, San Salvador	89W12	13N41	+ 3 12	+ 5 56 48
Santa Ana, Santa Ana	89W34	13N59	+ 1 44	+ 5 58 16
Santa Tecle see Nueva San Salvador				
San Vicente, San Vicente	88W48	13N38	+ 4 48	+ 5 55 12
Sonsenate, Sonsenate	89W44	13N43	+ 1 04	+ 5 58 56
Suchitoto, Cuscatlan	89W02	13N56	+ 3 52	+ 5 56 08
Usulutan, Usulutan	88W27	13N20	+ 6 12	+ 5 53 48
Zacatecoluca, La Paz	88W52	13N28	+ 4 32	+ 5 55 28

ELLICE OR ELLIS ISLANDS see Gilbert & Ellice Islands.

ELSASS-LOTHRINGEN see France.

ENGLAND see Great Britain.

EQUATEUR see Ecuador

ERDELY see Rumania

ERITREA see Italian East Africa.

ESPAGNE see Spain.

ESPANA see Spain.

ESTONIA. Capital: Tallinn. Republic, situated in Europe. Standard Time Meridian 30° EAST.

Arensburg see Kuressaar.				
Baltiski see Paldiski.				
Dorpat see Tarti.				
Elva, Tartumaa	25E26	58N14	-14 16	- 1 45 44
Haapsalu, Saaromaa	23E52	58N57	-25 52	- 1 34 08
Keina, Hiiumaa	22E47	58N49	-28 52	- 1 31 08
Kuivastu, Saaremaa	23E23	58N25	-26 28	- 1 33 32
Kuressaae, Saaremaa............	22E29...	58N15...	-30 04...	- 1 29 56
Narva, Virumaa	28E11	59N20	- 7 16	- 1 52 44
Paldiski	24E04	59N21	-23 44	- 1 36 16
Parnu, Parnumaa	24E29	58N24	-22 04	- 1 37 56
Pernau see Parnu				
Rakvere, Virumaa................	26E21...	59N21...	-14 36...	- 1 45 24
Reval see Tallinn				
Tallinn, Harjumaa	24E43	59N26	-21 08	- 1 38 52
Tapa, Jarvamaa	25E56	59N16	-16 16	- 1 43 44
Tartu, Tartumaa	26E44	58N23	-13 04	- 1 46 56

44

			L. M. T. VARIATION FROM S.T. M. S.	G. M. T. VARIATION FROM LMT h. m. s.
ESTONIA (Continued)				
Valga (Valk), Valgamaa	26E02	57N47	-15 52	- 1 44 08
Viljandi, Viljandimaa	25E35	58N23	-17 40	- 1 42 20
Voru, Vorumaa	26E59	57N51	-12 04	- 1 47 56

ESTABLISSEMENTS FRANCAISE DANS L'INDE see French Establismneuts in
   India

ESTABLISSEMENTS FRANCAIS DE L'OCEANIE   "   "   "   "   Oceania.

ETAT DE LA CITE DU VATICAN   see Vatican City State.

ETAT LIBRE D'IRLANDE see Eire.

ETATS MALAIS FEDERES see Malaya.

ETATS MALAIS NON-FEDERES see Malaya.

ETHIOPIA. Capital: Addis-Ababa. Empire, situated
    in Africa. Standard Time Meridian 45° EAST.

Addis Ababa	38E43	9N01	-25 08	- 2 34 52
Aduwa	38E54	14N10	-24 24	- 2 35 36
Aksum (Axum)	38E43	14N12	-25 08	- 2 34 52
Debra-Markos	37E49	10N16	-28 44	- 2 31 16
Debra-Tabor	38E04	11N51	-27 44	- 2 32 16
Dire Daue.....................	41E45....	9N37...	-13 00...	- 2 47 00
Gambeila	34E35	8N15	-41 40	- 2 18 20
Gondar	37E29	12N36	-30 04	- 2 29 56
Gorrahei	44E20	6N37	- 2 40	- 2 57 20
Harrar	42E02	9N21	-11 52	- 2 48 08
Makalle.....................	39E27	13N30	-22 12...	- 2 37 48
Sokota	39E03	12N39	-23 48	- 2 36 12

FAEROE ISLANDS. Capital: Torshaven. Danish
    possession in North Atlantic. Standard Time
    Meridian 0°.

Torshaven	6W45	62N01	-27 00	+ 0 27 00
Vaag	6W49	61N29	-27 16	+ 0 27 16

FALKLAND ISLANDS' Capital: Stanley. British
    Crown Colony situated in the South Atlantic.
    Standard Time Meridian 60° WEST.

Darwin	58W58	51S50	+ 4 08	+ 3 55 52
Port Albemarle	60W26	52S11	- 1 44	+ 4 01 44
Port Edgar	60W14	52S00	- 0 56	+ 4 00 56
Port Louis	56W10	51S33	+ 7 20	+ 3 52 40
San Carlos	58W59	51S30	+ 4 04	+ 3 55 56
Stanley	57W50	51S42	+ 8 40	+ 3 51 20

FANNING ISLAND see Gilbert & Ellice Islands.

FEDERATED MALAY STATES see Malaya.

FEDERATION INDOCHINOISE see French Indo-China.

FERNANDO PO see Spanish Guinea.

FIJI. Capital: Suva. British Crown Colony, sit-
    uated in the South Pacific. Standard Time
    Meridian 180° EAST.

Lambasa, Vanua Levu	179E24	16S26	- 2 24	-11 57 36
Lautoka, Viti Levu	177E27	17S37	-10 12	-11 49 48
Nambouwalu, Vanua Levu	178E42	16S59	- 5 12	-11 54 48
Rotuma Island	177E05	12S30	-11 40	-11 48 20
Suva, Viti Levu	178E26	18S09	- 6 16	-11 53 44

FINLAND. Capital: Helsinki. Republic situated in
    Northern Europe. Standard Time Meridian 30° EAST.

			L. M. T. VARIATION FROM S. T.		G. M. T. VARIATION FROM LMT.		
Abo see Turku.							
Bjorneborg see Pori.							
Borga see Porvoo.							
Brahestad see Rache.			m.	s.	h.	m.	s.
Ekenas, Uud.	23E26	59N58	-26	16	- 1	33	44
Forssa, Ham.	23E38	60N48	-25	28	- 1	34	32
Fredrikshamn see Hamina.							
Gamlakarleby see Kokkola.							
Homina, Vii.	27E12	60N34	-11	12	- 1	48	48
Heinola, Mikk.	26E02	61N13	-15	52	- 1	44	08
Haapajarvi, Oulu	24E52	60N13	-20	32	- 1	39	28
Hameenlinna, Ham..........	24E27...	61N00...	-22	12...	- 1	37	48
Hanko (Hango), Uud.	22E57	59N45	-28	12	- 1	31	48
Helsingfors see Helsinki.							
Helsinki, Uud.	24E58	60N09	-20	08	- 1	39	52
Hyvinaa, Uud.	24E50	60N38	-20	40	- 1	39	20
Idensalmi see Iisalmi							
Iisalmi, Kupio	27E11	63N34	-11	16	- 1	48	44
Ikaalinen, Turku	23E04	61N46	-27	44	- 1	32	16
Ikalis see Ikaolinen.							
Jakobstad see Pietarsaari.							
Jaensuu, Kuop.	29E44	62N36	- 1	04	- 1	58	56
Jyvaskyla, Vaasa	25E44	62N14	-17	04	- 1	41	56
Kajaani, Oulu	27E41	64N14	- 9	16	- 1	50	44
Kakisalmi, Vii.	30E08	61N02	+ 0	32	- 2	00	32
Karis, Uud.	23E40	60N05	-25	20	- 1	34	40
Karjaa see Karis.							
Kemi, Lap.	24E31	65N48	-21	56	- 1	38	04
Kemijarvi, Lap.	27E26	66N42	-10	16	- 1	49	44
Kexholm see Kakisalmi.							
Kokkola, Vaasa	23E08	63N50	-27	28	- 1	32	32
Kotka, Vii..........	26E55	60N28	-12	20	- 1	47	40
Kristiinankaupunki, Vaasa	21E23	62N16	-34	28	- 1	25	32
Kristinestad see Kristiinankaupunki.							
Kuopio, Kuopio	27E41	62N52	- 9	16	- 1	50	44
Kuusankoski, Uud.	26E39	60N55	-13	24	- 1	46	36
Lahti, Ham.........	25E39...	61N00...	-17	24...	- 1	42	36
Lappeenranta, Vii.	28E11	61N04	- 7	16	- 1	52	44
Lieksa, Kuop.	30E02	63N19	+ 0	08	- 2	00	08
Lohja, Uud.	24E04	60N15	-23	44	- 1	36	16
Loimaa, Turku	23E03	60N52	-27	48	- 1	32	12
Lopo see Lohja.							
Mikkeli, Mikkeli	27E15	61N41	-11	00	- 1	49	00
Nokia, Ham.	23E30	61N28	-26	00	- 1	34	00
Nyslott see Savolinna.							
Nystad see Uusikanpuski.							
Oulu, Oulu	25E28	65N01	-18	08	- 1	41	52
Petsamo (Petsmo), Oulu	31E15	69N33	+ 5	00	- 2	05	00
Pithenya see Petsamo.							
Pieksama, Mikk.	27E08	62N19	-11	28	- 1	48	32
Pietarsaari, Vaasa	22E42	63N40	-29	12	- 1	30	48

			L. M. T. VARIATION FROM S.T.	G. M. T. VARIATION FROM LMT.
			m. s.	h. m. s.
FINLAND. (Continued)				
Pori, Turku	21E47	61N29	-32 52	- 1 27 08
Porvoo, Uud.	25E40	60N22	-17 20	- 1 42 40
Rache, Oulu.....................	24E29...	64N40	-22 04....	- 1 37 56
Raima, Turku	21E30	61N08	-34 00	- 2 34 00
Riimaki, Hon.	24E46	60N44	-20 56	- 1 39 04
Rovaniemi, Lap.	25E45	66N31	-17 00	- 1 43 00
Salo, Turku	23E10	60N23	-27 20	- 1 32 40
Sankt Michel see Mikkeli				
Savolinna, Mikk.................	28E53...	61N52	...- 4 28.....	- 1 55 32
Seinajoki, Vaasa	22E49	62N47	-28 44	- 1 31 16
Tammisaari see Ekenas.				
Tampere, Ham.	23E43	61N29	-26 28	- 1 34 52
Tannerefore see Tampere.				
Tavastehus see Hameenlinna.				
Tornio, Lap.	24E08	65N51	-23 28	- 1 36 32
Turku, Turku	22E17	60N26	-30 52	- 1 29 08
Uleaborg see Oulu.				
Uusikanpuski, Turku	21E25	60N48	-34 20	- 1 25 40
Vaasa, Vaasa....................	21E36...	63N07	...-33 36....	- 1 26 24
Valkeakoski, Ham.	24E02	61N16	-23 52	- 1 36 08
Varkaus, Kuop.	27E52	62N20	- 8 32	- 1 51 28
Viborg see Viipuri.				
Viipuri, Viipuri	28E44	60N43	- 5 04	- 1 54 56
Villmanstrand see Lappeenranta.				

FLORES see Netherlands East Indies.

FORMOSA see Taiwan. Republic.

FOX ISLANDS see Alaska and Aleutian Islands.

FRANCE. Capital: Paris. Republic, situated in Europe.
Standard Time Meridian 0°, was adopted March 11,
1911, with the exception of Corsica where local time
prevails. 0ʰ34'57" EAST.

Aabbeville, Somme	1E50	50N07	+ 7 20	- 0 07 20
Agen, Lot-et-Gane	0E37	44N12	+ 2 28	- 0 02 28
Ajaccio, Corse (Corsico)	8E43	41N55		- 0 34 52
Albi, Tarn	2E09	43N56	+ 8 36	- 0 08 36
Alencon, Orne	0E06	48N26	+ 0 06	- 0 00 24
Ales, Gard......................	4E05...	44N07	...+16 20....	0 16 20
Amiens, Somme	2E18	49N54	+ 9 12	- 0 09 12
Angers, Maine-et-Loire	0W33	47N28	- 2 12	+ 0 02 12
Angouleme, Charente	0E09	45N39	+ 0 36	- 0 00 36
Annecy, Hte-Savoie	6E08	45N54	+ 24 32	- 0 24 32
Arles-sur-Rhone, B-du-Rhone......	4E38...	43N41..	+18 32....	- 0 18 32
Armentieres, Nord	2E52	50N42	+11 28	- 0 11 28
Arras, Pas-de-Calais	2E47	49N17	+11 08	- 0 11 08
Auch, Gers	0E35	43N39	+ 2 20	- 0 02 20
Auray, Mordiban	3W01	47N40	-12 04	+ 0 12 04
Aurillac, Cantal	2E27	44N56	+ 9 48	+ 0 09 48
Auxerre, Yonne..................	3E34...	47N48..	+14 16....	- 0 14 16
Avallon, Yonne	3E54	47N29	+15 36	- 0 15 36
Avignon, Vaucluse	4E48	43N57	+19 12	- 0 19 12

			L. M. T. VARIATION FROM S.T.	G. M. T. VARIATION FROM LMT.
			m. s.	h. m. s.
FRANCE. (Continued)				
Bar-le-Duc, Meuse	5E10	48N46	+20 40	- 0 20 40
Bayeux, Calvados	0W42	49N17	- 2 48	+ 0 02 48
Bayonne, Basses-Pyr.	1W29...	43N30....	- 1 29..	+ 0 05 56
Beauvais, Oise	2E05	49N26	+ 8 20	- 0 08 20
Belfort, Terr.	6E52	47N38	+27 28	- 0 27 28
Besancon, Doubs	6E01	47N15	+24 04	- 0 24 04
Biarritz, Basses-Pyr.	1W34	43N28	- 6 16	+ 0 06 16
Blois, Loire-et-Cher	1E20...	47N35....	+ 5 20..	- 0 05 20
Bordeaux, Gironde	0W35	44N50	- 2 20	+ 0 02 20
Boulogne-sur-Mer, Pas-de-Callais	1E37	50N44	+ 6 28	- 0 06 28
Bourges, Cher	2E24	47N05	+ 9 36	- 0 09 36
Brest, Finistere	4W29...	48N23....	-17 56..	+ 0 17 56
Brive-la-Gaillarde, Correze	1E32	45N09	+ 6 08	- 0 06 08
Caen, Calvados	0W21	49N11	- 1 24	+ 0 01 24
Calais, Pas-de-Calais	1E51	50N57	+ 7 24	- 0 07 24
Cambrai, Nord	5E14	50N11	+12 56	- 0 12 56
Cannes, Alpes Mmes.	7E00...	43N33....	+28 00..	- 0 28 00
Carcassone, Aude	2E21	43N13	+ 9 24	- 0 09 24
Castres, Tarn	2E15	43N36	+ 9 00	- 0 09 00
Chalon sur Saone, Saone-et Loire	4E51	46N47	+19 24	- 0 19 24
Chalons-sur-Marne, Marne	4E22...	48N57....	+17 28..	- 0 17 28
Chambery, Savoie	5E55	45N34	+23 40	- 0 23 40
Chartres, Eure-et-Loire	1E29	48N27	+ 5 56	- 0 05 56
Chateauroux, Indre	1E42	46N49	+ 6 48	- 0 06 48
Chateau-Thierry, Aisne	3E24	49N02	+13 36	- 0 13 36
Chaumont, Hte.-Marne	5E08...	48N07....	+20 32..	- 0 20 32
Cherbourg, Manche	1W37	49N39	- 6 28	+ 0 06 28
Claude, Jura	5E52	47N23	+23 28	- 0 23 28
Clermont-Ferrand, Puy-de-Dome	3E05	45N47	+12 20	- 0 12 20
Colmar, Haut-Rhin	7E21	48N05	+29 24	- 0 29 24
Compiegno, Oise	2E50	49N25....	+11 20..	- 0 11 20
Dieppe, Seine-Inf.	1E05	49N56	+ 4 20	- 0 04 20
Dijon, Cote-d'Or	5E05	47N19	+20 20	- 0 20 20
Douai, Nord	3E05	50N22	+12 20	- 0 12 20
Draguignan, Var	6E28	43N32	+25 52	- 0 25 52
Dunkerque, Nord	2E22...	51N02....	+ 9 28..	- 0 09 28
Epernay, Marne	3E57	49N03	+15 48	- 0 15 48
Epinal, Vosges	6E27	48N10	+25 48	- 0 25 48
Evreux, Eure	1E09	49N02	+ 4 36	- 0 04 36
Flers, Orne	0W33	48N45	- 2 12	+ 0 02 12
Foi . Ariege.	1E36...	42N58....	+ 6 24..	- 0 06 24
Gap, Htes-Alpes	6E05	44N34	+24 20	- 0 24 20
Granoble, Isere	5E44	45N11	+22 56	- 0 22 56
Hendaye, Basses-Pyr.	1W44	43N22	- 6 56	+ 0 06 56
Issodun, Indre	2E00	46N57	+ 8 00	- 0 08 00
Laon, Aisne	3E57...	49N34....	+14 28..	- 0 14 28
La Rochelle, Charents-Inf.	1W09	46N09	- 4 36	+ 0 04 36
La Roche sur Yon, Vendce	1W26	46N40	- 5 44	+ 0 05 44
Laval, Mayenne	0W46	48N04	- 3 04	+ 0 03 04

			L. M. T. VARIATION FROM S.T. m. s.	G. M. T. VARIATION FROM LMT. h. m. s.
FRANCE (Continued)				
Le Havre, Seine Inf.	0E07	49N29	+ 0 28	- 0 00 28
Le Creusot, Saone-et-Loire	4E26	46N48	+17 44	- 0 17 44
Le Mans, Sarthe....................	0E12...	48N00..	+ 0 48...	- 0 00 48
Le Puy, Haute-Loire	3E53	45N03	+15 32	- 0 15 32
Lillie, Nord	3E04	50N39	+12 16	- 0 12 16
Limoges, Haute-Vienne	1E16	45N50	+ 5 04	- 0 05 04
Lisieux, Calvados	0E14	49N09	+ 0 56	- 0 00 56
Lorient, Mordiban..................	3W21...	47N45..	-13 24...	+ 0 13 24
Lourdes, Hautes-Pyr.	0W02	43N07	- 0 08	+ 0 00 08
Luneville, M. & M.	6E30	48N36	+26 00	- 0 26 00
Lyon, Rhone	4E49	45N46	+19 16	- 0 19 16
Macon, S. & L.	4E50	46N18	+19 20	- 0 19 20
Marseille, B. -du-Rhone..........	5E23...	43N19..	+21 32....	- 0 21 32
Maubeuge, Nord	3E59	50N17	+15 56	- 0 15 56
Mende, Lozere	3E30	44N31	+14 00	- 0 14 00
Menton, Alpes-Mar.	7E30	43N47	+30 00	- 0 30 00
Metz, Moselle	6E10	49N07	+24 40	- 0 24 40
Meziers, Ardenne..................	4E13...	49N45...	+18 52...	- 0 18 52
Montauben, T. & G.	1E21	44N01	+ 5 24	- 0 05 24
Mont-de-Marsan, Landes	0W30	43N54	- 2 00	+ 0 02 00
Montpelier, Herault	3E50	43N37	+15 30	- 0 15 30
Moulins, Allier	3E20	46N34	+13 20	- 0 13 20
Mulhouse, Haut-Rhin...............	7E21...	46N45..	+29 24...	- 0 29 24
Nancy, M. & M.	6E11	48N42	+24 44	- 0 24 44
Nantes, Loire-Inf.	1W33	47N13	- 6 12	+ 0 06 12
Narbonne, Aude	3E00	43N11	+12 00	- 0 12 00
Nevers, Nievres	3E09	46N59	+12 36	- 0 12 36
Nice, (Nizza), Alpes-Mmes........	7E17....	43N42..	+29 08...	- 0 29 08
Nimes, Gard	4E21	43N51	+17 24	- 0 17 24
Niort, Deux-Sevres	0W28	46N19	- 1 52	+ 0 01 52
Orleans, Loiret	1E55	47N54	+ 7 40	- 0 07 40
PARIS AND ENVIRONS:				
Paris, Observatoire, Seine	2E20	48N50	+ 9 20	- 0 09 20
Argenteuil, S. & O.	2E15	48N57	+ 9 00	- 0 09 00
Asnieres, Seine	2E18	48N55	+ 9 12	- 0 09 12
Aubervillier, Seine	2E22	48N55	+ 9 28	- 0 09 28
Boulogne Billencourt, Seine	2E15	48N50	+ 9 00	- 0 09 00
Clichy-la-Garenne, Seine.......	2E18...	48N54..	+ 9 12...	- 0 09 12
Colombes, Seine	2E15	48N55	+ 9 00	- 0 09 00
Courbevoie, Seine	2E16	48N54	+ 9 04	- 0 09 04
Drancy, Seine	2E24	48N55	+ 9 36	- 0 09 36
Issy les Moulineaux, Seine	2E18	48N50	+ 9 12	- 0 09 12
Ivry-sur-Seine, Seine.........	2E24...	48N48..	+ 9 36...	- 0 09 36
Levallois-Perrett, Seine	2E19	48N54	+ 9 16	- 0 09 16
Maison Alfort, Seine	2E19	48N48	+ 9 16	- 0 09 16
Melun, S. & M.	2E40	48N33	+10 40	- 0 10 40
Montreuil s'Bois, Seine	2E27	48N51	+ 9 48	- 0 09 48
Montrouge, Seine.................	2E20...	48N49..	+ 9 20...	- 0 09 20
Nanterre, Seine	2E12	48N54	+ 8 48	- 0 08 48
Neuilly-sur-Seine, Seine	2E17	48N53	+ 9 08	- 0 09 08
Pantin, Seine	2E25	48N54	+ 9 40	- 0 09 40
Puteaux, Seine	2E15	48N53	+ 9 00	- 0 09 00

			L. M. T. VARIATION FROM S.T.	G. M. T. VARIATION FROM LMT.
			m. s.	h. m. s.

FRANCE (Continued)

PARIS AND ENVIRONS (Continued)

Saint-Cyr-l'Ecole, S. & O.	2E04	48N48	+ 8 16	- 0 08 16
Saint-Denis, Seine	2E22	48N56	+ 9 28	- 0 09 28
Saint-Germain-on-Laye, S&O	2E05	48N54	+ 8 20	- 0 08 20
Saint-Maure des Fosses, Seine...	2E29...	48N48...	+ 9 56...	- 0 09 56
Saint-Ouen, Seine	2E20	48N54	+ 9 20	- 0 09 20
Versailles, S. & O.	2E08	48N48	+ 8 32	- 0 08 32
Vincennes, Seine	2E27	48N51	+ 9 48	- 0 09 48
Pau, Basses-Pyr.	0W22	43N18	- 1 28	+ 0 01 28
Perigueux, Dordogne..............	0E43...	45N11...	+ 2 52...	- 0 02 52
Perpignan, P. O.	2E54	42N42	+11 36	- 0 11 36
Poitiers, Vienne	0E20	46N35	+ 1 20	- 0 01 20
Privas, Ardeche	4E36	44N44	+18 24	- 0 18 24
Quimper, Finistere	4W06	48N00	-16 24	+ 0 16 24
Reims, Marne....................	4E02...	49N15...	+16 08...	- 0 16 08
Rennes, Ille & Vil.	1W45	48N07	- 7 00	+ 0 07 00
Rochefort-s/Mer, Char. Inf.	0W58	45N56	- 3 52	+ 0 03 52
Rodez, Aveyron	2E35	44N21	+10 20	- 0 10 20
Roubaix, Nord	3E10	50N42	+12 40	- 0 12 40
Rouen, Seine-Inf................	1E08...	48N26...	+ 4 32...	- 0 04 32
Saint-Etienne, Loire	4E23	45N26	+17 32	- 0 17 32
Saint-Lo, Manche	1W06	49N07	- 4 24	+ 0 04 24
Saint-Malo, Ille & Vil.	2W01	48N39	- 8 04	+ 0 08 04
Saint-Nazaire, Loire-Inf.	2W12	47N16	- 9 48	+ 0 08 48
Saint-Omer, Pas-de-Calais........	2E15...	50N45...	+ 9 00...	- 0 09 00
Saint-Quentin, Aisne	3E18	49N51	+13 12	- 0 13 12
Sedan, Ardennes	4E57	49N42	+19 48	- 0 19 48
Soissons, Aisne	3E19	49N23	+13 16	- 0 13 16
Strasbourg (Strassburg), Bas-Rhin	7E46	48N35	+31 04	- 0 31 04
Tarbes, Htes-Pyr.................	0E05...	43N14...	+ 0 20...	- 0 00 20
Toulon, Var.	5E56	43N07	+23 44	- 0 23 44
Toulouse, Hte-Garonne	1E26	43N36	+ 5 44	- 0 05 44
Tours, Inre-et-L.	0E42	47N23	+ 2 48	- 0 02 48
Troyes, Aube	4E05	48N18	+16 20	- 0 16 20
Tulle, Correze..................	1E46...	45N16...	+ 7 04...	- 0 07 04
Valence, Drome	4E53	44N56	+19 32	- 0 19 32
Valenciennes, Nord	3E31	50N21	+14 04	- 0 14 04
Vannes, Morbihan	2W46	47N40	-11 04	+ 0 11 04
Vendoma, Loire-et-Cher	1E04	47N48	+ 4 16	- 0 04 16
Verdun-sur-Meuse, Meuse..........	5E24...	49N10...	+21 36...	- 0 21 36
Vesoul, Hte-Saone	6E09	47N37	+24 36	- 0 24 36
Vienne, Isere	1E22	47N32	+ 5 28	- 0 05 28

FRENCH EQUATORIAL AFRICA. Capital: Brazzaville.
French Colony situated in Africa. Standard
Time Meridian 15° EAST.

Abeche, Tchad	20E48	13N49	+23 12	- 1 23 12
Bembari, Ou.-Chari	20E36	5N40	+22 24	- 1 22 24
Bangui, Ou.-Chari	18E35	4N21	+14 20	- 1 14 20
Berberati, Ou.-Chard.............15E46...		4N16...	+ 3 04...	- 1 03 04
Brazzaville, Middle Congo	15E14	4S17	+ 0 56	- 1 00 56
Fort Archambault, Tchad	18E24	9N10	+13 36	- 1 13 36
Fort Lamy, Tchad	15E03	12N08	+ 0 12	- 1 00 12

			L. M. T. VARIATION FROM S.T.	G. M. T. VARIATION FROM LMT.
			m. s.	h. m. s.
FRENCH EQUATORIAL AFRICA. (Continued)				
Lambrene, Gabon	10E12	0S43	-19 12	- 0 40 48
Libreville, Gabon	9E26	0N23	-22 16	- 0 37 44
Mouila, Gabon..................	11E01....	1S08...	-15 56...	- 0 44 04
Moundou, Tchad	16E06	8N36	+ 4 24	- 1 04 24
Pointe Noire, Middle Congo	11E49	4S49	-12 44	- 0 47 16
Port Gentil, Gabon	8E46	0S44	-24 56	- 0 35 04
FRENCH ESTABLISHMENTS IN INDIA. Capital: Pondichery.				
French Colony, situated on the Indian subcontinent.				
Standard Time Meridian 82°30' EAST.				
Chandernagore, Bengal	88E22	22N52	+23 28	- 5 53 28
Karikal, Madras	79E51	10N55	-10 36	- 5 19 24
Mahe, Madras	75E32	11N42	-27 52	- 5 02 08
Pondichery, Madras............	79E50...	11N56...	-10 40...	- 5 19 20
Yanam (Yanaon), Madras	82E13	16N44	- 1 08	- 5 28 52
FRENCH ESTABLISHMENTS IN OCEANIA. Capital: Papeete.				
French Colony situated in the South Pacific.				
Standard Time Meridian 150° WEST. The French				
Establishments in Oceania consist of:				
1. The Society Islands;				
2. The Marquesas Islands;				
3. The Tuamotu Group;				
4. The French Leeward Islands (Iles sous le Vent);				
5. Gambier, Austral and Rapa Islands.				
The number following an entry indicates which of these				
five subdivisions to which a place belongs. Only in-				
habited islands have been listed.				
Afareaitu, Moorea 1	149W47	17S32	+ 9 52	+ 9 59 08
Ahurei, Rapa 5.................	144W18...27S36		+22 48...	+ 9 37 12
Atu Ana, Hiva-On 2	139W36	8S56	+41 36	+ 9 18 24
Bora Bora, Bora Bora 4	151W45	16S30	- 7 00	+10 07 00
Haka Mui, Ua-Pou 2	140W00	9S23	+40 00	+ 9 20 00
Mataura 5, Tubuai (Austral) 5	149W28	23S22	+ 2 08	+ 9 57 32
Papeete, Tahiti 1.............	149W34..	17S32...	+ 1 44...	+ 9 58 16
Pueu, Tahiti 1	149W13	17S44	+ 3 08	+ 9 56 52
Punaavia, Tahiti 1	149W36	17S37	+ 1 36	+ 9 58 24
Rikitea, Mangareva (Gambier) 5	134W57	23S08	+1^{h}00 12	+ 8 59 48
Rotoava, Fakarava Atoll 3	145W36	16S02	+17 36	+ 9 42 24
Taio Hae, Nukuhiva 2..........	140W05...	8S56...	+39 40...	+ 9 20 20
T eahupu, Tahiti 1	149W16	17S50	+ 2 56	+ 9 57 04
Uturea, Raiatea	151W26	16S44	+ 5 44	+10 05 44
FRENCH GUIANA. Capital: Cayene. French Colony				
situated in South America. Standard Time				
Meridian 60° WEST.				
Caux	52W02	4N26	+31 59	+ 3 28 08
Cayenne	52W20	4N57	+30 40	+ 3 29 29
Ile du Diable (Devil's Island),				
Southmost point	52W35	5N17	+29 40	+ 3 30 20
Forestiere.............	54W20	5N13	+22 40	+ 3 37 20
Mann	53W49	5N39	+24 16	+ 3 25 44
St. Laurent	54W03	5N30	+23 48	+ 3 36 12
FRENCH GUINEA See French West Africa.				

FRENCH INDO-CHINA. Capital: Saigon, : L. M. T. G. M. T.
    French Colony, situated in southeast Asia : VARIATION VARIATION
    Standard Time Meridian 105° EAST. For a : FROM S.T. FROM LMT.
    short time the standard time meridian :
    used was 120° EAST. : m. s. h. m. s.

Place			From S.T.	From LMT
Angtassom, Cambodia	104E11	11N01	- 3 16	- 6 56 44
Auke, Cambodia	106E03	9N52	+ 4 12	- 7 04 12
Bak Ninh, Tonkin	106E03	21N10	+ 4 12	- 7 04 12
Battambang, Cambodia	103E12	13N05	- 7 12	- 6 52 48
Ben Cat, Cochin China.........	106E35...	11N08...	+ 6 20...	- 7 06 20
Bianhoa, Cochin China	106E50	10N57	+ 7 20	- 7 07 20
Cao Bang, Tonkin	106E16	22N39	+ 5 04	- 7 05 04
Cholon, Cochin China	106E40	10N45	+ 6 40	- 7 06 40
Dinh Nam, Tonkin	106E09	20N26	+ 4 36	- 7 04 36
Hoabinh, Tonkin...............	105E19	20N49	+ 1 16	- 7 01 16
Hai Dzung (Hai Duong), Tonkin	106E19	20N56	+ 5 16	- 7 05 16
Haiphong, Tonkin	106E41	20N52	+ 6 44	- 7 06 44
Hanoi, Tonkin	105E50	21N02	+ 3 20	- 7 03 20
Ha Tinh, Annam	105E53	18N21	+ 3 32	- 7 03 32
Hue, Annam....................	107E34...	16N29...	+10 16...	- 7 10 16
Kampot, Cambodia	104E11	10N36	- 3 16	- 6 56 44
Kieng Khouang see Xieng Khouang.				
Kompong-Cham, Cambodia	105E28	12N00	+ 1 52	- 7 01 52
Kwinhon, Annam	109E14	13N46	+16 56	- 7 16 56
Laokay, Tonkin................	103E56...	22N30...	- 4 16	- 6 55 44
Long Xuyen, Cochin China	105E26	10N23	+ 1 44	- 7 01 44
Luang Prabang, Laos	102E08	19N54	-11 28	- 6 48 32
Mytho, Cochin China	106E22	10N21	+ 5 28	- 7 05 29
Nam Dinh see Dinh Nam.				
Pak Se, Laos..................	105E47...	15N07	+ 3 08	- 7 05 08
Phanthiet, Annam	108E06	10N55	+12 24	- 7 12 24
Phnom Penh, Cambodia	104E52	11N33	- 0 32	- 6 59 28
Quinhon see Kwinhon.				
Rach Gia, Cochin China	105E05	10N00	+ 0 20	- 7 00 20
Saigon, Cochin China.........	106E41...	10N47...	+ 6 44...	- 7 06 44
Sam Neua, Laos	104E02	20N28	- 3 52	- 6 56 08
Sarawane, Laos	106E25	15N43	+ 5 40	- 7 05 40
Savannakhet, Laos	104E45	16N33	- 1 00	- 6 59 00
Stung Trang, Cambodia	105E58	13N31	+ 3 52	- 7 03 52
Thak Hek, Laos...............	104E49...	17N24...	- 0 44...	- 6 59 16
Tourane, Annam	108E13	16N04	+12 52	- 7 12 52
Udon (Udonp), Cambodia	104E47	11N48	- 0 52	- 6 59 08
Vientiane, Laos	102E37	17N58	- 9 32	- 6 50 28
Wue see Hue.				
Xieng Khouang, Laos...........	103E22...	19N19...	- 6 32...	- 6 53 28

FRENCH LEEWARD ISLANDS see Frendh Establishments in Oceania
FRENCH MOROCCO see Morocco.
FRENCH SOMALILAND. Capital: Djibouti, French Colony sit-
    uated in East Africa. Standard Time Meridian 45° EAST

Place			From S.T.	From LMT
Djibouti	43E07	11N36	- 7 32	- 2 52 28
Obokh	43E16	11N57	- 6 56	- 2 53 04
Tadjoura (Tajura)	42E51	11N45	- 8 36	- 2 51 04

			L. M. T. VARIATION FROM S.T.	G. M. T. VARIATION FROM LMT.

FRENCH WEST AFRICA. Capital: Bakar. French
Colony situated in Africa. Standard Time
Meridians 0°, 15° EAST and 15° WEST.

Place	Long.	Lat.	m. s.	h. m. s.
Abidjan, Ivory Coast	4W01	5N19	-16 04	+ 0 16 04
Abomey, Dahomey.....................1E41.....		7N12....	+ 6 44...	- 0 06 44
Agades, Niger	7E58	16N59	-28 08	- 0 31 52
Bamako, French Sudan	7W59	12N39	-31 56	+ 0 31 56
Bingerville, Ivory Coast	3W54	5N20	-15 36	+ 0 15 36
Cotonou, Dahomey	2E27	6N27	+ 9 48	- 0 09 48
Dakar, Senegal.....................17W26...		14N40...	- 9 44...	+ 1 09 44
Conakry, French Guinea	13W43	9N30	+ 5 08	+ 0 54 52
Douala (Duala), Fr. Cam.	9E41	4N02	-21 16	- 0 38 44
Garoua, Fr. Cam.	13E24	9N18	- 6 24	- 0 53 36
Jaunde see Yaounde.				
Kankan, French Guinea.......... 9W17...		10N23...	+22 52...	+ 0 37 08
Kaolack, Senegal	16W05	14N08	- 4 20	+ 1 04 20
Kribi, Fr. Cam.	9E55	2N57	-20 20	- 0 39 40
Lome, French Togo	1E14	6N08	+ 4 56	- 0 04 56
Niamey, Niger	2E07	13N31	+ 8 28	- 0 08 28
Nioro, French Sudan.............. 9W36...		15N14...	-38 24...	+ 0 38 24
Ouagadougou, Ivory Coast.	1W31	12N22	- 6 04	+ 0 06 04
Port Etienne, Mauretania	17W03	20N55	- 8 12	+ 1 08 12
Porto Novo, Dahomey	2E37	6N29	+10 28	- 0 10 28
St. Louis, Mauretania	16W31	16N01	- 6 04	+ 1 06 04
Sokode, French Togo............ 1E10...		8N59...	+ 4 40...	- 0 04 40
Thies, Senegal	16W56	14N47	- 7 44	+ 1 07 44
Timbukto see Tombouctou.				
Tombouctou, Soudan	3W01	16N46	-12 04	+ 0 12 04
Yaounde, French Cameroons	11E32	3N51	-13 52	- 0 46 08
Zinder, Niger.................... 9E00...		13N48...	-24 00...	- 0 36 00

FRIENDLY ISLANDS see Tonga Island.

FRIESLAND see Netherlands.

FUTUNA ISLAND see New Caledonia.

GABON see French Equatorial Africa. Independent August 17, 1960

GALAPAGOS ISLANDS. Possession of Ecuador.
Standard Time Meridian 90° WEST.

Place	Long.	Lat.	m. s.	h. m. s.
Progreso	89W32	0S55	+ 1 52	+ 5 58 02
Puerto Chico, Isla San Cristobal	89W36	0S54	+ 1 36	+ 5 58 24
Villamil, Isla Isabel	91W01	0S58	- 4 04	+ 6 04 04

GALICIA see 1. Poland.
2. Spain.

GAMBIA. Capital: Bathurst. British Colony and Protectorate, situated in West Africa. Standard
Time Meridian 15° WEST.

Place	Long.	Lat.	m. s.	h. m. s.
Bathurst	16W34	13N27	- 6 16	- 1 06 16
Brikama	16W37	13N15	- 6 28	- 1 06 28
MacCarthy	14W46	13N31	+ 0 56	+ 0 59 04

GAMBIER ISLANDS see French Establishments in Oceania.

GEORGIAN S,S,R, see U. S. S. R.

GEORGIE DU SUD see Falkland Islands.

GERMAN EAST AFRICA see 1. Belgian Congo.
2. Tanganyika.

GERMAN NEW GUINEA see New Guinea.

GERMAN SAMOA see Western Samoa.

GERMAN SOLOMON ISLANDS see New Guinea

GERMANy. Federal Republic, September 21, 1949.

Capital Bonn. Also German Democratic Republic (East Germany) Oct. 7, 1949. Standard Time

Meridian 15° EAST.

			L. M. T. VARIATION FROM S.T. m. s.	G. M. T. VARIATION FROM LMT. h. m. s.
Aachen, Rheinprov. Pr.	6E05	50N47	-35 40	- 0 24 20
Aalen Wurtembert	10E06	48N50	-19 36	- 0 40 24
Abbach Bayern	12E00	48N55	-12 00	- 0 48 00
Abbehausen, Oldenburg..........	8E30...	53N29...	-26 00...	- 0 34 00
Aix la Chapelle see Aachen.				
Allenstein, Preussen	20E28	53N46	+21 52	- 1 21 52
Altona, Holstein, Pr.	9E48	53N34	-20 48	- 0 39 12
Apolda, Sachsen-Weimar	11E31	51N02	-13 56	- 0 46 04
Aschaffenburg, Bayern..........	9E09...	49N59...	-23 24...	- 0 36 36
Augsburg, Bayern	10E54	48N22	-16 24	- 0 43 36
Baden-Baden, Baden	8E14	48N46	-27 04	- 0 32 56
Bad Homburg, Hessen-Nassau	8E36	40N13	-25 36	- 0 34 24
Bad Nauheim, Hessen	8E44	50N22	-25 04	- 0 34 56
Bamberg, Bayern.,............11E54...		49N54....	-12 24....	- 0 47 36
Bayreuth, Bayern	11E36	49N57	-13 36	- 0 46 24
Berchtesgaden, Bayern	13E00	47N38	- 8 00	- 0 52 00
Berlin, Brand., Pr.	13E23	52N30	- 6 28	- 0 53 32
Berlin-Schoneberg, Brand., Pr.	13E22	52N28	- 6 32	- 0 53 28
Beuthen, Schlesien, Pr.........	18E56...	50N21....	+15 44....	- 1 15 44
Bielefeld, West., Pr.	8E31	52N01	-25 56	- 0 34 04
Bochum, Westf., Pr.	7E12	51N29	-31 12	- 0 28 48
Bonn, Rheinprov., Pr.	7E05	50N44	-31 40	- 0 28 20
Brandenburg, Preussen	12E34	52N24	- 9 44	- 0 50 16
Braunschweig, Braunschweig.....	10E32...	52N16...	-17 52...	- 0 42 08
Bremen, Bremen	8E48	53N05	-24 48	- 0 35 12
Bremerhaven, Bremen	8E32	53N34	-25 52	- 0 34 08
Breslau, Schlesien, Pr.	17E02	51N07	+ 8 08	- 1 08 08
Brunswick see Braunschweig.				
Charlottenburg, Brand., Pr.....	13E17...	52N30...	- 6 52...	- 0 53 08
Chemnitz, Sachsen	12E55	50N50	- 8 20	- 0 51 40
Coln see Koln.				
Cologne, see Koln.				
Cottbus, Brand., Pr.	14E20	51N46	- 2 40	- 0 57 20
Crefeld see Krefeld.				
Cuxhaven, Hamburg	8E42	53N52	-25 12	- 0 34 48
Dachau, Bayern.................	11E27...	48N16...	-14 12...	- 0 45 48
Danzig see DANZIG, FREE CITY OF				
Darmstadt, Starkenburg, Hessen	8E40	49N52	-25 20	- 0 34 40
Dessau, Anhalt	12E17	51N50	-10 52	- 0 49 08
Detmold, Lippe	8E53	51N56	-24 28	- 0 35 32
Dartmund, West., Pr.	7E30	51N31	-30 00	- 0 30 00
Dresden, Sachsen	13E44	51N03	- 5 04	- 0 54 56
Duisburg, Rheinprov., Pr.......	6E46...	51N26...	-32 56...	- 0 27 04
Duren, Rheinprov.	6E29	50N49	-34 04	- 0 25 56
Dusseldorf, Rheinprov.	6E49	51N12	-32 44	- 0 27 16
Eckernforde, Schleswig-Holstein	9E51	54N28	-20 36	- 0 39 24
Eisenach, Sachsen-Weimar	10E20	50N59	-18 40	- 0 41 20
Elberfeld, Rheinprov., Pr.......	7E10...	51N15...	-31 20...	- 0 28 40
Erfurt, Sachsen, Pr.	11E03	50N59	-15 48	- 0 44 12

			L. M. T. VARIATION FROM S.T.	G. M. T. VARIATION FROM LMT
			m. s.	h. m. s.
GERMANY (continued.				
Erlangen, Bayern	11E00	49N36	-15 00	- 0 44 00
Essen, Rheinprov., Pr.	7E00	51N27	-32 00	- 0 28 00
Flensburg, Schleswig-Holstein	9E26	54N47	-22 16	- 0 37 44
Fulda, Hessen-Nassau, Pr.	9E42	50N34	-21 12	- 0 38 48
Frankfurt am Main, Hessen-Nassau, Pr.	8E41	50N07	-25 16	- 0 34 44
Frankfurt a. d. Oder, Preussen..	14E33...	52N22...	- 1 48...	- 0 58 12
Freiburg i. B., Baden	7E50	47N59	-28 40	- 0 31 20
Furth, Bayern	12E52	49N19	- 8 32	- 0 51 28
Gelsenkirchen, Wesft., Pr.	7E06	51N31	-31 36	- 0 28 24
Gera, Reuss-Gera................	12E04...	50N53...	-11 44...	- 0 48 16
Giessen, Hessen	8E40	50N34	-25 20	- 0 34 40
Goerlitz, Schlesien, Pr.	15E00	51N09	- 0 00	- 1 00 00
Gotenhafen see Gdynia, Poland.				
Gotha, S.-K. Gotha	10E34	50N57	-17 08	- 0 42 52
Gottingen, Hannover, Pr.........	9E57...	51N32...	-20 12...	- 0 39 48
Gumbinnen, Preussen	22E09	54N35	+28 36	- 1 28 36
Hagen, Westf., Pr.	7E28	51N22	-30 08	- 0 29 52
Halle a. d. Saale, Sachsen,Pr.	11E58	51N30	-12 08	- 0 47 52
Hamburg, Hamburg	10E00	53N33	-20 00	- 0 40 00
Hannover, Hannover, Pr..........	9E44...	52N22...	-21 04...	- 0 38 56
Harburg-Wilhelmsburg,Hannover,Pr.	9E59	53N28	-20 04	- 0 39 56
Heidelberg, Baden	8E41	49N25	-25 16	- 0 34 44
Heilbronn, Wurtt.	9E13	49N08	-23 08	- 0 36 52
Halgoland, Heligoland.............	7E53...	54N11...	-28 20...	- 0 31 32
Hildesheim, Hannover, Pr.	9E57	52N09	-20 12	- 0 39 48
Hindenburg, Schlesien, Pr.	18E47	50N19	+15 08	- 1 15 08
Hof, Bayern	11E55	50N19	-12 20	- 0 47 40
Insterburg, Preussen	21E47	54N38	+27 08	- 1 27 08
Kaiserslautern, Pfalz.............7E47...		49N27...	-29 52...	- 0 31 08
Karlsruhe, Baden	8E24	49N00	-26 24	- 0 33 36
Kassel, Hessen-Nassau, Pr.	9E30	51N19	-22 00	- 0 39 00
Kiel, Schleswig-Holstein	10E07	54N19	-19 32	- 0 40 28
Koblenz, Rheinprov., Pr.	7E35	50N22	-29 40	- 0 30 20
Koburg, Sachsen-Koburg-Gotha....	10E58...	50N16...	-16 08...	- 0 43 52
Koln (Cathedral), Rheinprov. Pr.	6E58	50N57	-32 08	- 0 27 52
Konigsberg, Preussen	20E31	54N42	+22 04	- 1 22 04
Konstenz, Baden	9E10	47N39	-23 20	- 0 36 40
Kopenick, Brand., Pr.	13E35	52N26	- 5 40	- 0 54 20
Krefeld, Rheinprov., Pr.........	6E34....	51N20....	-33 44...	- 0 26 16
Leipzig, Sachsen	12E24	51N20	-10 24	- 0 49 36
Lubeck, Lubeck	10E41	53N52	-17 16	- 0 42 44
Ludwigshafen, Pfalz	8E26	49N29	-26 16	- 0 33 44
Magdeburg, Sachsen, Pr.	11E39	52N08	-13 24	- 0 46 36
Mainz, Rheinhessen, Hessen......	8E16...	50N00...	-26 56...	- 0 33 04
Mannheim, Baden	8E28	49N29	-26 08	- 0 33 52
Marburg, Hessen-Nassau	8E46	50N49	-24 56	- 0 35 04
Mayence see Mainz.				
Meissen, Sachsen	13E29	51N10	- 6 04	- 0 53 56
Memel, Preussen.................	21E07...	55N43...	+24 28...	- 1 24 28
Munich see Munchen.				
Munchen, Bayern	11E33	48N09	-13 48	- 0 46 12
Munchen-Gladbach, Rheinpr., Pr.	6E27	51N11	-34 12	- 0 25 48

				L. M. T. VARIATION FRCM S. T.	G. M. T. VARIATION FROM LMT
				m. s.	h. m. s.
GERMANY (Continued)					
Munster, West., Pr.	7E38	51N58		-29 28	- 0 30 32
Neumunster, Schleswig-Holstein,Pr.9E59...		54N05...		-20 04...	- 0 39 56
Nurnberg, Bayern	11E05	49N26		-15 40	- 0 44 20
Oberammergau, Bayern	11E03	47N35		-15 48	- 0 44 12
Oldenburg, Oldenburg............	8E13...	53N08...		-27 08...	- 0 32 52
Oppeln, Schlesien, Pr.	17E56	50N41		+11 44	- 1 11 44
Oranienburg, Brand., Pr.	13E14	52N46		- 7 04	- 0 52 56
Osnabruck, Hannover, Pr.	8E03	52N17		-27 48	- 0 32 12
Pforzheim, Baden	8E42	48N54		-25 12	- 0 34 48
Pirmasens, Pfalz	7E36	49N12		-29 36	- 0 30 24
Plauen, Sachsen	12E08	50N30		-11 28	- 0 48 32
Potsdam, Brand., Pr............	13E04...	52N23...		- 7 44...	- 0 52 16
Ratibor, Schlesien, Pr.	18E13	50N06		+12 52	- 1 12 52
Ratisbon see Regensburg.					
Regensburg, Bayern	12E06	49N01		-11 36	- 0 48 24
Remscheid, Rheinprov., Pr.	7E11	51N11		-31 16	- 0 28 44
Reutlingen, Wurtt...............	9E12...	48N29...		-23 12...	- 0 36 48
Rostock, Meckl.-Schw.	12E08	54N06		-11 28	- 0 48 32
Saarbrucken, Rheinprov., Pr.	6E59	49N14		-32 04	- 0 27 56
Schleswig, Schleswig-Holstein	9E33	54N30		-21 48	- 0 38 12
Schneidemuhl, Preussen	16E45	53N09		+ 7 00	- 1 07 00
Schweinfurt, Bayern............	10E14...	50N03...		-19 04...	- 0 40 56
Schwerin, Meckl.-Schw.	11E25	53N38		-14 20	- 0 45 40
Solingen, Rheinprov., Pr.	7E04	51N10		-31 44	- 0 28 16
Spandau, Brand., Pr.	13E14	52N31		- 7 04	- 0 52 56
Speyer, Pfalz	8E26	49N19		-26 16	- 0 33 44
Starnberg, Bayern.............	11E20...	47N59...		-14 40...	- 0 45 20
Stettin, Preussen	14E34	53N26		- 1 44	- 0 58 16
Stolp, Preussen	17E01	54N28		+ 8 04	- 1 08 04
Stralsund, Preussen	13E05	54N19		- 7 40	- 0 52 20
Stuttgart, Wurtt.	9E11	48N47		-23 16	- 0 36 44
Tilsit, Preussen...............	21E53---	55N05...		+27 32...	- 1 27 32
Treves see Trier.					
Trier, Rheinprov. Pr.	6E39	49N46		-33 24	- 0 26 36
Ulm, Wurtt.	10E00	48N24		-20 00	- 0 40 00
Weimer, Sachsen-Weimar	11E20	50N59		-14 40	- 0 45 20
Wesermunde, Bremen-............	8E33...	53N32...		-25 48...	- 0 34 12
Wiesbaden, Hessen-Nassau,Pr.	8E14	50N05		-27 04	- 0 32 56
Wilhelmshaven, Hannover, Pr.	8E07	53N31		-27 32	- 0 53 28
Wittenberg, Sachsen, Pr.	12E38	51N52		- 9 28	- 0 50 32
Wolfenbuttel, Braunschweig	10E33	52N09		-17 48	- 0 42 12
Worms, Rheinhessen, Hessen......	8E22...	49N38...		-26 32...	- 0 33 28
Wurzburg, Bayern	9E57	49N48		-20 12	- 0 39 48
Zittau, Sachsen	14E49	50N53		- 0 44	- 0 59 16
Zwickau, Sachsen	12E31	50N43		- 9 56	- 0 50 04
Ghana see Togoland.					
GIBRALTAR. British Crown Colony, situated in					
Southern Europe. Standard Time Meridian 0°					
Gibraltar	5W21	36N09		-21 24	+ 0 21 24

GILBERT AND ELLICE ISLANDS., Capital: Ocean
Island. British Colony, situated in the
South Pacific. Some Islands are possessions
of the United States, others are
claimed by the U. S., as indicated.
Standard Time Meridian 165° WEST
and 180° EAST.

			L. M. T. VARIATION FROM S. T.	G. M. T. VARIATION FROM L.M.T.
			m. s.	h. m. s.
Apaiang	172E53	1N58	-28 08	-11 31 32
Baker Island (U.S.A.)	176W28	0N13	+14 08	+11 45 52
Banaba Island see Ocean Island.				
Butaritari, Makin	172E48	3N02	-28 48	-11 31 12
Canton Island (Claimed by U.S.)	171W43	2S50	-26 52	-11 26 52
Charlotte Island see Apaiang.				
Cook Island see Tarawa.				
Drummond Island see Tapeteuea.				
Enderbury Island, Phoenix Group				
(Claimed by U.S.A.)	171W05	3S08	-24 20	+11 24 20
English Harbor, Fanning	159W22	3N51	+22 32	+10 37 28
Holland Island see Howland Island.				
Howland Island (U.S.A.)	176W38	0N48	+13 28	+11 46 32
Mary Island see Canton Island.				
New Nantucket Island see Baker Island.				
New York Island see Washington Island.				
Ocean Island	169E35	0S53	+18 20	-11 18 20
Paanoba Island see Ocean Island.				
Phoebe Island see Baker Island.				
Sydney Island, Phoenix Group	171W16	4S27	-25 04	+11 25 04
Tapeteuea Island	175E11	1S29	-19 16	-11 40 44
Tarawa	173E00...	1N30...	-28 00...	-11 32 00
Tracy Island see Vaitupu.				
Vaitupu	178E41	7S28	- 5 16	-11 54 44
Washington Island, Village	160W26	4N43	+18 16	+10 41 44

GOA see Portuguese India.

GOLD COAST COLONY WITH ASHANTI AND NORTHERN TERRITORIES, AND
TOGOLAND. Capital: Accra. British Colony
situated in Africa. StandardTime Meridian 0°.

Accra, Gold Coast	0W14	5N31	- 0 56	+ 0 00 56
Ashanti, Ashanti	0E32	6N55	+ 2 08	- 0 02 08
Bawku, N. T.	0W13....	11N05...	- 0 52...	+ 0 00 52
Bekwai, Ashanti	1W35	6N28	- 6 20	+ 0 06 20
Cape Coast, Gold Coast	1W14	5N06	- 4 56	+ 0 04 56
Coomassie see Kumasi.				
Korofidua, Gold Coast	0W15	6N05	- 1 00	+ 0 01 00
Kumasi, Ashanti	1W38....	6N43...	- 6 32...	+ 0 06 32
Salaga, N. T.	0W31	8N33	- 2 04	+ 0 02 04
Sekondi, Gold Coast	1W44	4N56	- 6 56	+ 0 06 56
Tamale, N. T.	0W50	9N24	- 3 20	+ 0 03 20
Wa, N. T.	2W27....	10N04...	- 9 48...	+ 0 09 48
Yendi, Togoland	0E01	9N27	- 0 04	- 0 00 04

GRANDE BRETAGNE see Great Britain.

GREAT BRITAIN, AND NORTHERN IRELAND.

Capital: London. United Kingdom, including
Scotland (Capital, Edinburgh), Northern Ire- : L. M. T.   G. M. T.
land (Capital, Belfast), the Channel Islands :VARIATION   VARIATION
and the Isle of Man. Situated on the British:FROM S.T.   FROM LMT.
Isles in Europe. Standard Time Meridien 0°. :   m. s.   h. m. s.

Place	Long	Lat	LMT m.s.	GMT h.m.s.
Aberdare, Glamorgan	3W26	51N43	-13 44	+ 0 13 44
Aberdeen, Aberdeen	2W06	57N09	- 8 24	+ 0 08 24
Accrington, Lancashire	2W22	53N45	- 9 28	+ 0 09 28
Acton, Middlesex...............	0W16...	51N30..	- 1 04....	+ 0 01 04
Aldershot, Hampshire	0W46	51N15	- 3 04	+ 0 03 04
Alexandria, Dumbarton	4W35	56N00	-18 20	+ 0 18 20
Alloa, Clackmannan	3W47	56N07	-15 08	+ 0 15 08
Antrim, Antrim	6W13	54N43	-24 52	+ 0 24 52
Armagh, Armagh...............	6W39...	54N20...	-26 36...	+ 0 26 36
Ayr, Ayr	4W38	55N28	-18 32	+ 0 18 32
Banff, Banff	2W32	57N40	-10 08	+ 0 10 08
Ballymena, Antrim	6W17	54N52	-25 08	+ 0 25 08
Banbridge, Down	6W16	54N21	-25 04	+ 0 25 04
Bangor, Down..................	5W41...	54N39...	-22 44....	+ 0 22 44
Barnes, Surrey	0W15	51N29	- 1 00	+ 0 01 00
Barnsley, Yorkshire	1W29	53N53	- 5 29	+ 0 05 29
Barrhead, Renfrew	4W24	55N48	-17 36	+ 0 17 36
Barrow-in-Furness, Lancashire	3W14	54N07	-12 56	+ 0 12 56
Barry, Glamorgan...............	3W16...	51N25...	-13 04....	+ 0 13 04
Barvas, Ross & Cromarty	6W31	58N21	-26 04	+ 0 26 04
Bath, Somerset	2W22	51N23	- 9 28	+ 0 09 28
Bathgate, West Lothian	3W38	55N54	-14 32	+ 0 14 32
Bedford, Bedford	0W29	52N08	- 1 56	+ 0 01 56
Belfast, Antrim...............	5W55...	54N36...	-23 40....	+ 0 23 40
Bellshill, Lanark	4W01	55N49	-16 04	+ 0 16 04
Birkenhead, Cheshire	3W03	53N23	-12 12	+ 0 12 12
Birmingham, Warwick	1W54	53N28	- 7 36	+ 0 07 36
Blackburn, Lancashire	2W28	53N45	-9 52	+ 0 09 52
Blackpool, Lancashire..........	3W03...	53N49...	-12 12....	+ 0 12 12
Bolton, Lancashire	2W26	53N34	- 9 44	+ 0 09 44
Bonhill, Dumbarton	4W34	55N59	-16 16	+ 0 16 16
Borrowstounness, West Lothian	3W36	56N01	-14 24	+ 0 14 24
Rothwell, Lanark	4W04	55N48	-16 16	+ 0 16 16
Bournemouth, Hampshire.........	1W53...	50N43...	- 8 32...	+ 0 08 32
Bradford, Yorkshire	1W45	53N48	- 7 00	+ 0 07 00
Brighton, Sussex	0W08	50N50	- 0 32	+ 0 00 32
Bristol, Gloucester	2W36	51N27	-10 24	+ 0 10 24
Bromley, Kent	0E01	51N25	+ 0 04	- 0 00 04
Burnley, Lancashire............	2W15...	53N46...	- 9 00....	+ 0 09 00
Burton-upon-Trent, Stafford	1W38	52N48	- 6 32	+ 0 06 32
Bury, Lancashire	2W17	53N36	- 9 08	+ 0 09 08
Cambridge, Cambridge	0E08	53N12	+ 0 32	- 0 00 32
Cambuslang, Lanark	4W10	55N49	-16 40	+ 0 16 40
Canterbury, Kent..............	1E05...	51N17...	+ 4 20....	- 0 04 20
Cardiff, Glamorgan	3W10	51N29	-12 40	+ 0 12 40
Carlisle, Northumberland	2W57	54N53	-11 48	+ 0 11 48
Carmarthen, Carmarthen	4W18	51N51	-16 56	+ 0 16 56
Chatham, Kent	0E32	51N23	+ 2 08	- 0 02 08

58

			L. M. T. VARIATION FROM S.T.	G. M. T. VARIATION FROM LMT.
			m. s.	h. m. s.
GREAT BRITAIN (Continued)				
Cheltenham, Gloucester	2W06	51N54	- 8 24	+ 0 08 24
Chesterfield, Derby	1W25	53N14	- 5 40	+ 0 05 40
Clydebank, Dumbarton............	4W24...	55N54...	-17 36...	+ 0 17 36
Coatbridge, Lanark	4W02	55N52	-16 08	+ 0 16 08
Colchester, Essex	0E54	51N53	+ 3 36	- 0 03 36
Coleraine, Londonderry	6W40	54N08	-26 40	+ 0 26 40
Cookstown, Tyrone	6W45	54N39	-27 00	+ 0 27 00
Coventry, Warwick..............	1W31...	53N25...	- 6 04...	+ 0 06 04
Crewe, Cheshire	2W26	53N06	-10 44	+ 0 10 44
Cromarty, Ross & Cromarty	4W03	57N41	-16 12	+ 0 16 12
Croydon, Surrey	0W06	51N22	- 0 24	+ 0 00 24
Darlington, Durham	1W33	54N32	- 6 12	+ 0 06 12
Derby, Derby...................	1W29....	52N55...	- 5 56...	+ 0 05 56
Derry See Londonderry.				
Doncaster, York	1W08	53N31	- 4 32	+ 0 04 32
Douglas, Isle of Man	4N30	54N09	-10 00	+ 0 10 00
Dover, Kent	1E19	51N08	+ 5 16	- 0 05 16
Dudley, Worcester.............	2W05...	52N30...	- 8 20...	+ 0 08 20
Dumbarton, Dumbarton	4W34	55N57	-18 16	+ 0 18 16
Dumfries, Dumfries	3W36	55N04	-14 24	+ 0 14 24
Dundee, Angus	2W59	57N28	-11 56	+ 0 11 56
Dunfermline, Fife	3W28	56N04	-13 52	+ 0 13 52
Dungannon, Tyrone.............	6W46...	54N30...	-27 04...	+ 0 27 04
Duncon, Argyle	4W56	55N57	-19 44	+ 0 19 44
Durham, Durham	1W34	54N46	- 6 16	+ 0 06 16
Ealing, Middlesex	0W18	51N31	- 1 12	+ 0 01 12
East Ham, Essex	0E05	51N32	+ 0 20	- 0 00 20
Eastbourne, Sussex.............	0E17...	50N46...	+ 1 08...	- 0 01 08
Ebbw Vale, Monmouth	3W12	51N46	-12 48	+ 0 12 48
Edinburgh, Midlothian	3W11	55N57	-12 44	+ 0 12 44
Elgin, Elgin	3W19	57N39	-13 16	+ 0 13 16
Enfield, Middlesex	0W05	51N39	- 0 20	+ 0 00 20
Enniskillen, Fermanagh.........	6W38...	54N21...	-26 32...	+ 0 26 32
Epsom, Surrey	0W16	51N20	- 1 04	+ 0 01 04
Eton, Bucks.	0W36	51N29	- 2 24	+ 0 02 24
Exeter, Devon	3W31	50N43	-14 04	+ 0 14 04
Falkirk, Stirling	3W47	56N00	-15 08	+ 0 15 08
Folkestone, Kent..............	1E11....	51N05...	+ 4 44...	- 0 04 44
Forfar, Angus	2W53	56N39	-11 32	+ 0 11 32
Forres, Elgin	3W37	57N37	-14 28	+ 0 14 28
Fraserburgh, Aberdeen	2W00	57N42	- 8 00	+ 0 08 00
Galashiels, Selkirk	2W49	55N37	-11 16	+ 0 11 16
Gateshead, Durnam..............	1W36...	54N57...	- 6 24...	+ 0 06 24
Gillingham, Kent	0E33	51N23	+ 2 12	- 0 02 12
Glamis, Angus	3W00	56N37	-12 00	+ 0 12 00
Glasgow, Lanark	4W16	55N51	-17 04	+ 0 17 04
Gloucester, Gloucester	2W15	51N52	- 9 00	+ 0 09 00
Gravesend, Kent................	0E22...	51N26...	+ 1 28...	- 0 01 28
Great Yarmouth, Norfolk	1E44	52N37	+ 6 56	- 0 06 56
Greenock, Renfrew	4W46	55N57	-19 04	- 0 19 04
Grimsby, Lincoln	0W05	53N34	- 0 20	+ 0 00 20
Guilford, Surrey	0W34	51N14	- 2 16	+ 0 02 16

			L. M. T. VARIATION FROM S. T.	G. M. T. VARIATION FROM LMT
			m. s.	h. m. s.
GREAT BRITAIN (Continued)				
Halifax, Yorkshire	1W52	53N43	- 7 28	+ 0 07 28
Hamilton, Lanark	4W02	55N47	-16 08	+ 0 16 08
Harrogate, Yorkshire..............	1W33...	53N59...	- 6 12...	+ 0 06 12
Hastings, Sussex	0E54	50N51	+ 0 36	- 0 03 36
Hawick, Roxburgh	2W47	55N26	-11 08	+ 0 11 08
Hereford, Hereford	2W43	52N03	-10 52	+ 0 10 52
Hertford, Hertford	0W04	51N48	- 0 16	+ 0 00 16
Hornsey, Middlesex..............	0W08...	51N35...	- 0 32...	+ 0 00 32
Hove, Sussex	0W11	50N50	- 0 44	+ 0 00 44
Huddersfield, Yorkshire	1W47	53N39	- 7 08	+ 0 07 08
Hull, York see Kingston upon Hull.				
Ilford, Essex	0E06	51N33	+ 0 24	- 0 00 24
Inverness, Inverness..............	4W14...	57N29...	-16 56...	+ 0 16 56
Ipswich, Suffolk	1E10	53N03	+ 4 40	- 0 04 40
Irvine, Ayr	4W40	55N37	-18 40	+ 0 18 40
Johnstone, Renfrew	4W30	55N50	-10 00	+ 0 10 00
Keighley, Yorkshire	1W55	53N52	- 7 40	+ 0 07 40
Kilmarnock, Ayrshire..............	4W30...	55N37...	-18 00...	+ 0 18 00
Kingston upon Hull, Yorkshire	0W20	53N45	- 1 20	+ 0 01 20
Kingston-upon.Thames, Surrey	0W17	51N25	- 1 08	+ 0 01 08
Kirkcaldy, Fife	3W10	56N07	-12 40	+ 0 12 40
Kirkintilloch, Dumbarton	4W09	55N56	-16 36	+ 0 16 36
Kirkwall, Orkney.................	2W58...	58N59...	-11 52...	+ 0 11 52
Lanark, Lanark	3W47	55N41	-15 08	+ 0 15 08
Lancaster, Lancashire	2W48	53W03	-11 12	+ 0 11 12
Larne, Antrim	5W49	54N50	-23 16	+ 0 23 16
Largs, Ayr	4W52	55N48	-19 28	+ 0 19 28
Lasswade, Midlothian..............	3W07...	55N53...	-12 28...	+ 0 12 28
Leeds, Yorkshire	1W32	53N48	- 6 08	+ 0 06 08
Leicester, Leicester	1W03	53N39	- 4 32	+ 0 04 32
Leigh, Lancashire	2W30	53N30	-10 00	+ 0 10 00
Leith, Midlothian	3W11	55N58	-12 44	+ 0 12 44
Lerwick, Shetland Islands........	1W09...	60N10...	- 4 36...	+ 0 04 36
Lesmahagow, Lanark	3W53	55N39	-15 32	+ 0 15 32
Lincoln, Lincoln	0W32	53N13	- 2 08	+ 0 02 08
Linlithgow, West Lothian	3W36	55N59	-14 24	+ 0 14 24
Lisburn, Antrim	6W04	54N31	-24 16	+ 0 24 16
Liverpool, Lancashire............	2W58...	53N25...	-11 52...	+ 0 11 52
LONDON--Consists of 28 Buroughs as given. When the Borough				
is unknown use the coordinates of				
St. Paul's Cathedral	0W06	51N31	- 0 24	+ 0 00 24
Battersea	0W10	51N28	- 0 40	+ 0 00 40
Bermondsey......................	0W05...	51N30...	- 0 20...	+ 0 00 20
Bethnal Green	0W03	51N32	- 0 12	+ 0 00 12
Camberwell	0W05	51N27	- 0 20	+ 0 00 20
Chelsea	0W10	51N29	- 0 40	+ 0 00 40
Deptford	0W02	51N29	- 0 08	+ 0 00 08
Finsbury.......................	0W05...	51N31...	- 0 20...	+ 0 00 20
Fulham	0W13	51N28	- 0 52	+ 0 00 52
Greenwich	0W00	51N29	- 0 00	0 00 00
Hackney	0W03	51N33	- 0 12	+ 0 00 12

			L. M. T. VARIATION FROM S. T.		G. M. T. VARIATION FROM LMT.		
GREAT BRITAIN (Continued)			m.	s.	h.	m.	s.
London (Continued)							
Hammersmith	OW13	51N30	- 0	52	+ 0	00	52
Hampstead	OW11	51N34	- 0	44	+ 0	00	44
Holborn	OW07	51N31	- 0	28	+ 0	00	28
Islington	OW06	51N33	- 0	24	+ 0	00	24
Kensington	OW12	51N30	- 0	48	+ 0	00	48
Lambeth	OW06	51N28	- 0	24	+ 0	00	24
Lewisham	OW01	51N27	- 0	04	+ 0	00	04
Paddington	OW12	51N32	- 0	48	+ 0	00	48
Poplar	OW10	51N31	- 0	40	+ 0	00	40
St. Marylebone	OW09	51N31	- 0	36	+ 0	00	36
St. Pancras	OW07	51N32	- 0	28	+ 0	00	28
Shoreditch	OW05	51N32	- 0	20	+ 0	00	20
Southwark	OW06	51N30	- 0	24	+ 0	00	24
Stepney	9W02	51N31	- 0	08	+ 0	00	08
Stoke Newington	OW05	51N34	- 0	20	+ 0	00	20
Wandsworth	OW12	51N28	- 0	48	+ 0	00	48
Westminster	OW09	51N30	- 0	36	+ 0	00	36
Woolwich	OW05	51N29	+ 0	20	- 0	00	20
London--Other Points.							
City	OW05	51N31	- 0	20	+ 0	00	20
Crystal Palace	OW04	51N25	- 0	16	+ 0	00	16
Buckingham Palace	OW08	51N30	- 0	32	+ 0	00	32
Dalston	OW05	51N33	- 0	20	+ 0	00	20
Hornsey	OW06	51N33	- 0	24	+ 0	00	24
Houses of Parliament	OW07	51N30	- 0	28	+ 0	00	28
Kensington Palace	OW08	51N30	- 0	32	+ 0	00	32
Whitechapel	OW04	51N31	- 0	16	+ 0	00	16
Londonderry, Derry	7W20	55N00	-29	20	+ 0	29	20
Lowestoft, Suffolk	1E45	52N29	+ 7	00	- 0	07	00
Lurgan, Armagh	6W20	54N28	-25	20	+ 0	25	20
Luton, Bedfordshire	OW25	51N53	- 1	40	+ 0	01	40
Macclesfield Chesire	2W08	53N16	- 8	36	+ 0	08	32
Macduff, Banff	2W30	57N40	-10	00	+ 0	10	00
Maidstone, Kent	0E31	51N17	+ 2	04	- 0	02	04
Manchester, Lancashire	2W15	53N29	- 9	00	+ 0	09	00
Mansfield, Nottinghamshire	1W12	53N09	- 4	48	+ 0	04	48
Merthyr Tydfil, Glamorgan	3W22	51N45	-13	28	+ 0	13	28
Middleborough, York	1W14	54N34	- 4	56	+ 0	04	56
Mitcham, Surrey	OW10	51N24	- 0	40	+ 0	00	40
Monmouth, Monmouthshire	2W43	51N49	-10	52	+ 0	10	52
Motherwell, Lanark	4W00	55N49	-16	00	+ 0	16	00
Nairn, Nairn	3W52	57N35	-15	28	+ 0	15	28
Newcastle-upon-Tyne, Northumb	1W36	54N58	- 6	24	+ 0	06	24
Newport, Isle of Wight	1W18	50N42	- 5	12	+ 0	05	12
Newport, Monmouthshire	3W00	51N35	-12	00	+ 0	12	00
Newry, Down	6W20	54N11	-25	20	+ 0	25	20
Newtownarde, Down	5W42	54N35	-22	48	+ 0	22	48
Northampton, Northampton	OW52	52N13	- 3	28	+ 0	03	28
Norwich, Norfolk	1E18	52N38	+ 5	12	- 0	05	12
Nottingham, Nottingham	1W09	52N57	- 4	36	+ 0	04	36
Oldham, Lancashire	2W07	53N32	- 8	28	+ 0	08	28
Omagh, Tyrone	7W19	54N36	-29	16	+ 0	29	16

				L. M. T. VARIATION FROM S.T. m. s.	G. M. T. VARIATION FROM LMT h. m. s.
GREAT BRITAIN (Continued)					
Oxford, Oxford	1W15	51N45		- 5 00	+ 0 05 00
Paisley, Renfrew	4W25	55N51		-17 40	+ 0 17 40
Peebles, Peebles...................	3W11...	55N39...		-12 44...	+ 0 12 44
Pembroke, Pembroke	4W55	51N40		-19 40	+ 0 19 40
Perth, Perth	3W26	56N24		-13 44	+ 0 13 44
Peterhead, Aberdeen	1W46	57N30		- 7 04	+ 0 07 04
Plymouth, Devon	4W08	50N22		-16 32	+ 0 16 32
Pontypridd, Glamorgan.............	3W21...	51N35...		-13 24...	+ 0 13 24
Portadown, Armagh	5W27	54N25		-25 48	+ 0 25 48
Port Glasgow, Renfrew	4W41	55N56		-18 44	+ 0 18 44
Portglenone, Antrim	6W28	54N52		-25 52	+ 0 25 52
Portabello, Midlothian	3W07	55N57		-12 28	+ 0 12 28
Portsmouth, Hampshire.............	1W05...	50N47...		- 4 20...	+ 0 04 20
Port Talbot, Glamorgan	3W45	51N35		-15 00	+ 0 15 00
Preston, Lancashire	2W42	53N46		-10 48	+ 0 10 48
Reading, Berkshire	0W58	51N27		- 3 52	+ 0 03 52
Redhill Surrey	0W10	51N14		- 0 40	+ 0 00 40
Reigate, Surrey...................	0W12...	51N14...		- 0 12...	+ 0 00 48
Renfrew, Renfrew	4W25	55N53		-17 32	+ 0 17 32
Rhayader, Radnor	5W51	52N18		-23 24	+ 0 23 24
Rhonda, Glamorgan	3W31	51N39		-14 04	+ 0 14 04
Richmond, Surrey	0W18	51N27		- 1 12	+ 0 01 12
Rochdale, Lancashire..............	2W09...	53N37...		- 8 36...	+ 0 08 36
Rochester, Kent	0E30	51N23		+ 2 00	- 0 02 00
Rotherham, Yorkshire	1W21	53N26		- 5 24	+ 0 05 24
Saint Albans (Verulamium), Hertfordshire..............	0W20...	51N45...		- 1 20...	+ 0 01 20
St. Andrews, Fife	2W48	56N21		-11 12	+ 0 11 12
St. Helens, Lancashire	2W44	53N27		-10 56	+ 0 10 56
St. Melier, Jersey Island	2W06	49N11		- 8 24	+ 0 08 24
St. Peter Port, Guernsey Is.	2W32	49N28		-10 08	+ 0 10 08
Salisbury, Wiltshire	1W48	51N04		- 7 12	+ 0 07 12
Salford, Lancashire..............	2W18...	53N29...		- 9 12...	+ 0 09 12
Saltcoats, Ayr	4W47	55N38		-19 08	+ 0 19 08
Scarborough, Yorkshire	0W24	54N17		- 1 36	+ 0 01 36
Sevenoaks, Kent	0E12	51N16		+ 0 48	- 0 00 48
Sheffield, Yorkshire	1W29	53N23		- 5 56	+ 0 05 56
Shrewsbury, Shropshire...........	2W45...	52N42...		-11 00...	+ 0 11 00
Slough, Buckinham	0W36	51N31		- 2 24	+ 0 02 24
Southampton, Hampshire	1W23	50N54		- 5 32	+ 0 05 32
Southend-on-Sea, Essex	0E43	51N32		+ 2 52	- 0 02 52
Southport, Lancashire	3W00	53N39		-12 00	+ 0 12 00
South Shields, Durham............	1W26...	54N59...		- 5 44...	+ 0 05 44
Stafford, Stafford	2W07	52N48		- 8 28	+ 0 08 28
Stamford, Rutland	0W29	52N39		- 1 56	+ 0 01 56
Stirling, Stirling	3W56	56N07		-15 44	+ 0 15 44
Stockport, Cheshire	2W09	53N24		- 8 36	+ 0 08 36
Stockton-on-Tees, Durham.........	1W18...	54N34...		- 5 12...	+ 0 05 12
Stoke-upon-Trent, Stafford	2W11	53N00		- 8 44	+ 0 08 44
Strabane, Tyrone	7W28	54N50		-29 52	+ 0 29 52
Stratford-upon-Avon, Warwick	1W08	52N24		- 4 32	+ 0 04 32

			L. M. T. VARIATION FROM S. T. m. s.	G. M. T. VARIATION FROM LMT. h. m. s.
GREAT BRITAIN (Continued)				
Sunderland, Durham.	1W23	54N55	- 5 32	+ 0 05 32
Sutton, Surrey	0W12	51N21	- 0 48	+ 0 00 48
Swansea, Glamorgan	3W57	51N38	-15 48	+ 0 15 48
Swindon, Wiltshire	1W47	51N34	- 7 08	+ 0 07 08
Teddington, Middlesex	0W20	51N26	- 1 20	+ 0 01 20
Tipton, Stafford	2W04	52N32	- 8 16	+ 0 08 16
Tonbridge, Kent	0E16	51N11	+ 1 04	- 0 01 04
Tewksbury, Gloucestershire	2W03	52N00	- 8 12	+ 0 08 12
Torquay, Devon	3W32	50N28	-14 08	+ 0 14 08
Troon, Ayr	4W40	55N33	-18 40	+ 0 18 40
Tunbridge Wells, Kent	0E16	51N08	+ 1 04	- 0 01 04
Twickenham, Middlesex	0W20	51N27	- 1 20	+ 0 01 20
Tynemouth, Northumberland	1W26	55N01	- 5 44	+ 0 05 44
Wakefield, Yorkshire	1W30	53N41	- 6 00	+ 0 06 00
Wallasey, Cheshire	3W04	53N25	-12 16	+ 0 12 16
Walsall, Staffordshire	1W59	52N35	- 7 56	+ 0 07 56
Walthamshow, Essex	0W02	51N34	- 0 08	+ 0 00 08
Warrington, Lancashire	2W36	53N24	-10 24	+ 0 10 24
West Bromwich, Staffordshire	2W00	52N32	- 8 00	+ 0 08 00
West Ham, Essex	0E01	51N31	+ 0 04	- 0 00 04
West Hartlepool, Durham	1W12	54N41	- 4 48	+ 0 04 48
Wigan, Lancashire	2W38	53N33	-10 32	+ 0 10 32
Wimbledon, Surrey	0W13	51N25	- 0 52	+ 0 00 52
Windsor, Berkshire	0W37	51N29	- 2 28	+ 0 02 28
Wishaw, Lanark	3W55	55N47	-15 40	+ 0 15 40
Wolverhampton, Staffordshire	2W07	52N35	- 8 28	+ 0 08 28
Worcester, Worcestershire	2W13	52N11	- 2 13	+ 0 08 52
Worksop, Nottinghamshire	1W08	53N18	- 4 32	+ 0 04 32
York, Yorkshire	1W05	53N57	- 4 20	+ 0 04 20
GRECE see Greece.				
GREECE. Capital Athinai (Athens). Kingdom, situated in Southeastern Europe. Standard Time Meridian 30° EAST.				
Aigina (Aegina), A-V	23E26	37N45	-26 16	- 1 33 44
Aigion, Achaia	22E05	38N14	-31 40	- 1 28 20
Alexandroupolis, Hevros	25E51	40N50	-16 36	- 1 43 24
Amphissa, F.-F.	22E22	38N31	-30 32	- 1 29 28
Andros, Kyklades	24E57	37N50	-20 12	- 1 39 48
Argos, Argolis	22E43	37N38	-29 08	- 1 30 52
Argostolion, Kephallenia X	20E29	38N11	-38 04	- 1 21 56
Arkansa, Karpathos, Dod.	27E08	35N28	-11 28	- 1 48 32
Athinai (Athens), A-V	23E43	37N59	-25 08	- 1 34 52
Castelrosso see Kastellprizo.				
Coo see Koos.				
Corfu see Kerkyra.				
Corinth see Korinthos.				
Dede-Agatch see Alexandroupolis.				
Delphi see Khryson.				
Drama, Drama	24E09	41N08	-23 24	- 1 36 36
Edessa, Pelli	22E03	40N48	-31 48	- 1 28 12
Elefsis (Eleusis) A-V	23E33	36N03	-25 48	- 1 34 12
Eraklion, Crete, Crete	25E08	35N20	-19 28	- 1 40 32

			L. M. T. VARIATION FROM S.T.	G. M. T. VARIATION FROM LMT.
			m. s.	h. m. s.
GREECE (Continued)				
Ermoupolis, Syros	24E57	37N27	-20 12	- 1 39 48
Florina, Florina	21E25	40N47	-34 20	- 1 25 40
Gumuljina see Komotini				
Igoumenitsa, Ioannina	20E15	39N30	-39 00	- 1 21 00
Ioannina, Ioannina	20E50	39N40	-36 40	- 1 23 20
Ithaki (Ithica), Kephallenia....	20E43...	38N21...	-37 08...	- 1 22 52
Kalamata see Kalame.				
Kaleme, Massinia	22E08	37N03	-31 28	- 1 28 32
Kandia see Eraklion.				
Kanea, see Khania.				
Karlovassi, Samos	26E42	37N48	-13 12	- 1 46 48
Karyai, Agion Oros	24E14	40N14	-23 04	- 1 36 56
Kastellorizo, Dodecanese........	29E35...	36N07...	- 1 40...	- 1 58 20
Kastron, Limnos	25E04	39N52	-19 44	- 1 40 16
Kavalla, Kavalla	24E25	40N56	-22 20	- 1 37 40
Khalkis, Evvia	23E36	38N28	-25 36	- 1 34 24
Khania, Khania	24E01	35N32	-23 56	- 1 36 04
Khios, Khios....................	26E08....	38N22...	-15 28...	- 1 44 32
Khryson, A.-A.	22E27	38N28	-30 12	- 1 29 48
Komotini, Rodhopi	25E25	41N07	-18 20	- 1 41 40
Koos, Dodecanese	27E09	36N53	-11 24	- 1 48 36
Korinthos, Korinthos	22E55	37N56	-28 20	- 1 31 40
Kozani, Kozani.................	21E47...	40N18...	-32 52...	- 1 27 08
Lamia, Phthiosis	22E26	38N54	-30 16	- 1 29 44
Larisa (Larissa), Larisa	22E25	39N38	-30 20	- 1 29 40
Lepanto, see Nafpaktos.				
Leros see Porto Lago.				
Madraki see Kastellorizo.				
Marathon, A.-V.	23E57	38N10	-24 12	- 1 35 48
Megara, A.-V.	23E20	38N00	-26 40	- 1 33 20
Mesolonghion (Missolounghi).A&A	21E25	38N23	-34 20	- 1 25 40
Mt. Athos see Karyai.				
Mytilini, Lesvos................	26E32...	39N06...	-13 52...	- 1 46 08
Nafpaktos, A.-A.	21E50	38N24	-32 40	- 1 27 20
Naxos, Kyklades	25E23	37N06	-18 28	- 1 41 32
Patmos, Patmos	26E33	36N19	-13 48	- 1 46 12
Patrai (Patras), Achaia	21E44	38N15	-33 04	- 1 26 56
Pireefs (Piraeus), A.-V.........	23E39...	37N57...	-25 24...	- 1 34 36
Polygyros, Khalkis	23E26	40N22	-26 16	- 1 33 44
Porto Lago, Leros, Dodecanese	26E51	37N09	-12 36	- 1 47 24
Preveza, Preveza	20E45	38N57	-37 00	- 1 23 00
Paerimos, Pserimos, Dodecanese	27E09	36N56	-11 24	- 1 48 36
Pyrgos, Ilia	21E28...	37N41...	-34 08...	- 1 25 52
Rethimi, Rethimi	24E30	35N22	-22 00	- 1 38 00
Rhodes see Rodi.				
Rodi, Rodi, Dodecanese	28E16	36N27	- 6 56	- 1 53 04
Salamis, A.-V.	23E29	37N58	-26 04	- 1 33 56
Salonica see Thessaloniki.				
Salona see Amphissa.				
Samothraki, Evros	25E32	40N28	-17 52	- 1 42 08
Serrai (Seres), Serrai	23E32	41N04	-25 52	- 1 34 08
Sparta, Lakonia	22E26	37N05	-30 16	- 1 29 44

			L. M. T. VARIATION FROM S. T.	G. M. T. VARIATION FROM LMT.

GREECE. (Continued)
  Thebe see Thivai
  Thebes see Thiyai

			m. s.	h. m. s.
Thessalonika, Thessalonika	22E56	40N38	-28 16	- 1 31 44
Thivai, A.-V.............	23E19...	38N20...	-26 44...	- 1 33 16
Trikkala, Trikkala	21E45	39N33	-33 00	- 1 27 00
Tripolis, Ardakia	22E23	37N30	-26 28	- 1 33 32
Vathy, Samos	26E59	37N44	-12 04	- 1 47 56
Volos, Thessalonika	22E56	39E22	-28 16	- 1 31 44

  Yannina see Ioannina.

| Zakynthos (Zante), Zakynthos | 20E54 | 37N47 | -36 24 | - 1 23 36 |

GREENLAND. Capital: Godhavn. Danish Colony, sit-
    uated in the Arctic Ocean. Standard Time
      Meridians 30°,45°, 60° and 75° WEST.

Angmagssalk	37W38	65N37	+29 28	+ 2 30 32
Christianshab	51W11	68N50	-24 44	+ 3 24 44
Egesminde	52W53	68N43	-31 32	+ 3 31 32
Etah	72W39	78N18	+ 9 24	+ 4 50 36
Frederikshab..................	49W44...	62N00...	-18 56 ..	+ 3 18 56
Godhavn	53W32	69N15	-34 08	+ 3 34 08
Godthaab	51W43	64N11	-26 52	+ 3 26 52
Holsteinborg	53W36	66N56	-34 24	+ 3 34 24
Ivigtut	48W10	61N12	-12 40	+ 3 12 40
Jakobshavn..................	51W02...	69N13...	-24 08...	+ 3 24 08
Julianehaab	46W06	60N43	- 4 24	+ 3 04 24

  Kap York see Thule.
  Lievely see Gothavn.

| Ritenbank | 51W19 | 69N46 | -25 16 | + 3 25 16 |
| Scoresby Sund.................. | 21W57... | 70N30... | +32 12... | + 1 27 48 |

  Sisimut see Holsteinborg.

Sukkertoppen	52W53	65N24	-31 32	+ 3 31 32
Thule	68W50	76N33	+24 40	+ 4 35 20
Umanak	52W08	70N40	-28 32	+ 3 28 32
Upurhivik..................	56W11...	72N47...	-44 44...	+ 3 44 44

GRENADA see British West Indies.
GRENADINES see British West Indies.
GROENLANDE see Greenland.'
GUADELOUPE AND DEPENDENCIES. Capital: Basse Terre.
    French Colony situated in Lesser Antilles.
    Standard Time Meridian 60° WEST.

Basse-Terre	60W44	16N00	- 2 56	+ 4 02 56
Bourg, Iles des Saintes	61W36	15N52	- 6 20	+ 4 06 20
Goyave	61W35	16N08	- 6 20	+ 4 06 20
Brand Bourg, Marie Galante.......	61W19...	15N53...	- 5 16...	+ 4 05 16
Grande Anse, Desirade	61W05	16N18	- 4 20	+ 4 04 20
Gustavia, St. Barthelemy	62W51	17N54	-11 24	+ 4 11 24
Marigot, St. Martin	63W06	18N04	-12 24	+ 4 12 24
Pointe a Pitre	61W35	16N14	- 6 12	+ 4 06 12
Port Louis..................	61W32...	16N25...	- 6 08...	+ 4 06 08
Sainte-Rose	61W42	16N20	- 6 48	+ 4 06 48

GUAHANI (GUAJAN) see Guam.

GUAM. Capital: Agana. A possession of United States, situated in the Mariana Islands, in the North Pacific. Standard Time Meridian 150° EAST.	:	L. M. T. VARIATION FROM S.T.	G. M. T. VARIATION FROM LMT.
	:	m. s.	h. m. s.
Agana	144E45	13N28	-21 00	- 9 39 00
Agat..........................	144E40 ..	13N24...	-21 20...- 9 38 40
Apra Harbor	144E38	13N27	-21 28	- 9 38 32
Asan	144E43	13N28	-21 08	- 9 38 52
Dededo	144E49	13N31	-20 44	- 9 39 16
Inarajan	144E45	13N17	-21 00	- 9 39 00
Merizo.......................	144E50..	13N15...	-20 40...- 9 39 20
Piti	144E41	13N28	-21 16	- 9 38 44
Port Apra see Apra Harbor.				
Sinajaro	144E45	13N28	-21 00	- 9 39 00
Umatac	144E40	13N18	-21 20	- 9 38 40
Yona.........................	144E47...13N25...	-20 52...- 9 39 08

GUATAMALA. Capital: Guatamala, Republic, situated in Central America. Standard Time Meridian 90° WEST.

Amatitlan, Guatamala	90W38	14N28	- 2 32	+ 6 02 32
Antigua, Sacatepequez...........	90W44...	14N34...	- 2 56...+ 6 02 56
Chimaltanango, Chimaltenango	90W50	14N38	- 3 20	+ 6 03 20
Chiquimula, Chiquimula	89W32	14N49	- 1 52	+ 6 58 08
Coban, Alta Verapaz	90W20	15N29	- 1 20	+ 6 01 20
Cuajiniquilapa, Santa Rosa	90W17	14N16	- 1 08	+ 6 01 08
Escuintla, Escuintle............	90W47...	14N17...	- 3 08..+ 6 03 08
Flores, El Peten	89W53	16N56	+ 0 28	+ 5 59 32
Guatemala, Guatemala	90W31	14N38	- 2 04	+ 6 02 04
Huehuetenanga, Huehuetenango	91W28	15N19	- 5 52	+ 6 05 52
Jalapa, Jalapa	89W59	14N38	+ 0 04	+ 5 59 56
Jutiapa, Jutiapa................	89W53...	14N17...	+ 0 28...+ 5 59 32
La Libertad, El Peten	90W07	16N47	- 0 28	+ 6 00 28
Livingston, Izabel	88W45	15N49	+ 5 00	+ 5 55 00
Mazatenango, Suchitepeque	91W30	14N32	- 6 00	+ 6 06 00
Progreso, El Progreso	90W04	14N50	- 0 16	+ 6 00 16
Puerto Barrios,Izabel............88W36...	15N43...	+ 5 36...+ 5 54 24
Quezaltenango, Quezaltenango	91W31	14N50	- 6 04	+ 6 06 04
Retalhueleu, Retalhueleu	91W40	14N31	- 6 40	+ 6 06 40
Salama, Baja Verapaz	90W16	15N06	- 1 04	+ 6 01 04
San Marcos, San Marcos	91W48	14N57	- 7 12	+ 6 07 12
Santa Cruz de Quiche, El Quiche..	91W07...	15N02...	- 4 28...+ 6 04 28
Solola, Solola	91W11	14N45	- 4 44	+ 6 04 44
Totonicapan, Totonicapan	91W22	14N54	- 5 28	+ 6 05 28
Zacapa, Zacapa	89W31	14N59	+ 1 56	+ 5 58 04

GRIQUALAN, EAST AND WEST see Union of South Africa.

QUIANA see British, French Guiana and Surinam.

GUIENA see 1. French West Africa. Independent Oct. 2, 1958.
　　　　　　2. Portuguese West Africa.
　　　　　　3. Spanish Guinea.

GUINEE ESPAGNOLE see Spanish Guinea.

GUINEE FRANCAISE see French West Africa.

GUINEE PORTUGAISE see Portuguese West Africa.

GUYANNE BRITANNIQUE see British Guiana.

GUYANNE FRANCAISE see French Guiana
GUYANNE HOLLANDAISE see Surinam.
HAITI. Capital: Port-au-Prine. Republic,
        situated in the Greater Antilles.
        Standard Time Meridian 75° WEST.

			L. M. T. VARIATION FROM S.T. m. s.	G. M. T. VARIATION FROM LMT. h. m. s.
Anse-a-Veau, Sud	73W21	18N40	+ 6 36	+ 4 53 24
Aux Cayes see Les Cayes.				
Cap Haitien. Nord	72W13	19N47	+11 08	+ 4 48 52
Gonaive, Atr	72W40	19N27	+ 9 20	+ 4 50 40
Jacmel, Ouest...................	72W32...	18N14...	+ 9 52...	+ 4 50 08
Jeremie, Sud	74W07	18N39	+ 3 32	+ 4 56 28
Le Limbe, Nord	72W22	19N44	+10 32	+ 4 49 28
Le Mole St. Nicholas, Nord-Ouest	73W23	19N49	+ 6 28	+ 4 53 32
Les Cayes, Sud...................	73W44...	18N12...	+ 5 04...	+ 4 54 56
Los Coteaux, Sud	74W02	18N12	+ 3 52	+ 4 56 08
Port-au-Prince, Ouest	72W20	18N33	+10 40	+ 4 49 20
Port de Paix, Nord-Ouest	72W47	19N58	+ 8 52	+ 4 51 08
Saint Marc. Atr.	72W42	19N07	+ 9 12	+ 4 50 48

HACHEMITE, ROYAUME see Trans-Jordan.
HASHEMITE KINGDOM see Trans-Jordan.
HAUTE VOLTA see French West Africa.
HEBRIDES ISLANDS see Great Britain.
HEDJAZ, HEJAZ see Saudi Arabia.
HERVEY ISLANDS see Cook Islands.
HERZEGOVINA see Yugoslavia.
HOLLAND see The Netherlands.
HONDURAS. Capital: Tegucigalpa. Situated
        in Central America. Standard Time
        Meridian 90° WEST.

Alianza, Valle....................	87W44...	13N31...	+ 9 04...	+ 5 50 56
Choluteca, Choluteca	87W13	13N17	+11 08	+ 5 48 52
Comayagua, Comayagua	87W38	14N24	+ 9 28	+ 5 50 32
Gracias, Gracias	88W38	14N34	+ 5 28	+ 5 54 32
Juticalpa, Olancho	86W16	14N39	+14 56	+ 5 45 04
La Ceiba, Atlantida.............	86W50...	15N46...	+12 40...	+ 5 47 20
La Esperanza, Inticuba	88W19	14N19	+ 6 44	+ 5 53 16
La Paz, La Paz	87W40	14N16	+ 9 20	+ 5 50 40
Nacaome, Valle	87W29	13N31	+10 04	+ 5 49 56
Nueva Valladolid see Comayagua.				
Ocotepeque, Ocotepeque...........	89W13...	14N24...	+ 3 08...	+5 56 52
Pespire, Choluteca	87W21	13N35	+10 36	+ 5 49 24
Progreso, Yoro	87W49	15N22	+ 9 24	+ 5 51 16
Puerto Cabellos see Puerto Cortes.				
Puerto Cortes, Cortes	87W56	15N51	+ 8 16	+ 5 52 44
Roatan, Islas de la Bahia	86W31	16N20	+13 56	+ 5 46 04
San Francisco, Morazan...........	88W07...	13N41...	+ 7 32..	+ 5 52 28
San Juan de Flores, Fr. Morazan	87W02	14N15	+11 52	+ 5 48 08
San Lorenzo, Valle	87W27	13N34	+10 12	+ 5 49 48
San Pedro Sula, Cortes	88W02	15N27	+ 7 52	+ 5 52 08
Santa Barbara, Santa Barbara	88W17	14N51	+ 6 52	+ 5 53 08
Santa Rosa de Copan, Copan.......	88W50...	14N45...	+ 4 40..	+ 5 55 20
Tegucigalpa, Honduras	87W13	14N06	+11 08	+ 5 48 52
Tela, Atlantida	87W30	15N46	+10 00	+ 5 50 00

		L. M. T. VARIATION FROM S.T.	G. M. T. VARIATION FROM LMT.

HONDURAS (Continued)

			m. s.	h. m. s.
Trujillo, Colon	86W00	15N55	+16 00	+ 5 44 00
Yoro, Yoro	87W08	15N08	+11 28	+ 5 48 32
Yuscaran, Paraiso	86W49	13N55	+12 44	+ 5 47 16

HONDURAS BRITANNIQUE see British Hondura.

HONGKONG. British Crown Colony, situated in the South China Sea. Standard Time Meridian 120° EAST.

Hong Kong	114E10	22N16	-23 20	- 7 36 40
Victoria (British)	114E09	22N17	-23 24	- 7 36 36

HONGRIE see Hungary.

HOORN OR HORN ISLANDS see New Caledonia and Dependencies.

HUNGARY. Capital: Budapest. Kingdom, situated in Central Europe. Standard Time Meridian 15° EAST. Places marked * have been recaptured by Czechoslovakia in 1945.

Aszod, Pest	19E30	47N39	+18 00	- 1 18 00
Baja, Bacs-Bodrog	18E57	46N11	+15 48	- 1 15 48
Balassagyarmat, Nograd-Hont	19E18	48N04	+17 12	- 1 17 12
Bekescsaba, Bekes	21E05	46N41	+24 20	- 1 24 20
Beregszasz, B. & U. *	22E38	48N13	+31 32	- 1 31 32
Berettyoujfalu, Bihar	21E32	47N13	+26 08	+ 1 26 08
Budapest, Pest	19E05	47N30	+16 20	- 1 16 20
Cegled, Pest	19E49	47N10	+19 16	- 1 19 16
Csongrad, Csongrad	20E09	46N43	+20 36	- 1 20 36
Debrecen, Hajdu	21E38	47N32	+26 32	- 1 26 32
Eger, Heves	20E22	47N54	+21 28	- 1 21 28
Ersekujvar, Ny. & P. *	18E10	47N59	+12 40	- 1 12 40
Esztergom, Kom-Eszt.	18E45	47N48	+15 00	- 1 15 00
Felsogalla, Kom.-Eszt	18E27	47N32	+13 48	- 1 13 48
Fuenfkirchen see Pecs				
Gran see Esztergom.				
Guens see Koszeg.				
Galanta, Ny. & P. *	17E44	48N12	+10 56	- 1 10 56
Gyoma, Bekes	20E50	46N57	+23 20	- 1 23 20
Gyongyos, Heves	19E56	47N47	+19 44	- 1 19 44
Gyor, Gyor-Moson	17E39	47N41	+10 36	- 1 10 36
Gyula, Bekes	21E16	46N39	+25 04	- 1 25 04
Hajduboszormeny, Hajdu	21E31	47N41	+26 04	- 1 26 04
Hatvan, Heves	19E40	47N39	+18 40	- 1 18 40
Hodmezovasarhely, Csongrad	20E19	46N25	+21 16	- 1 21 16
Jaszbereny, Szolnok	19E56	47N30	+19 44	- 1 19 44
Kalocsa, Pest	18E59	46N32	+13 56	- 1 13 56
Kaposvar, Somogy	17E54	46N22	+11 36	- 1 11 36
Karcag, Szolnok	20E56	47N19	+23 44	- 1 23 44
Kassa (Kaschau), Abauj *	21E16	48N43	+25 04	- 1 25 04
Kecskemet, Pest	19E42	46N54	+18 48	- 1 18 48
Keszthely, Zala	17E15	46N47	+ 9 00	- 1 09 00
Kiskoros, Pest	19E17	46N37	+17 08	- 1 17 08
Kiskunhalas, Pest	19E29	46N26	+17 56	- 1 17 56

			L. M. T. VARIATION FROM S.T.		G. M. T. VARIATION FROM LMT.		
			m.	s.	h.	m.	s.

HUNGARY (Continued)

Place			m.	s.	h.	m.	s.
Kismarton see Eisenstadt, Austria.							
Komarom, Kom.-Eszt.*	18E08	47N44	+12	32	- 1	12	32
Koszeg, Vas	16E32	47N24	+ 6	08	- 1	06	08
Losonc, Nograd *	19E41	48N20	+18	44	- 1	18	44
Magyarovar see Mosonmagyarovar.							
Mako, Csanad	20E29	46N13	+21	56	- 1	21	56
Matoszalka, Sz.-B.	22E20	47N57	+29	20	- 1	29	20
Mezokovesd, Bor.-Gom.	20E34	47N49	+22	16	- 1	22	16
Miskolc, Bor.-Gom.	20E47	48N06	+23	08	- 1	23	08
Mohacs, Baranya	18E41	45N59	+14	44	- 1	14	44
Mosonmagyarovar, Gy.-M.	17E16	47N52	+9	04	- 1	09	04
Munkacs, B. & U. *	22E43	48N26	+30	52	- 1	30	52
Nagykanizsa, Zala	17E00	46N28	+ 8	00	- 1	08	00
Nagykoros, Pest	19E47	47N02	+19	08	- 1	19	08
Nyiregyhaza, Szabolos	21E43	47N58	+26	52	- 1	26	52
Ofen-Pest see Budapest							
Odenburg see Sopron							
Papa, Veszpram	17E29	47N20	+ 9	56	- 1	09	56
Pecs, Baranya	18E14	46N05	+12	56	- 1	12	56
Pest see Budapest.							
Raab see Gyor.							
Rimaszombat, G. & Kishont *	20E02	48N23	+20	08	- 1	20	08
Salgotarjan, Nograd	19E49	48N06	+19	16	- 1	19	16
Satoraljaujhely, Zemplen	21E39	48N24	+26	36	- 1	26	36
Siklos, Baranya	18E19	45N51	+13	16	- 1	13	16
Siofok, Veszprem	18E04	46N54	+12	16	- 1	12	16
Sopron, Sopron	16E36	47N42	+ 6	24	- 1	06	24
Steinamanger see Szombathely.							
Stuhlweissenburg see Szekesfehervar.							
Sszarvas, Bekes	20E33	46N52	+22	12	- 1	22	12
Szecseny, Nograd-Hont	19E32	48N05	+18	08	- 1	18	08
Szeged, Csongrad	20E09	46N15	+20	36	- 1	20	36
Szekesfehervar, Fejer	18E25	47N12	+13	40	- 1	13	40
Szekszard, Tolna	18E43	46N21	+14	52	- 1	14	52
Szentendre, Pest	19E04	47N41	+16	16	- 1	16	16
Szentes, Csongrad	20E16	46N39	+21	04	- 1	21	04
Szigetvar, Somogy	17E49	46N03	+11	16	- 1	11	16
Szolnok, Szolnok	20E12	47N10	+20	48	- 1	20	48
Szombathely, Vas.,,,	16E37	47N14	+ 6	28	- 1	06	28
Torokszentmiklos, Szolnok	20E26	47N11	+21	44	- 1	21	44
Ujpest, Pest	19E07	47N35	+16	28	- 1	16	28
Ung. Altenburg see Mosonmagyarovar.							
Ungvar, B. & U.	22E19	48N37	+29	16	- 1	29	16
Vac, Pest	19E08	47N47	+16	32	- 1	16	32
Vasvar, Vas	16E48	47N03	+ 7	12	- 1	07	12
Veszprem, Veszprem	17E54	47N06	+11	36	- 1	11	36
Visegrad, Pest	18E55	47N48	+15	40	- 1	15	40
Weitzen see Vac.							
Wieselburg see Mosonmagyarovar.							
Zalaegerszeg, Zala	16E51	46N51	+ 7	24	- 1	07	24

			L. M. T. VARIATION FROM S.T.	G. M. T. VARIATION FROM LMT.
			m. s.	h. m. s.

ICELAND. Capital: Reykjavik. Sovereign State situated in the North Atlantic. Standard Time Meridian 15° WEST.

Akranes	22W06	64N10	-28 24	+ 1 28 24
Akureyri........................	18W06...	65N40..	-12 24..	+ 1 12 24
Hafnarfjordur	21W42	64N04	-26 48	+ 1 26 48
Isafjordur	23W08	66N04	-32 22	+ 1 32 32
Nes see Akranes.				
Olafsvik	23W43	64N54	-34 53	+ 1 34 53
Reykjavik.......................	21W57...	64N09..	-27 48..	+ 1 27 48
Seydisfjordur	14W00	65N08	+ 4 00	+ 0 56 00
Siglufjordur	18W55	66N04	-15 40	+ 1 15 40
Vatneyri	24W00	65N39	-36 00	+ 1 36 00
Vestmannaeyer	20W18	63N18	-21 12	+ 1 21 12

IFNI. Spanish Colony in West Africa. Standard Time Meridian 0°.

Sidi Ifni	10W10	29N23	-40 40	+ 0 40 40

INDE BRITANNIQUE see Indian.

INDE NEERLANDAISE See 1. Netherlands East or 2, West Indies.

INDE PORTUGAISE see Portuguese India.

INDIA. Capital: Delhi. During the publication of this volume, India, an empire under British rule, situated in Asia, is undergoing political changes, dividing the country into two nations -- Hindustan and Pakistan. Indepentent August 15, 1947.
While at this time (1948) all India standard Time is based on meridian 82°30' EAST, calculations herein for LMT are based on 82°30' EAST, except for the Province of Bengal which has heretofore used Meridian 97°30', except the City of Calcutta which used LMT.

Adayar, (Adyar), Madras	80E15	13N01	- 9 00	- 5 21 00
Agartala, Tripura................	91E17...	23N49..	+35 08..	- 6 05 08
Agra, United Provinces	78E00	27N11	-18 00	- 5 12 00
Ahmadabad, Baroda	72E35	23N02	-39 40	- 4 50 20
Ahmadnagar, Bombay	74E44	19N06	-31 04	- 4 58 56
Ajmer, Ajmer	74E39	26N28	-31 24	- 4 58 36
Aligarh, United Provinces........	78E05...	27N54..	-17 40..	- 5 12 20
Allahabad, United Provinces	81E50	25N27	- 2 40	- 5 27 20
Ambala, Punjab States	76E47	30N23	-22 52	- 5 07 08
Amraoti, Central Provinces	77E45	20N59	-19 00	- 5 11 00
Amritsar, Punjab	74E52	31N37	-30 32	- 4 59 28
Aurangabad, Hyderabad	75E39	19N53	-27 24	- 5 02 36
Balasore, B. & O.	86E56	21N30	+17 44	- 5 47 44
Bangalore, Mysore................	77E36...	12N59..	-19 36..	- 5 10 24
Bannu, Northwest Province	70E36	33N00	-47 36	- 4 42 24
Bareilly, United Province	79E26	28N21	-12 16	- 5 17 44
Baroda, Baroda	73E20	22N19	-36 40	- 4 53 20
Belgaum, Bombay	74E30	15N52	-32 00	- 4 58 00
Bencres, United Province........	83E00	25N19	+ 2 00	- 5 32 00
Berhampore, Bengal	88E16	24N06	-36 56	- 5 53 04

			L. M. T. VARIATION FROM S.T.	G. M. T. VARIATION FROM LMT.
			m. s.	h. m. s.

INDIA. (Continued)

Bhagalpur, B. & O.	88E58	25N14	+17 52	- 5 47 52
Bhaunagar, Western India	72E09	21N46	-41 24	- 4 48 36
Bhopal, Central India	77E24	23N16	-20 24	- 5 09 36
Bihar, B. & O.	85E32	25N12	+12 08	- 5 42 08
Bikaner, Rajputana	73E18	28N10	-36 48	- 4 53 12
Bombay, Bombay	72E50	19N57	-38 40	- 4 51 20
Buddha-Gaya, B. & O.	85E01	24N48	+10 04	- 5 40 04
Calcutta, Bengal	88E20	22N34	+23 20.8	- 5 53 20.8
(Prior to 1948 Calcutta was used LMT.)				
Calicut, Madras	75E47	11N15	-26 52	- 5 03 08
Campbellpore (Campbellpur) Attock	72E22	33N46	-41 32	- 4 49 28
Cawnpore, United Province	80E20	26N28	- 8 40	- 5 21 20
Chanda, Central Province	79E18	19N57	-12 48	- 5 17 12
Chitor, Rajputana	74E38	24N54	-31 28	- 4 58 32
Chittagong, Bengal	91E50	22N21	-22 40	- 6 07 20
Coimbatore, Madras	76E58	11N00	-22 08	- 5 07 52
Conjeevaram, Madras	79E43	12N50	-11 08	- 5 18 52
Cuddalore, South Arcot	79E45	11N43	-11 00	- 5 19 00
Cuttack, B. & O.	85E52	20N28	+13 28	- 5 43 28
Dacca, Bengal	90E25	23N43	-28 20	- 6 01 40
Darbhanga, Bihar	85E54	26N09	+13 36	- 5 43 36
Darjeeling, Bengal	88E17	27N03	-36 52	- 5 53 08
Delhi, Delhi	77E14	28N39	-21 04	- 5 08 56
Dera Ismail Khan, N.W.Frontier	70E55	31N50	-46 20	- 4 43 40
Dharwar, Bombay	75E01	15N44	-29 56	- 5 00 04
Dinajpore, Bengal	88E38	25N38	-35 28	- 5 54 32
Ellora, Hyderabad	75E10	20N02	-29 20	- 5 00 40
Farrukhabad, United Province	79E34	27N24	-11 44	- 5 18 16
Ferozepore, Punjab	74E37	30N55	-31 32	- 4 58 28
Fort Sandeman, Baluchistan	69E27	31N21	-52 12	- 4 37 48
Fyzabad, United Province	82E08	26N46	- 1 28	- 5 28 32
Gangtak, Sikkim	88E39	27N19	+24 36	- 5 54 36
Gaya see Buddha-Gaya				
Gilgit, Kashmir	74E18	35N55	-32 48	- 4 57 12
Gorakhpur, United Province	83E22	26N46	+ 3 28	- 5 33 28
Guadur (Gwadur), Baluchistan	62E20	25N08	- 1h20 40	- 4 09 20
Gwalior, Gwalior	78E09	26N12	-14 36	- 5 15 24
Howrah, Bengal	88E20	22N37	-36 40	- 5 53 20
Hubli, Bombay	75E09	15N21	-29 24	- 5 00 36
Hyderabad, Hyderabad	68E22	25N24	-56 32	- 4 33 28
Indore, Central Provinces	75E51	22N43	-26 36	- 5 03 24
Imphal, Manipur	93E56	24N51	+45 44	- 6 15 44
Indore, Rajputana	75E53	22N43	-26 28	- 5 03 32
Jaipur, Rajputana	75E50	26N55	-26 10	- 5 03 40
Jamkhandi, Bombay	75E17	16N30	-28 58	- 5 01 08
Jhansi, Gwalior	78E34	25N28	-15 44	- 5 14 16
Jodhpur Rajputana	73E02	26N17	-37 52	- 4 52 08
Jubbulpore, Central Provinces	79E57	23N10	-10 12	- 5 19 48
Jullundur, Punjab	75E34	31N19	-27 44	- 5 02 16
Kalat, Baluchistan	66E35	29N02	-1h03 40	-4 26 20
Karachi, Sind	67E02	24N52	-1h01 52	- 4 28 08
Katmandu, Nepal	85E19	27N43	-11 16	- 5 41 16

			L. M. T. VARIATION FROM S.T.		G. M. T. VARIATION FROM LMT		
			m.	s.	h.	m.	s.
INDIA (Continued)							
Kohat, N. W. Province	71E26	33N35	-44	16	- 4	45	44
Koil see Aligarh.							
Kolharpur, Deccan States	74E13	16N42	-33	08	- 4	56	52
Lahore, Punjab..................	74E20...	31N34..	-32	40....	- 4	57	20
Larkana, Sind	68E12	27N32	-57	12	- 4	32	48
Lashkar, G lior	78E08	26N12	-17	28	- 5	12	32
Loralai, Baluchistan	68E24	30N22	-56	24	- 4	33	36
Lucknow, United Province	80E56	26N51	- 6	16	- 5	23	44
Lyallpur, Punjab..............	73E05...	31N25..	-37	40....	- 4	52	20
Madras, Madras	80E17	13N05	- 9	52	- 5	21	08
Madura, Madras	78E08	9E55	-17	28	- 5	12	32
Mahabalipuram, Madras	80E13	12N38	- 9	08	- 5	20	52
Mangalore, Madras	74E51	12N52	-30	36	- 4	59	24
Meerut, United Province........	77F42...	29N00..	-19	12....	- 5	10	48
Midnapore, Bengal	87E20	22N25	-40	40	- 5	49	20
Mirzapur, United Province	82E35	25N09	+ 0	20	- 5	30	20
Monghyr, B. & O.	86E29	25N23	+15	56	- 5	45	56
Moradabad, United Province	78E47	28N51	-14	52	- 5	15	08
Multan, Punjab.................	71E28...	30N11...-44	08,....	- 4	45	52
Muttra, United Province	77E40	27N30	-19	20	- 5	10	40
Muzaffarabad, Kashmir	73E28	34N22	-36	08	- 4	53	52
Mysore, Mysore	76E40	12N19	-23	20	- 5	06	40
Nagpur, Central Provinces	79E04	21N09	-13	44	- 5	16	16
Nellore, Madras...............	79E59...	14N26..	-10	04....	- 5	19	56
New Delhi, Delhi	77E13	28N38	-21	08	- 5	08	52
Ormara, Baluchistan	64E38	25N12	-1h11	28	- 4	18	32
Panjgar, Baluchistan	64E06	26N58	-1h13	36	- 4	16	24
Pasni, Baluchistan	63E29	25N16	-1h16	04	- 4	13	56
Patiala, Punjab................	76E25...	30N19..	-24	20....	- 5	05	40
Patna, B. & O.	85E14	25N34	+10	56	- 5	40	56
Peshawar, Peshawar	71E31	34N00	-43	56	- 4	46	04
Poona, Bombay	73E52	18N31	-34	32	- 4	55	28
Punaka, Bhutan	89E52	27N37	+29	28	- 5	59	28
Purnea, B. & O................	87E30...	25N48..	+20	00...	- 5	50	00
Quetta, Baluchistan	67E00	30N13	-1h02	00	- 4	28	00
Rajahmundri, Madras	81E46	17N00	- 2	56	- 5	27	04
Rajkot, Kathiawar	70E47	22N19	-46	52	- 4	43	08
Rajpur, Central Provinces	81E38	21N14	- 3	28	- 5	26	32
Ramoswaram, Madras.............	79E19....	9N17...-12	44....	- 5	17	16
Ramnad, Ramnad	78E50	9N22	-14	40	- 5	15	20
Ranchi, B. & O.	85E19	23N22	+11	16	- 5	41	16
Rawalpindi, Punjab	73E04	33N36	-37	44	- 4	52	16
Saharanpur, United Provinces	76E34	29N58	-23	44	- 5	06	16
Salem, Madras	78E10	11N39	-17	20	- 5	12	40
Shahjanpur, United Provinces...	79E55...	27N52....-10	20...	- 5	19	40
Shillong, Assam	91E53	25N34	+37	32	- 6	07	32
Sholapur, Bombay	75E54	17N40	-26	24	- 5	03	36
Sialkot, Kashmir	74E33	32N29	-31	48	- 4	58	12
Simla, Punjab..................	77E10...	31N06..	-21	20....	- 5	08	40

			L. M. T. VARIATION FROM S. T.	G. M. T. VARIATION FROM LMT.
			m. s.	h. m. s.
INDIA. (Continued)				
Sirajganj, Assam.	89E44	24N28	+28 56	▼ 5 58 56
Sitapur, United Provinces	80E41	27N34	- 7 16	- 5 22 44
Srinagar, Kashmir	74E48	34N05	-30 48	- 4 59 12
Sukkur, Sind	68E50	27N41	-54 40	- 4 35 20
Surat, Baroda	72E50	21N12	-38 40	- 4 51 20
Tonk, Rajputana...............	75E47...	26N10...	-26 52...	- 5 03 08
Trinichopoly, Trinichopoly	78E43	10N50	-15 08	- 5 14 52
Trivandrum, Travancore	76E57	8N29	-22 12	- 5 07 48
Udaipur, Rajputana	73E42	24N35	-35 12	- 4 54 48
Ujjain, Gwalior	75E50	23N11	-26 40	- 5 03 20
Vizagapatam, Madras............	83E18...	17N42...	+ 3 12...	- 5 33 12

INDO-CHINA see French Indo-China.

INDO-CHINESE FEDERATION see French Indo-China.

INDONESIA, see Netherlands East Indies. Independent Dec. 27, 1949

ININI see French Guiana.

INNER MONGOLIA see China.

IRAN. Capital: Tehran. Kingdom, situated in Western Asia. Standard Time Meridian 52°30' EAST.

Ardobil (Ardabil), Azerb.	48E18	38N14	-16 48	- 3 13 12
Arak, Hamadan	49E41	34N05	-11 16	- 3 18 44
Babul, Mazanderan...............	52E42...	36N34...	+ 0 48...	- 3 30 48
Balfurush see Babul.				
Bandar adu Shehr see Bushire.				
Birjand, Khurasan	59E13	32N52	+26 52	- 3 26 52
Bushire, Fars	50E50	28N59	- 6 40	- 3 23 20
Daulatab see Malayer.				
Duzdad see Zehidan.				
Ghazvin see Qazvin.				
Gulpaigan, Isfahan	50E18	33N27	- 8 48	- 3 21 12
Gurgan, Astorabad	54E29	36N50	+ 7 56	- 3 37 56
Hamadan, Hamadan...............	48E30...	34N48...	-16 00...	- 3 14 00
Isfahan (Ispahan), Isfahan	51E38	32N40	- 3 28	- 3 26 32
Kashan, Kashan	51E29	33N59	- 4 04	- 3 25 56
Kazvin see Qazvin.				
Khom see Qum.				
Korman, Korman.................	57E05...	30N17...	+18 20...	- 3 48 20
Kermanshah, Kermanshah	47E04	34N19	-21 44	- 3 08 16
Khurramabad, Luristan	48E20	33N30	-16 40	- 3 13 20
Khurremshahr, Khuzistan	48E12	30N27	-17 12	- 3 12 48
Malayer, Luristan	48E50	34N17	-14 40	- 3 15 20
Meshed (Mashad), Khurasan.......	59E36...	36N18...	+28 24...	- 3 58 24
Qazvin, Qazvin	50E00	36N16	-10 00	- 3 20 00
Qum, Teheran	50E54	34N39	- 6 24	- 3 23 36
Resht, Gilan	49E35	37N16	-11 40	- 3 18 20
Rizaiyeh, Azerb.	45E04	37N34	-29 44	- 3 00 16
Sabzawar, Khurasan	57E39	36N12	+20 36	- 3 50 36
Samnan (Semnan), Semnan-Damghan	53E24	35N33	+ 3 36	- 3 33 36
Saveh, Qazvin	50E19	35N01	- 8 44	- 3 21 16
Shahsawar see Sabzawar.				
Shiraz, Fars	53E32	29N36	+ 4 08	- 3 34 08

			L. M. T. VARIATION FROM S.T m. s.	G. M. T. VARIATION FROM LMT. h. m. s.

IRAN (Continued)

Shushtar , Khurzistan	48E51	32N03	-14 36	- 3 15 24
Sostra see Shushtar.				
Sultanabad see Arak.				
Tabriz, Azerb..............	46E18...	38N05...	-24 48,...	- 3 05 12
Tehran (Teheran), Tehran	51E26	35N40	- 4 16	- 3 25 44
Urmida see Rizaiyeh.				
Yezd (Yazd), Yezd	54E25	31N54	+ 7 40	- 3 37 40
Zenjan, Khamseh	48E29	36N40	-16 04	- 3 13 56
Zahidan, Kerman	60E52	39N30	+33 28	- 4 03 28

IRAQ. Capital: Baghdad. Kingdom situated in
Western Asia. Standard Time Meridian
45° EAST.

Arbil, Arbil	43E59	36N11	- 4 04	- 2 55 56
Amarah, Amarah	47E10	31N51	+ 8 40	- 3 08 40
Babil (Babylon), Hillah	44E26	32N33	- 2 16	- 2 57 44
Badra, Kut-al-Imara............	45E58...	33N07...	+ 3 52...	- 3 03 52
Baghdad, Baghdad	44E24	33N20	- 2 24	- 2 57 36
Baquba, Diyalah	44E41	33N44	- 1 16	- 2 58 44
Basrah (Bassorah), Basarah	47E50	30N30	+11 20	- 3 11 20
Erbil see Arbil.				
Habaniya.......................	43E34...	33N23...	- 5 44...	- 2 54 16
Hillah, Hillah	44E25	32N30	- 2 20	- 2 57 40
Hit, Dulaim	42E50	33N36	- 8 40	- 2 51 20
Karbala (Kerbela), Karbala	44E02	32N37	- 3 52	- 2 56 08
Kirkuk, Kirkuk	44E23	35N28	- 2 28	- 2 57 32
Kut-el-Imara, Kut-al-Imara......	45E50...	32N30...	+ 3 20...	- 3 03 20
Muqdadiyah see Shahraban.				
Mosul, Mosul	43E08	36N20	- 7 28	- 2 52 32
Nasiriya, Muntafiq	46E15	31N01	+ 5 00	- 3 05 00
Palmyra see Tudmur.				
Ramadi, Dulaim.....,...........	43E21...	33N25...	- 6 36...	- 2 53 24
Samarra, Baghdad	43E54	34N12	- 4 24	- 2 55 36
Shahraban, Diyalah	44E59	33N58	- 0 04	- 2 59 56
Sulaimani, Sulaimani	45E26	35N33	+ 1 44	- 3 01 44
Tudmur	38E15	34N32	-27 00	- 2 33 00

IRELAND see Eire.

IRISH FREE STATE see Eire.

IRELAN (E) see Eire.

ISLAND see Iceland.

ISRAEL see Palestine. Independent May 14, 1948.

ISTRIA see Italy.

ITALIAN EAST AFRICA. Italian Colonies, situated in East
Africa. ETHIOPIA, annexed by Italy on May 9, 1936,
has become Independent. See ETHIOPIA. ERITREA,
Capital Asmara. Italian Somaliland, capital
MOGADISCIA. Standard Time Meridian 45° EAST.

Abardeb, Eritrea	37E03	16N06	-31 48	- 2 28 12
Agordat, Eritria..............,	37E53...	15N33,...	-28 28...	- 2 31 32
Asmara, Eritrea	38E56	15N21	-24 16	- 2 35 44
Assab, Eritrea	42E44	13N01	- 9 04	- 2 50 56

			L. M. T. VARIATION FROM S.T.		G. M. T. VARIATION FROM LMT.		
			m.	s.	h.	m.	s.

ITALIAN EAST COAST

Belet Uen, Somaliland	45E13	4N44	+ 0	52	- 3	00	52
Bender Cassim, Somaliland	49E11	11N17	+16	44	- 3	16	44
Cheren, Eritrea..............	38E27...	15N46...	-26	12...	- 2	33	48
Chisimaio, Somaliland	42E32	00S22	- 9	52	- 2	50	08
Duca degli Abrussi, Somali	45E30	2N46	+ 2	00	- 3	02	00
Gallacaio see Rocca Littorio.							
Isha Badoia, Somaliland	43E39	3N08	- 5	24	- 2	54	36
Karora, Eritrea...............	38E22...	17N43...	-26	32...	- 2	33	28
Keren see Cheren.							
Kisimayu see Chisimaio.							
Margherita, Somililand	42E45	0N03	- 9	00	- 2	51	00
Massua, Eritrea	39E29	15N37	-22	04	- 2	37	56
Meeca, Bonadir...............	44E46...	1N42...	- 0	56...	- 2	59	04
Mogadiscio, Somaliland	45E21	2N02	+ 1	24	- 3	01	24
Rocca Littorio, Somaliland	47E26	6N46	+ 9	44	- 3	09	44

ITALIAN SOMALILAND see Italian East Africa.

ITALY. Capital: Roma. Republic, situated in Europe. Standard Time Meridian 15°EAST.

Abbazia, Fiume	14E19	45N21	- 2	44	- 0	57	16
Aderno (Adrano), Catania	14E50	37N40	+ 0	40	- 0	59	20
Agrigento see Girganti.							
Alessandria, Alessandria........	8E38...	44N54...	-25	28...	- 0	34	32
Ancona, Ancona	13E31	43N37	- 5	56	- 0	54	04
Anzio, Roma	12E39	41N27	- 9	24	- 0	50	36
Aosta, Torino	7E20	45N44	-30	40	- 0	29	20
Aquila degli Abruzzi, Aquila	13E24	42N24	- 6	24	- 0	53	36
Arezzo, Arezzo................	11E53...	43N28...	-12	28...	- 0	47	32
Ascoli, Piceno, Ascoli Piceno	13E36	42N52	- 5	36	- 0	54	24
Assissi, Perugia	12E38	43N05	- 9	28	- 0	50	32
Asti, Alessandria	8E12	44N54	-27	12	- 0	32	48
Avellino, Campania	14E48	40N54	- 0	48	- 0	59	12
Bari, Bari...................	16E53...	41N07...	+ 7	32...	- 1	07	32
Belluno, Belluno	12E13	46N08	-11	08	- 0	48	52
Benevento, Benevento	14E48	41N07	- 0	48	- 0	59	12
Bergamo, Bergamo	9E39	45N42	-21	24	- 0	38	36
Bologna, Bologna	11E20	44N30	-14	40	- 0	45	20
Bolzano, Belzano..............	11E20...	46N30...	-14	40...	- 0	45	20
Bozon see Bolzano.							
Brescia, Brescia	10E12	45N32	-19	12	- 0	40	48
Brindisi, Lecce	17E56	40N39	+11	44	- 1	11	44
Cagliari, Cagliari	9E06	39N13	-23	36	- 0	36	24
Caltagirone, Catania	14E31	37N14	- 1	56	- 0	58	04
Caltanisetta, Caltanisetta......	14E04	37N29	- 3	44	- 0	56	16
Campobasso, Campobasso	14E40	41N34	- 1	20	- 0	58	40
Capri, Napoli	14E15	40N32	- 3	00	- 0	57	00
Carrara, Massa & Carrara	10E06	44N05	-19	36	- 0	40	24
Cassino, Caserta	13E50	41N30	- 4	10	- 0	55	20
Castellammaro del Golfo, Trapani	12E53	38N01	- 8	28	- 0	51	32

				L. M. T. VARIATION FROM S.T.		G. M. T. VARIATION FROM LMT.		
				m.	s.	h.	m.	s.
ITALY (Continued)								
Castrogiovanni, Caltanisetta	14E17	37N33		- 2	52	- 0	57	08
Catania, Catania	15E05	37N30		+ 0	20	- 1	00	20
Catanzaro, Catanzaro	16E35	38N54		+ 6	20	- 1	06	20
Chieti, Chieti..................	14E11...	42N21...		- 3	16...	- 0	56	44
Civita Vecchia, Roma	11E47	42N05		-12	52	- 0	47	08
Como, Como	9E05	45N49		-23	40	- 0	36	20
Cosenza, Cosanza	16E15	39N17		+ 5	00	- 1	05	00
Cremona, Cremona	9E01	45N08		-23	56	- 0	36	04
Crotone, Catanzaro.............17E08...		39N05...		+ 8	32...	- 1	08	32
Cuneo, Cuneo	7E33	44N23		-29	48	- 0	30	12
Enna see Costrogiovanni.								
Faenza, Ravenna	11E53	44N17		-12	28	- 0	47	38
Ferrara, Ferrara	11E38	44N50		-13	28	- 0	46	32
Firenze (Florence) Firence......	11E16...	43N46...		-14	56...	- 0	45	04
Fiume, Fiume	14E27	45N20		- 2	12	- 0	57	48
Foggia, Foggia	15E34	41N28		+ 2	16	- 1	02	16
Forli, Forli	12E02	44N13		-11	52	- 0	48	08
Frosinone, Roma	13E22	41N39		- 6	32	- 0	53	28
Genova (Genua), Genova..........	8E55...	44N25...		-24	20...	- 0	35	40
Girgenti, Girgenti	13E55	37N18		- 5	40	- 0	54	20
Gorizia (Goerz), Gorizia	13E37	45N57		- 5	32	- 0	54	28
Grosetto, Grosetto	11E07	42N46		-15	32	- 0	44	28
Iglesias, Cagliari	9E32	39N18		-21	52	- 0	38	04
Imperia, Imperia................	8E02...	43N54...		-27	52...	- 0	32	08
La Spezia, Genoa	9E49	44N06		-20	44	- 0	39	16
Lecce, Lecce	18E10	40N21		+12	40	- 1	12	40
Leghorn see Liverno								
Lipari, Messina	14E57	38N28		- 0	12	- 0	59	48
Littoria, Littoria.............12E54...		41N28...		- 8	24..	- 0	51	36
Liverno, Liverno	10E19	43N33		-18	44	- 0	41	16
Lodi, Milano	9E30	45N18		-22	00	- 0	38	00
Lucca, Lucca	10E30	43N50		-18	00	- 0	42	00
Lussingrande, Pola	14E31	44N31		- 1	56	- 0	58	04
Mailand see Milano.								
Mantova (Mantua), Mantova	10E47	45N09		-16	52	- 0	43	08
Marsala, Trapani	12E26	37N48		-10	16	- 0	49	44
Mantera, Mantera	16E37	40N41		+ 6	28	- 1	06	38
Merano, Bolzano	11E10	46N41		-15	20	- 0	44	40
Messina, Messina...............15E33...		38N11...		+ 2	12...	- 1	02	02
Milano, Milano	9E12	45N28		-23	12	- 0	36	48
Modena, Modena	10E56	44N38		-16	16	- 0	43	44
Modica, Ragusa	14E58	36N48		- 0	08	- 0	59	52
Monza, Milano	9E15	45N35		-23	00	- 0	37	00
Napoli, (Naples), Napoli	14E16	40N52		- 2	56	- 0	57	04
Nettuna, Roma..................	12E41...	41N28...		- 9	16...	- 0	50	44
Novara, Novara	8E36	45N27		-25	36	- 0	34	24
Nuoro, Nuoro	9E20	40N20		-22	40	- 0	37	20
Padova (Padua), Padova	11E52	45N23		-12	32	- 0	47	28
Palermo, Palermo	13E22	38N07		- 6	32	- 0	53	28
Palestrina, Roma...............12E54...		41N50...		- 8	24	- 0	51	36

			L. M. T. VARIATION FROM S.T.	G. M. T. VARIATION FROM LMT.
ITALY (Continued)			m. s.	h. m. s.
Parma, Parma	10E10	44N48	-18 44	- 0 41 16
Pavia, Pavia	9E09	45N11	-23 24	- 0 36 36
Perugia, Perugia	12E23	43N07	-10 28	- 0 49 32
Posaro, Posaro & Urbino	12E55	43N55	- 8 20	- 0 51 40
Poscara, Chioti................	14E13...	42N28...	- 3 08...	- 0 56 52
Piacenza, Piacenza	9E42	45N03	-21 12	- 0 38 48
Pisa, Pisa	10E24	43N43	-18 24	- 0 41 36
Pistoia, Firenze	10E55	43N56	-16 20	- 0 43 40
Pola, Pola	13E51	44N52	- 4 36	- 0 55 24
Porto Ferraio, Elba...........	10E20...	43N49....	-18 40...	- 0 41 20
Potenza, Potenza	15E49	40N38	+ 3 16	- 1 03 16
Rapallo, Genova	9E14	44N20	-23 04	- 0 36 56
Ravenna, Ravenna	12E12	44N25	-11 12	- 0 48 48
Reggio di Calabria, R. di C.	15E39	38N06	+ 2 36	- 1 02 36
Reggio nell' Emilia, R.n.E......	10E38...	44N41...	-17 26...	- 0 42 32
Rimini, Forli	12E35	44N03	- 9 40	- 0 50 20
Roma (Rome), Roma	12E29	41N54	-10 04	- 0 49 56
Salerno, Campenia	14E46	40N41	- 0 56	- 0 59 04
San Remo, Imporia	7E47	43N49	-28 52	- 0 31 08
Sassari, Sassari................	8E33...	40N44...	-25 48...	- 0 34 12
Savona, Genoa	8E29	44N18	-26 04	- 0 33 56
Sestri Levante, Genoa	9E23	44N16	-22 28	- 0 37 32
Siena, Siena	11E18	43N19	-14 48	- 0 45 12
Siracusa, Siracusa	15E17	37N04	+ 1 08	- 1 01 08
Sorrento, Napoli................	14E23...	40N37...	- 2 28...	- 0 57 32
Taranto, Lecco	17E15	40N28	+ 9 00	- 1 09 00
Tampio Pausania, Sassari	9E05	40N54	-23 40	- 0 36 20
Teramo, Teremo	13E43	42N39	- 5 08	- 0 54 52
Terni, Perugia	12E39	42N34	- 9 24	- 0 50 36
Tivoli, Roma...................	12E48...	41N58...	- 8 48...	- 0 51 12
Torino, Torino	7E42	45N04	-29 12	- 0 30 48
Trapani, Trapani	12E32	38N01	- 9 52	- 0 50 08
Trento, Trento	11E08	46N03	-15 28	- 0 44 32
Treviso, Treviso	12E15	45N40	-11 00	- 0 49 00
Trient see Trento				
Trieste (Triest), Trieste	13E46	45N39	- 4 56	- 0 55 04
Turin see Terino				
Udine, Udine	13E14	46N03	- 7 04	- 0 52 56
Urbino, Pesaro & Urbino	12E38	43N44	- 9 28	- 0 50 52
Varoso, Como..................	8E49...	45N50...	-24 44...	- 0 35 16
Venezia (Venice), Venezia	12E20	45N26	-10 40	- 0 49 20
Verona, Verona	11E00	45N26	-16 00	- 0 44 00
Viconza, Viconza	11E32	45N32	-13 52	- 0 46 08
Viterbo, Roma	12E07	42N25	-11 32	- 0 48 28
Voghera, Pavia	9E01	44N59	-23 56	- 0 36 04
Zara, Zara	15E14	44N07	+ 0 56	- 1 00 56

IVORY COAST see French West Africa.
      Independent August 7, 1960
JAMAICA (JAMAIQUE) see British West Indies.

JAPAN. Capital: Tokyo. Empire, situated Eastern Asia. Standard Time Meridian 135° EAST.			L. M. T. VARIATION FROM S.T.	G. M. T. VARIATION FROM LMT.
			m. s.	h. m. s.
Aihama, Karafuto	142E40	47N31	+30 40	- 9 30 40
Akashi, Hyogo	135E00	34N39	0 00	- 9 00 00
Akita, Akita	140E07	39N41	+20 29	- 9 20 28
Amagasaki, Hyogo............	135E25...	34N42...	+ 1 40...	- 9 01 40
Aomori, Aomori	140E44	40N47	+22 56	- 9 22 56
Asahikawa, Hokkaido	142E25	43N47	+29 40	- 9 29 40
Boppu, Oita	131E28	33N15	-14 08	- 8 45 52
Bofu, Yamagushi	131E34	34N03	-13 44	- 8 46 16
Chiba, Chiba..................	140E07...	35N35...	+20 28...	- 9 20 28
Cheshi, Chiba	140E51	35N42	+23 24	- 9 23 24
Fujisawa, Kauagawa	139E28	35N18	+17 52	- 9 17 52
Fukui, Fukui	136E14	36N03	+ 4 56	- 9 04 56
Fukuoka, Fukuoka	130E23	33N34	-18 28	- 8 41 32
Fukushima, Fukushima..........	140E29...	37N45...	+21 56...	- 9 21 56
Fukuyama, Hireshima	133E22	34N28	- 6 32	- 8 53 28
Fuse, Osaka	133E35	34N37	+ 2 20	- 9 02 20
Gifu, Gifu	136E47	35N23	+ 7 08	- 9 07 08
Hachinohe, Aomori	141E32	40N29	+26 08	- 9 26 08
Hachioji, Tokyo..............	139E20...	35N38...	+17 20...	- 9 17 20
Hakodato, Hokkaido	140E44	41N42	+22 56	- 9 22 56
Hamamatsu, Shizuoka	137E42	34N42	+10 56	- 9 10 56
Himoji, Hyogo	134E43	34N49	- 1 08	- 8 58 52
Hiroshima, Hiroshima	132E25	34N24	-10 20	- 8 49 40
Ichinomiya, Aichi............	136E47...	35N16...	+ 7 08...	- 9 07 08
Isahaya, Nagasaki	130E03	32N50	-19 48	- 8 40 12
Kagoshima, Kagoshima	130E34	31N40	-17 44	- 8 42 16
Kanazawa, Ishikawa	136E40	36N34	+ 6 40	- 9 06 40
Kataoka, Chishima	156E11	50N43	+1h24 44	-10 24 44
Kawaguchi, Saitama............	139E44...	35N47...	+18 56	- 9 18 56
Kawasaki, Kanagawa	139E42	35N29	+18 48	- 9 18 48
Kiryu, Gumma	139E20	36N24	+17 20	- 9 17 20
Kobe, Hyogo	135E11	34N40	+ 0 44	- 9 00 44
Kochi, Kochi	133E31	33N32	- 5 56	- 8 54 04
Kofu, Yamanashi..............	138E35...	35N37...	+14 20...	- 9 14 20
Kokura, Fukuoka	130E52	33N52	-16 32	- 8 43 28
Koriyama, Fukushima	140E28	37N28	+21 52	- 9 21 52
Kumamoto, Kumamoto	130E13	32N47	-19 08	- 9 40 52
Kure, Hiroshima	132E32	34N13	- 9 52	- 8 50 08
Kurume, Fukuoka..............	130E30...	33N18...	-18 00...	- 8 42 00
Kushiro, Hokkaido	144E23	42N58	+37 32	- 9 37 32
Kyoto, Kyoto	135E45	34N58	+ 3 00	- 9 03 00
Maebashi, Gumma	139E03	36N23	+16 12	- 9 16 12
Mako, Bokoto	119E32	23N55	-1h01 52	- 7 58 08
Matsue, Shimane	133E04	35N26	- 7 44	- 8 52 16
Matsumoto, Nagano	137E58	36N13	+11 52	- 9 11 52
Matsuyama, Enime.............	132E46...	33N51...	- 8 56...	- 8 51 04
Mito, Ibaraki	140E28	36N21	+21 52	- 9 21 52
Miyazaki, Miyazaki	131E26	31N54	-14 16	- 8 45 44
Moji, Fukuoka	130E58	33N55	-16 08	- 8 43 52
Morioka, Iwate	141E09	39N42	+24 36	- 9 24 36

			L. M. T. VARIATION FROM S.T.		G. M. T. VARIATION FROM LMT.		
			m.	s.	h.	m.	s.
JAPAN (Continued)							
Muroran, Hokkaido	140E58	42N20	+23	52	- 9	23	52
Nagano, Nagano	138E12	36N37	+12	48	- 9	12	48
Nagaoka, Niigata	138E52	37N25	+15	28	- 9	15	28
Nagasaki, Nagasaki	129E52	32N43	-20	32	- 8	39	28
Nagoya, Aichi	136E55	35N08	+ 7	40	- 9	07	40
Naha, Okinawa.....................	127E40....	26N12...	-29	20...	- 8	30	40
Nara, Nara	135E50	34N40	+ 3	20	- 9	03	20
Niigata, Niigata	139E03	37N55	+16	12	- 9	16	12
Nishinomiya, Hyogo	135E20	34N47	+ 1	20	- 9	01	20
Nobeoka, Miyazaki	131E40	32N34	-13	20	- 8	46	40
Numazu, Shizuoka.................	138E52...	35N05...	+15	28...	- 9	15	28
Oita, Oita	131E37	33N13	-13	32	- 8	46	28
Okayama, Okayama	133E54	34N37	- 4	24	- 8	55	36
Okazaki, Aichi	137E10	34N56	+ 8	40	- 9	08	40
Omuta, Fukuoka	130E26	33N02	-18	16	- 8	41	44
Onomichi, Hiroshima.............	133E11...	34N24...	- 7	16...	- 8	52	44
Osaka, Osaka	135E29	34N39	+ 1	56	- 9	01	56
Otaru, Hokkaido	141E01	43N10	+24	04	- 9	24	04
Otome-wan, Chishima	154E00	48N48	+1h16	00	-10	16	00
Otsu, Shiga	135E52	34N59	+ 3	28	- 9	03	28
Saga, Saga.....................	130E16....	33N15...	-18	56...	- 8	41	04
Sakai, Osaka	135E28	34N34	+ 1	52	- 9	01	52
Sapporo, Hokkaido	141E19	43N03	+25	16	- 9	25	16
Sasebo, Nagasaki	129E40	33N10	-21	20	- 8	38	40
Sendai, Miyagi	140E53	38N15	+23	32	- 9	23	32
Shikuka, Karafuto.............	143E04,...	49N13...	+32	16...	- 9	32	16
Shimizu, Shizuoka	138E29	34N57	+13	56	- 9	13	56
Shizuoka, Shizuoka	138E24	34N57	+13	36	- 9	13	36
Shomonoseki, Yamagushi	130E55	33N58	-16	20	- 8	43	40
Takamatsu, Kagowa	134E03	34N19	- 3	48	- 8	56	12
Takaoka, Toyama.................	137E00...	36N44...	+ 8	00...	- 9	08	00
Takasaki, Gumma	139E01	36N19	+16	04	- 9	16	04
Tamoriuro, Karafuto	142E04	47N47	+28	16	- 9	28	16
Tobata, Fukuoka	130E50	33N53	-16	40	- 8	43	20
Tokushima, Tokushima	135E00	34N02	0	00	9	00	00
Tokuyama, Yamagushi.............	131E50...	34N03...	-12	40...	- 8	47	20
Tokyo, Tokyo	139E45	35N40	+19	00	- 9	19	00
Tottori, Tottori	134E15	33N27	- 3	00	- 8	57	00
Toyama, Toyama	137E11	36N40	+ 8	44	- 9	08	44
Toyohashi, Aichi	137E23	34N39	+ 9	32	- 9	09	32
Tsu, Mie.......................	136E31....	34N42...	+ 6	04...	- 9	06	04
Ube, Yamagushi	131E16	33N56	-14	56	- 8	45	04
Ujiyamada, Mie	136E43	34N28	+ 6	32	- 9	06	32
Urawa, Saitama	139E39	35N50	+18	36	- 9	18	36
Utsunomiya, Tochigi	140E18	36N20	+21	12	- 9	21	12
Uwajima, Ehide	132E35	33N13	- 9	40	- 8	50	20
Wakamatsu, Fukuoka	130E48	33N55	-16	48	- 8	43	12
Wakayama, Wakayama.............	135E11....	34N13...	+ 0	44...	- 9	00	44
Yamagata, Yamagata	140E20	38N15	+21	20	- 9	21	20
Yamagushi, Yamagushi	131E28	34N10	-14	08	- 8	45	52

			L. M. T. VARIATION FROM S.T.	G. M. T. VARIATION FROM LMT.
			m. s.	h. m. s.
JAPAN (Continued)				
Yawata, Fukuoka	130E48	33N50	-16 48	- 8 43 12
Yokkaichi, Mie	136E12	35N05	+ 4 48	- 9 04 49
Yokohama, Kaganawa..............	139E38...	35N25..	+18 32...	- 9 18 32
Yokusuka, Kanagawa	139E40	35N15	+18 40	- 9 18 40
Yonezawa, Yamagata	140E07	37N55	+20 28	- 9 20 28

JARVIS ISLAND.. British possession, situated
        in the South Pacific. Also claimed
        by U. S. A. Standard Time Meridian
        165° WEST

Jarvis Island (Radio Towers)	160W02	0S22	+19 52	+10 40 08

JAVA see Netherlands East Indies.

JEBEL DRUZE see Levant States.

JOHNSTON ISLAND. U. S. possession situated
        in North Pacific. Standard Time
        Meridian 157°30' WEST.

Johnston Island	169W30	16N45	-48 00	+11 18 00

JOHORE see Malaya.

JORDAN see Trans-Jordan. Independent May 22, 1946.

JUDEA see Palestine.

JUTLAND see Denmark.

KAISER WILHELMLAND   see Papua.

KARAFUTO see Japan.

KAZAK AUTONOMOUS S. S. R. see U.S.S.R.

KEDAH see Malaya.

KELANTAN see Malaya.

KENYA. Capital: Nairobi. British Colony
        and Protectorate, situated in
        East Africa. Standard Time
        Meridian 41°15' EAST.

Fort Hall, Fort Hall	37E09	0s43	-16 24	- 2 28 36
Kisumu, Nyasza Province	34E45	0S06	-26 00	- 2 19 00
Malindi, Malindi	40E07	3S13	- 4 32	- 2 40 28
Mombasa, Seydie	39E41	4S03	- 6 16	- 2 38 44
Mvita see Mombasa				
Nairobi, Ukamba	36E48	1S17	-17 48	- 2 27 12
Nakuru, Rift Valley Province	36E04	0S17	-20 44	- 2 24 16

KERMADEC ISLANDS. Dependency of New Zealand,
        situated in South Pacific. Standard
        Time Meridian 172°30' EAST. Beginning
        Nov. 24, 1945, changed to 180° EAST.

Denham Flagstaff, Raoul (Sunday) Is.	177E57	29S16	+21 48	-11 51 48

KERGUELEN ISLANDS. Capital: Port Jeanne d'Arc.
        Dependency of Madagascar, situated in
        Indian Ocean. Standard Time Meridian 75EAST.

Port Jeanne d'Arc	69E49	49S33	-20 44	- 4 39 16

KINGSMILL ISLANDS   see Gilbert & Ellice Islands.

KIRGIZ AUTONOMOUS S.S.R. see U.S.S.R.

			L. M. T. VARIATION FROM S.T. m. s.	G. M. T. VARIATION FROM LMT. h. m. s.
KOREA. Republic of, Aug. 15, 1948, and : KOREA DEMOCRATIC PEOPLES REPUBLIC: September 12, 1948. Capital: : Seoul. Formerly Japanese terri-; tory, situated in Eastern Asia. ; Standard Time Meridian 135°EAST.;				
Chemulpo see Inchon.				
Chinnampo	125E25	38N43	-38 20	- 8 21 40
Chongjin	129E51	41N46	-20 36	- 8 39 24
Chongju	127E29	36N39	-30 04	- 8 29 56
Chunchon	127E44	37N54	-29 04	- 8 30 56
Fusan see Pusan.				
Hamhung......................	127E30...	39N55...	-30 00...	- 8 30 00
Heijo see Phyongyang.				
Hoeju	125E42	36N04	-37 12	- 8 22 48
Inchon	126E36	37N27	-33 36	- 8 26 24
Jinsen see Inchon.				
Kaishu see Hoeju.				
Kanko see Hamhung.				
Keijo see Seoul.				
Koshu see Kwangju.				
Kwangju	126E56	35N08	-32 16	- 8 27 44
Kyongsong see Seoul.				
Mokpo (Moppo)	126E22	34N48	-34 32	- 8 25 28
Najin	130E17	42N12	-18 52	- 8 41 08
Phyongyang	126E45	39N00	-37 00	- 8 23 00
Pusan	129E03	35N06	-23 48	- 8 56 12
Pyong-Yang see Phyongyang.				
Rashin see Najin.				
Seishin see Chongjin.				
Seishu see Chongju.				
Seoul (Seool)	126E57	37N32	-32 12	- 8 27 48
Shingishu see Sinuiju.				
Shunsen see Chunchon.				
Sinuiju	124E20	40N05	-42 40	- 8 17 20
Taegu	128E36	35N53	-25 36	- 8 34 24
Taejan	127E25	36N18	-30 20	- 8 29 40
Taiden see Taejan.				
Taikyu see Taegu.				

KURIL OR KURILI ISLANDS   see Japan.
KURLAND see 1. Latvia.
         2. Lithuania.
KUSTENLAND see Italy.
KUWAIT see Saudi Arabia.
KWANTUNG LEASED TERRITORY see China.

LABRADOR see Canada.
LABUAN see Malaya.
LACCADIVE ISLANDS see India.
LADRONE ISLANDS see South Sea Mandated Territory.
LAGOON ISLANDS see Gilbert & Ellice Islands.
LAOS see French Indo-China. Independent December 29, 1954.
LATAKIA see Levant States.

			L. M. T. VARIATION FROM S.T.	G. M. T. VARIATION FROM LMT.

LATVIA. Capital: Riga. Republic, situated in
Northern Europe (now part of U.S.S.R.)
Standard Time Meridian 30° EAST.

			m. s.	h. m. s.
Aizpute, Aizpute	21E37	56N44	-33 32	- 1 26 28
Bauska, Bauska	24E10	56N24	-23 20	- 1 36 40
Cecis, Northern District........	25E17...	57N19...	-18 52...	- 1 41 08
Daugavpils, Daugavpils	26E33	55N53	-13 48	- 1 46 12
Dvinak see Daugavpils.				
Frauenburg see Saldus.				
Goldingen see Kuldiga.				
Grobina, Liepaja...............	21E10	56N32...	-35 20...	- 1 24 40
Hasenpot see Aizpute.				
Jakobstadt see Jakabpils.				
Jaunlatgale, Jaunlatgale	27E56	57N04	- 8 16	- 1 51 44
Jekabpils, Jekabpils	25E52	56N29	-16 32	- 1 43 28
Jelgava, Jelgava..............	23E43...	56N39...	-25 08...	- 1 34 52
Kuldiga, Kuldiga	21E59	56N59	-32 04	- 1 27 56
Libau see Liepaja.				
Liepaja, Liepaja	21E01	56N32	-35 56	- 1 24 04
Ludza (Lucyu), Ludza	27E44	56N33	- 9 04	- 1 50 56
Madona, Madona................	26E13...	56N51...	-15 08...	- 1 44 52
Mitau see Jelgava.				
Rezekne, Rezekne	27E20	56N31	-10 40	- 1 49 20
Riga, Riga	24E07	56N55	-23 32	- 1 36 28
Rigas Jurmala	23E46	56N58	-24 56	- 1 35 04
Rositen see Rezekne				
Saldus	22E30	56N40	-30 00	- 1 30 00
Talsi (Talsen), Ralsi	22E07	57N14	-29 32	- 1 30 28
Tukums (Tukkum), Tukums	23E10	56N58	-27 20	- 1 32 40
Valmiera, Valmiera	25E26	57N33	-18 16	- 1 41 44
Ventspils, Ventspils...........	21E34...	57N24...	-33 44...	- 1 26 16
Wenden see Cecis.				
Windau see Ventspils.				
Wolmar see Valmiera.				

LEASED TERRITORY OF KWANTUNG see China.
LEBANON see Levant States.
LEEWARD ISLANDS see 1. British West Indies.
                    2. French Establishments in Oceania.
LETTONIE see Latvia.
LAVANT STATES: 1. SYRIA. Capital: Damas (Damascus).
                   2. LEBANON. Capital: Beyrouth.
                   3. LATAKIA. Capital Latakia (Laodice).
                   4. JEBEL DRUZE. Capital: Soueida (Es-Suweideh).
   Republics situated in Western Asia.
   Standard Time Meridian 30° EAST.

Alep (Aleppo), Syria	37E09	36N11	+28 36	- 2 28 36
Antakiveh (Antiochia), Syria	36E09	36N12	+24 36	- 2 24 36
Baalbeck, Lebanon	36E12	34N01	+24 48	- 2 24 48
Banyas, Syria	35E57	35N11	+23 48	- 2 23 48
Beyrouth, Lebanon..............	35E28...	35N54...	+21 52...	- 2 21 52
Damas (Damascus), Syria	36E18	33N30	+25 12	- 2 25 12
Deir-es-Zor, Syria	40E08	35N21	+40 32	- 2 40 32
Deraa	36E06	32N37	+24 24	- 2 24 24

			L. M. T. VARIATION FROM S.T.	G. M. T. VARIATION FROM LMT.
			m. s.	h. m. s.
LEVANT STATES (Continued)				
Djerablous, Syria	38E02	36N50	+32 08	2 32 08
Dimeshk see Damas (Damascus).				
Epiphania see Hama.				
Es.Seweidea see Soueida.				
Fik, Syria	35E42	32N48	+22 48	- 2 22 48
Haffe, Syria	36E02	35N36	+24 08	- 2 24 08
Haleb see Alep				
Hama, Syria.....................	36E45...	35N08...	+ 27 00...	- 2 27 00
Heliopolis see Baalbeck.				
Hemesa see Homs.				
Homs, Syria	36E43	34N44	+26 52	- 2 26 52
Idlib, Syria	36E37	35N55	+26 28	- 2 26 28
Iaodice see Latakia.				
Latakia, Syria	35E45	35N31	+23 00	- 2 23 00
Massyaf, Syria	36E20	35N04	+25 20	- 2 25 20
Mardjayoun, Lebanon	35E36	33N21	+22 24	- 2 22 24
Onoranie see Massyaf.				
Safita, Syria...................	36E07...	34N49...	+24 28...	- 2 24 28
Saida, Lebanon	35E22	33N34	+21 28	- 2 21 28
Sidon see Saida.				
Soueida, Jebel Druse	36E34	32N43	+26 16	- 2 26 16
Sur, Lebanon	35E11	33N17	+20 44	- 2 20 44
Tarabulus see Tripoli.				
Tripoli, Lebanon	35E50	34N27	+23 20	- 2 23 20
Tyre see Sur.				
Zahle, Lebanon	35E54	33N51	+23 36	- 2 23 36
Zebdani, Syria	36E06	33N44	+24 24	- 2 24 24

LIBAN see Levant States.

LIBERIA. Capital: Monrovia. Republic situated in Western Africa. Standard Time Meridian 11° WEST.

Buchanan see Grand Bassa.				
Grand Bassa, Central Province	10W57	5N52	+ 0 12	+ 0 43 48
Greenville see Sino.				
Harper, Eastern Province	7W43	4N22	+13 08	+ 0 30 52
Kolahun, Western Province	10W03	8N18	+ 3 46	+ 0 40 12
Marshall, Central Province	10W23	6N08	+ 2 28	+ 0 41 32
Monrovia, Central Province......	10W48...	6N20...	+ 0 48...	+ 0 43 12
River Cess, Central Province	9W42	5N34	+ 5 12	+ 0 38 48
Robertsport, Western Province	11W20	6N42	- 1 20	+ 0 45 20
Sanoquelli (Sanokwele),				
Central Province	8W43	7N24	+ 9 08	+ 0 34 52
Sino, Eastern Province..........	9W04...	5N01...	+ 7 44...	+ 0 36 16
Tappi, Central Province	8W54	6N29	+ 8 24	+ 0 35 36
White Plains, Central Prov.	10W43	6N29	+ 1 08	+ 0 42 52

LIBYA. Capital: Tripoli. Formerly Italian Colony, situated in North Africa. Independent Dec. 24, 1951. Standard Time Meridian 15° EAST

Agebadia, Bengasi	20E14	30N46	+20 56	- 1 20 56
Apollonia, Derna	21E58	32N54	+27 52	- 1 27 52
Arinoe Cleopatride see Tocra.				

			L. M. T. VARIATION FROM S.T.	G. M. T. VARIATION FROM LMT.
			m. s.	h. m. s.
LIBYA. (Continued)				
Barce, Bengasi	20E54	32N30	+23 36	- 1 23 36
Bardia, Derna	25E06	31N42	+40 24	- 1 40 24
Bengasi, Bengasi................	20E05...	32N06...	+20 20...	- 1 20 20
Berenico see Bengasi.				
Beni Ulid, Misurata	14E00	31N44	- 4 00	- 0 56 00
Derna, Derna	22E39	32N46	+30 36	- 1 30 36
El Azizia, Tripoli	13E02	32N32	- 7 52	- 0 52 08
El Gusbat, Misurata..............14E02...		32N34...	- 3 52...	- 0 56 08
Euhesperide see Bengasi.				
Gadamos, Tripoli	9E29	30N08	-22 04	- 0 37 56
Garian, Tripoli	13E00	32N10	- 8 00	- 0 52 00
Homs, Misurata	14E17	32N39	- 2 52	- 0 57 08
Lebda see Homs.				
Misurata, Misurata	15E06	32N23	+ 0 24	- 1 00 24
Sirte, Misurata	16E36	31N11	+ 6 24	- 1 06 24
Sliten, Misurata	14E34	32N28	- 1 44	- 0 58 16
Soluch, Bengasi	20E15	31N40	+21 00	- 1 21 00
Tarhuna, Tripoli................	13E38...	32N27...	- 5 28...	- 0 54 32
Teuchira see Tocra.				
Tripoli, Tripoli	13E10	32N54	- 7 20	- 0 52 40
Tobruk, Derna	23E58	32N06	+35 52	- 1 35 52
Zaafran see Sirte.				
Zephyrion see Derna.				
Zliton see Sliten.				
LICHTENSTEIN. Capital: Vaduz. Principality,				
situated in Central Europe. Standard				
Time Meridian 15° EAST.				
Balzera	9E30	47N04	-22 00	- 0 38 00
Ruggel	9E32	47N15	-21 52	- 0 38 08
Schaan	9E31	47N10	-21 56	- 0 38 04
Vaduz	9E31	47N08	-21 56	- 0 38 04
LITHUANIA. Capital: Kaunas. Republic, situated in				
Northern Europe (Now a part of U.S.S.R.) Standard				
Time Meridian 15° EAST, although time has been ad-				
vanced 1 hour throughout entire year (as in U.S.S.R.)				
Alytus, Alytus	24E04	54N25	+36 16	- 1 36 16
Augustavas see Augustow, Poland.				
Birzai (Birsche)	24E45	56N13	+39 00	- 1 39 00
Gardinas see Grodno, Poland.				
Kaisiadorys, Trakai	24E28	54N52	+37 52	- 1 37 52
Kaunas, Kaunas	23E55	54N54	+35 40	- 1 35 40
Kedainiai, Kedainiai...........	23E58...	55N17...	+35 52...	- 1 35 52
Kiejdany see Kedainiai.				
Klaipeda see Memol, Germany.				
Koschedary see Kaisiadorys.				
Kovno (Kowno) see Kaunas.				
Kretinga (Kretingen) Kretinga	21E13	55N54	+24 52	- 1 24 52
Mazeikiai, Mazeikiai	22E20	56N19	+29 20	- 1 29 20
Mosneiki see Mazeikiai.				
Murajevo see Mazeikiai.				

			L. M. T. VARIATION FROM S.T.	G. M. T. VARIATION FROM LMT.
			m. s.	h. m. s.

LITHUANIA, (Continued)

Olita see Alytus.				
Panevezys, Panevezys	24E22	55N44	+ 37 28	- 1 37 28
Poniewiez see Panevezys.				
Rakischki see Rokiskis.				
Rasseniai, Rasseniai	23E07	55N23	+ 32 28	- 1 32 28
Rokiskis, Rokiskis	25E36	55N57	+ 42 24	- 1 42 24
Rossieny see Rasseniai.				
Savalkai see Suwalki, Poland.				
Savli see Siauliai.				
Schaulen see Siauliai.				
Schoden see Skuedas.				
Siauliai, Siauliai	23E18	55N56	+ 33 12	- 1 33 12
Taurage (Tauroggen), Taurage	22E17	55N15	+ 29 08	- 1 29 08
Telsiai (Telsche), Telsiai......	22E14...	55N59...	+ 28 56...	- 1 28 56
Ukmerge, Ukmerge	24E46	55N14	+ 39 04	- 1 39 04
Utena, Utena	25E37	55N29	+ 42 28	- 1 42 28
Uzjany see Utena.				
Vilkaviskis, Vilkaviskis	23E03	54N39	+ 32 12	- 1 32 12
Vilnius see Wilno, Poland.				
Wilkomierz see Ukmerge.				
Wilkowischki see Vilkaviskis.				

LOMBARDIA see Italy.

LOYALTY ISLANDS see New Caledonia.

LUANG-PRABANG see French Indo-China.

LUXEMBOURG. Capital: Luxembourg. Grand Duchy situated
in Central Europe. Standard Time Meridian 15° EAST.

Clervaux, Gaz.	6E02	50N03	- 35 52	- 0 24 08
Diekirch, Diekirch...............	6E10...	49N53...	- 35 20..	- 0 24 40
Echternach, Gaz.	6E25	49N48	- 34 20	- 0 25 40
Grevenmacher, Gaz.	6E26	49N41	- 34 16	- 0 25 44
Luxembourg, Luxembourg	6E10	49N38	- 35 20	- 0 24 40
Wiltz, Gaz.	5E56	49N58	- 36 16	- 0 23 44

MACAO see Portuguese India.

MACASSAR see Netherlands East Indies.

MACEDONIA see 1. Bulgaria.
          2. Greece.
          3. Yugoslavia.

MADAGASCAR AND DEPENDENCIES. Capital: Tananarive.
French Colony situated in the Indian Ocean.
Standard Time Meridian 45° EAST.

Andoveranto	49E09	18S56	+16 36	- 3 16 36
Andramaimbo	49E11	12S13	+16 44	- 3 16 44
Antsirana see Diego Suarez.				
Diego Suarez	49E18	12S17	+17 12	- 3 17 12
Dzaoudzi, Mayete	45E17	12S47	+ 1 08	- 3 01 08
Fenerive	49E24	17S22	+17 36	- 3 17 36
Fomboni, Moheli	43E45	12S17	- 5 00	- 2 55 00
Fort Dauphin.................47E01		25S01	+ 8 04	- 3 08 04
Hellville	48E18	13S24	+13 12	- 3 13 12
Johanna see Mutsamudu.				
Maevatanava	46E47	16S54	+ 7 08	- 3 07 08

			L. M. T. VARIATION FROM S.T.	G. M. T. VARIATION FROM LMT.

MADAGASCAR & DEPENDENCIES.

			m. s.	h. m. s.
Majunga see Mojanga				
Mojanga	46E20	15S44	+ 5 20	- 3 05 20
Morendava	44E18	20S19	- 2 48	- 2 57 12
Moroni, Grande Comore............	43E14...	11S40...	- 7 04...	- 2 52 56
Mutsamudu	44E24	19S09	- 2 24	- 2 57 36
Pomoni Harbor, Comore Islands	44E25	12S15	- 2 20	- 2 57 40
Port Choiseul	49E51	15S24	+19 24	- 3 19 24
Tananarive	47E30	18S54	+10 00	- 3 10 00
Tulear........................	43E38...	23S20...	- 5 28...	- 2 54 32
Vatomandri	49E02	19S18	+16 08	- 3 16 08
Windsor Castle see Andramaimbo.				

MADEIRA ISLANDS.   Capital: Funchai. Portuguese
    Colony situated in the North Atlantic Ocean.
    Standard Time Meridian 15° WEST.

Calhota, Funchal	17W12	32N44	- 8 48	+ 1 08 48
Funchal, Funchal	16W54	32N38	- 7 36	+ 1 07 36
Porto Santo, Porto Santo	16W19	33N03	- 5 16	+ 1 05 16
Sao Vicente, Funchal	17W03	32N47	- 8 12	+ 1 08 12

MADOERA (MADURA) see Netherlands East Indies.

MAEHREN see Czechoslovakia.

MAKASSAR see Netherlands East Indies.

MALABAR COAST See 1. India.
                2. Portuguese India.

MALACCA see Malaya.

MALAGASY, Formerly MADAGASCAR. Independent June 26, 1960.

MALAYA. Capital: Singapore. Formerly British Crown Colony.
    situated in South Asia. Independent Aug. 31, 1957.
    It includes the colony of Singapore; the Malayan
    Union comprising the former Straits Settlements
    (Malacca, Penang and Province Wellesley), the Fed-
    erated Malay States (Negri Sembilan, Pahang and
    Selangor), the Unfederated Malay States (Johore,
    Kedah, Kelantan, Perlis and Trengganu) and Labuan.
    Standard Time Meridian 110° EAST, with the exception
    of Labuan where 120° EAST prevails.

Alor Star Kedah	100E22	6N07	-38 32	- 6 41 28
Bandar Maharani, Johore	103E33	2N03	-25 48	- 6 54 12
Georgetown, Ponang.............	100E20....	5N25...	-38 40...	- 6 41 20
Ipoh, Porak	101E05	4N35	-35 40	- 6 44 20
Johore Bahru, Johore	103E46	1N27	-24 56	- 6 55 04
Kangar, Perlis	100E12	6N26	-39 12	- 6 40 48
Khota Baru, Kelantan	102E14	6N08	-31 04	- 6 48 56
Klang, Solangor................	101E27...	3N03...	-34 12...	- 6 45 48
Kuala Lipis, Pahang	102E03	4N11	-31 48	- 6 48 12
Kuala Lumphur, Selanger	101E42	3N10	-33 12	- 6 46 48
Kuala Trengganu, Trengganu	103E09	5N20	-27 24	- 6 52 36
Kuantan, Kuantan	103E20	3N48	-26 40	- 6 53 20
Lumut, Dindings, Perak........	100E38...	4N14...	-37 28...	- 6 42 32
Malacca, Malacca	102E15	2N12	-31 00	- 6 49 00
Muar see Bandar Maharani				
Port Dickson, Negri Sembilan	101E48	2N31	-32 48	- 6 47 12
Port Swettenham. Selangor	101E23	3N00	-34 28	- 6 45 32

			L. M. T. VARIATION FROM S.T.	G. M. T. VARIATION FROM LMT.
			m. s.	h. m. s.

MALAYA. (Continued)

Prai, Pr. Wellesley	100E23	5N23	-38 28	- 6 41 32
Seremban, Negri Semblan	101E56	2N44	-32 16	- 6 47 44
Singapore, St. Settlements	103E51	1N16	-24 36	- 6 55 24
Taiping, Perak..................	100E45...	4N51...	-37 00...	- 6 43 00
Telok Anson, Perck	101E02	4N01	-35 52	- 6 44 08
Victoria Town, Pulau Labuan	115E15	5N17	-19 00	- 7 41 00

(Incorporated into British North Borneo in 1946)

MALAY STATES see Malaya.

MALAYAN UNION see Malaya

MALDIVE ISLANDS. Capital: Male. British Dependency
situated in the Indian Ocean. LMT used based
on Meridian 73°30' EAST.

Male	73E30	4N10		- 4 54 00

MALI. See French West Africa. Independent June 20, 1960.

MALTA. Capital: La Valletta. British Colony situated in the Mediterranean. Standard Time
Meridian 15° EAST.

Citta Vocchia, Malta	14E24	35N53	- 2 24	- 0 57 36
La Valletta, Malta..............	14E31...	35N54...	- 1 56...	- 0 58 04
Medina see Citta Vecchia.				
Notabile see Citta Vecchia.				
Rabat, Gozo	14E14	36N32	- 3 04	- 0 56 56
Vittoriosa see La Valletta.				
Zeitun, Malta	14E32	35N51	- 1 52	- 0 58 08

MALVINAS, MALVINE ISLANDS see Falkland Islands.

MANCHUKUO see China.

MANCHURIA see China.

MANDCHOURIE see China.

MANDATED TERRITORY OF NEW GUINEA see New Guinea.

MANITOBA see Canada.

MARCUS ISLAND. Possession of the United States, situated in the North Pacific. Standard Time
Meridian 150° EAST.

Marcus Island	154E00	24N14	+16 00	-10 16 00

MARIANNE ISLANDS see South Sea Mandated Territories.

MAROC see Morocco.

MARQUESAS ISLANDS see French Establishments in Oceania.

MARSHALL ISLANDS see South Sea Mandated Territories.

MARTINIQUE. Capital: Fort de France. French Colony, situated in the West Indies. Standard Time Meridian 60° WEST.

Carbet	61W11	14N43	- 4 44	+ 4 04 44
Diamant	61W02	14N29	- 4 08	+ 4 04 08
Fort de France	61W05	14N36	- 4 20	+ 4 04 20
Lamentin	61W04	14N47	- 4 16	+ 4 04 16
Marin	60W53	14N28	- 3 32	+ 4 03 32
St. Esprit	60W57	14N34	- 3 48	+ 4 03 48
Trinite	60W58	14N44	- 3 52	+ 4 03 52

MASKAT see Saudi Arabia.

MATABELELAND see Rhodesia.

MAURICE, L'ILE see Mauritius.

MAURITANIA see French West Africa. Independent Nov. 28, 1960.

			L. M. T. VARIATION FROM S.T.	G. M. T. VARIATION FROM LMT.
			m. s.	h. m. s.

MAURITIUS. Capital: Port Louis. British
Colony, situated in the Indian Ocean.
Standard time Meridian 60° EAST.

Mahebourg	57E42	20S24	- 9 12	- 3 50 48
Port Louis	57E30	20S09	-10 00	- 3 50 00
Royal Alfred Observatory	57E33	20S06	- 9 48	- 3 50 12

MENDANA ISLAND see Wake Island.

MESOPOTAMIA see Iraq.

MEXICO. Capital: Mexico, D.F. Republic, situated in
North America. Central Standard Time (90° WEST)
used since November 12, 1945, with the exception
of the States of Nayarit, Sinaloa and Sonora
using 120° WEST and the northern part of the
Territory of Baja California using 105° WEST,
while the southern part of the same Territory
uses meridian 105° WEST.

Acapulco, Gro.	99W56	16N51	-39 44	+ 6 39 44
Aguascalientes, Agu.	102W18	21N53	-49 12	+ 6 49 12
Azcapotzalco, D.F.	99W11	19N29	-36 44	+ 6 36 44
Campeche, Camp.	90W34	19N21	- 2 16	+ 6 02 16
Calaya, Gto.	100W48	20N31	-43 12	+ 6 43 12
Chetumal, Q.R.	88W18	18N30	+ 6 48	+ 5 53 12
Chihuahua, Chi.	106W05	26N38	-1h04 20	+ 7 04 20
Chilpancingo, Gro.	99W30	17N33	-38 00	+ 6 38 00
Ciudad del Carmen, Cam.	91W50	18N38	- 7 20	+ 6 07 20
Ciudad de Valles, S.L.P.	99W01	22N00	-36 04	+ 6 36 04
Ciudad Guzman, Jal.	103W30	19N42	-54 00	+ 6 54 00
Ciudad Juarez, Chih.	106W29	31N44	-1h05 56	+ 7 05 56
Ciudad Victoria, Tam.	99W08	23N44	-36 32	+ 6 36 32
Coatzacoalcos, Ver.	94W25	18N09	-17 40	+ 6 17 40
Colima, Colima	103W43	19N14	-54 52	+ 6 54 52
Cuernavaca, Mor.	99W14	18N55	-36 56	+ 6 36 56
Culiacan, Sin.	107W24	24N49	- 9 36	+ 7 09 36
Durango, Dur.	104W40	24N02	-58 40	+ 6 58 40
Ensenada, B. Cfa. S.	116W37	31N52	+13 32	+ 7 46 28
Gomez Palacio, Dur.	103W30	25N34	-54 00	+ 6 54 00
Guadalajara, Jal.	103W21	20N40	-53 24	+ 6 53 24
Guanajuato, Gto.	101W15	21N01	-45 00	+ 6 45 00
Gustavo Madero, D.F.	99W07	20N29	-36 28	+ 6 36 28
Hermosillo, Son.	110W58	29N05	-23 52	+ 7 23 52
Hidalgo del Parral, Chih.	105W39	26N56	-1h02 36	+ 7 02 36
Ixtacalco, D.F.	99W07	19N23	-36 28	+ 6 36 28
Ixtapalapa, D.F.	99W05	19N22	-36 20	+ 6 36 20
Jalapa, Ver.	96W55	19N32	-27 40	+ 6 27 40
Juchitan, Oax.	95W01	16N27	-20 04	+ 6 20 04
La Paz, B. Cfa., S.	110W18	24N09	-21 12	+ 7 21 12
Leon, Gto.	101W41	21N08	-46 44	+ 6 46 44
Matameros, Tam.	97W30	25N53	-30 00	+ 6 30 00
Mazatlan, Sin.	106W25	23N12	- 5 40	+ 7 05 40
Merida, Yuc.	89W38	20N58	+ 1 28	+ 5 58 32
Mexicali, B. Cfa. N.	115W29	32N38	+18 04	+ 7 41 56
Mexico, D.F. (Mexico City)	99W09	19N24	-36 36	+ 6 36 36
Minatitlan, Ver.	94W33	17N59	-18 12	+ 6 18 12
Monterrey, N. L.	100W18	25N41	-41 12	+ 6 41 12

			L. M. T. VARIATION FROM S.T.		G. M. T. VARIATION FROM LMT.		
			m.	s.	h.	m.	s.
MEXICO (Continued)							
Morelia, Mich	101W07	19N42	-44	28	+ 6	44	28
Oaxaca de Juarez, Oax	96W43	17N04	-26	52	+ 6	26	52
Orizaba, Ver.	97W06	18N51	-28	24	+ 6	28	24
Pachuca, Hgo.	98W44	20N08	-34	56	+ 6	34	56
Parral see Hidalgo del Parral.							
Progreso, Yuc........	89W40...	21N17...	+ 1	20...	+ 5	58	40
Puebla, Puebla	98W12	19N03	-32	48	+ 6	32	48
Queretara, Qro.	100W23	20N36	-41	32	+ 6	41	32
Saltillo, Coah.	101W00	25N26	-44	00	+ 6	44	00
San Luis Potosi, S. L. P.	100W59	22N09	-43	56	+ 6	43	56
Santa Cruz de Bravo, Q.R.......	88W02...	19N35...	+ 7	52...	+ 5	52	08
Santa Rosalita, B. Cfa. N.	112W44	27N19	-30	56	+ 7	30	56
Tacubaya, D.F.	99W11	19N21	-36	44	+ 6	36	44
Tampico, Tam.	97W51	22N13	-31	24	+ 6	31	24
Tepic, Nay.	104W54	21N31	+ 0	24	+ 6	59	36
Tijuana, B.Cfa. N.............	117W02...	32N32...	+11	52...	+ 7	48	08
Tlalpam, D.F.	99W10	19N17	-36	40	+ 6	36	40
Tlalpujahua, Mich.	100W10	19N48	-40	40	+ 6	40	40
Tlaxcala, Tlax.	98W14	19N19	-32	56	+ 6	32	56
Toluca, Mex.	99W39	19N18	-38	36	+ 6	38	36
Tonala, Chis..................	93W45...	16N05...	-15	00...	+ 6	15	00
Torreon, Coah.	103W27	25N33	-53	48	+ 6	53	48
Tuxtla Gutierrez, Chis.	93W07	16N45	-12	28	+ 6	12	28
Uruapan, Mich.	101W57	19N25	-47	48	+ 6	47	48
Valladolid, Yuc.	88W13	20N41	+ 7	08	+ 5	52	52
Veracruz, Ver.................	96W08...	19N11...	-24	32...	+ 6	24	32
Villa Hermosa, Tab.	92W58	18N00	-11	52	+ 6	11	52
Xochimilco, D.F.	99W06	19N16	-36	24	+ 6	36	24
Zacatecas, Zac.	102W34	22N46	-50	16	+ 6	50	16

MEXIQUE see Mexico.

MIDDLE CONGO see French Equatorial Africa.

MIDWAY ISLANDS. Attached to the Territory of Hawaii,
under administration of the United States of
America. Situated in the North Pacific. Standard
Time Meridian 157°30' WEST. At this time, however, (1948) 165° WEST Meridian being used.

Walles Harbor, Sand Island	177W23	28N13	-1h19 32	+11 49 32

MIQUELON see St. Pierre & Miquelon.

MOLDAVIA see Rumania.

MOLUCCAS see Netherlands East Indies.

MONACO. Capital: Monaco. Principality situated
in Southern Europe. Standard Time
Meridian 0°.

Monaco	7E26	43N44	+29 44	- 0 29 44
Monte Carlo	7E25	43N45	+29 40	- 0 29 40

MONGOLIA see China.

MONTENEGRO see Yugoslavia.

MONTSERRAT see British West Indies.

MORAVIA see Czechoslavakia.

MOROCCO.. Empire, situated in North Africa, Independent March 2, 1956
    1. French Zone, capital: Rabat.   :
    2. International Zone, capital: Ranger.:   L. M. T.   G. M. T.
    3. Spanish Zone, capital: Melilla.   :   VARIATION   VARIATION
    Standard Time Meridian 0°   :   FROM S.T.   FROM LMT.

			m. s.	h. m. s.
Agadir	10W37	30N26	- 42 28	+ 0 42 28
Berguent	2W02	34N01	- 8 08	+ 0 08 08
Casablanca	7W37	33N37	- 30 28	+ 0 30 28
Fes (Fez)	4W58	34N03	- 19 52	+ 0 19 52
Kenitra see Port Lyautev.				
Marrakesh.........................	7W59...	31N37...	- 31 56...	+ 0 31 56
Mazagan	8W30	33N16	- 34 00	+ 0 34 00
Meknes	4W58	33N54	- 19 52	+ 0 19 52
Mogador	9W45	31N31	- 39 00	+ 0 39 00
Oudjda	1W55	34N41	- 7 40	+ 0 07 40
Oued Zem	6W33...	32N53...	- 26 20...	+ 0 26 20
Ouezzane	5W35	34N48	- 22 20	+ 0 22 20
Port Lyautey	6W35	34N17	- 26 20	+ 0 26 20
Rabat	6W51	34N01	- 27 24	+ 0 27 24
Safi	9W14	32N18	- 36 56	+ 0 36 56
Settat.........................	7W37...	33N00...	- 30 28...	+ 0 30 28
Taourirt	2W55	34N25	- 11 32	+ 0 11 32
Taza	4W01	34N13	- 16 04	+ 0 16 04
Ceuta	5W19	35N54	- 21 16	+ 0 21 16
Larache (Spanish Zone)	6W08	35N12	- 24 32	+ 0 24 32
Melilla (" ")	2W56...	35N17...	- 11 44...	+ 0 11 44
Tetuan (" ")	5W22	35N35	- 21 28	+ 0 21 28
Tanger (Tangier)(Int. Zone)	5W48	35N47	- 25 12	+ 0 23 12

MOZAMBIQUE   see Portuguese East Africa.
MUANG THAI   see Siam.
MUNI see Spanish Guinea
MUSCAT and OMAN see Saudi Arabia
NAMALAND see Union of South Africa.
NAMAQUALAND see Union of South Africa
NASHONALAND see Rhodesia
NATAL   see Union of South Africa
NAURU ISLANDS British Mandate in the South Pacific.
    Standard Time Meridian 172°30' EAST

Nauru Island, Gov't. station	166E55	0S32	- 22 20	- 11 07 40
Yangor, Nauru	166E54	0S31	- 22 24	- 11 07 36

NAVARRE   see Spain
NAVAGATORS ISLAND see Western Samoa
NECKER ISLAND see Hawaii
NEGRI SEMBLAN see Malaya
NEJD see Saudi Arabia
NEPAL   Nepal see India
NETHERLANDS.   Capital: 's Gravenhague (The Hague)
    Standard Time Meridian from May 1, 1909 to 1947
    was Meridian of Amsterdam, 4°53' 02' EAST.
    Reported that C. Eu. T. was S.T. Meridian in
    1953 and subsequently.

			L. M. T. VARIATION FROM S.T.	G. M. T. VARIATION FROM LMT.
			m. s.	h. m. s.
NETHERLANDS (Continued)				
Alkmear, Noordholland	4E45	52N38	-41 00	- 0 19 00
Almelo, Overijsel	6E47	52N21	-32 52	- 0 27 08
Amersfoort, Utrecht............	5E24...	52N09...	-38 24...	- 0 21 36
Amsterdam, Noordholland	4E53	52N23	-40 28	- 0 19 32
Apeldoorn, Gelderland	5E58	52N12	-36 08	- 0 23 52
Arnhem, Gelderland	5E55	51N59	-36 20	- 0 23 40
Breda, Noordbrabant	4E46	51N35	-40 56	- 0 19 04
Bussum, Noordholland	5E10...	52N16...	-39 20...	- 0 20 40
Delft, Zuidholland	4E22	52N00	-42 32	- 0 17 28
Den Helder, Noordholland	4E46	52N58	-40 56	- 0 19 04
Deventer, Overijsel	6E10	52N16	-35 20	- 0 24 40
Dordrecht, Zuidholland	4E40	51N48	-41 20	- 0 18 40
Eindhoven, Noordbrabant........	5E29...	51N26...	-38 04...	- 0 21 56
Emmen, Drente	6W14	52N30	-35 04	- 0 24 56
Enschedo, Overijsel	6E53	52N47	-31 28	- 0 27 32
Flushing see Vlissingen.				
Gouda, Zuidholland	4E43	52N00	-41 08	- 0 18 52
Groningen, Groningen............	6E32...	53N13...	-33 52...	- 0 26 08
Hague see 's Gravenhague.				
Hearlem, Noordholland	4E38	52N23	-41 28	- 0 18 32
Hengelo, Overijsel	6E18	52N03	-34 48	- 0 25 12
Hilversum, Noordholland	5E11	52N13	-39 16	- 0 20 44
Leeuwarden, Friesland...........	5E48...	53N12...	-36 48...	- 0 23 12
Leiden, Zuidholland	4E30	52N10	-42 00	- 0 18 00
Maastricht, Limburg	5E41	50N51	-37 16	- 0 22 44
Middelburg, Zeeland	3E36	51N30	-45 36	- 0 14 24
Nijmegen (nimegue), Noordbrab	5E52	51N50	-36 32	- 0 23 28
Roosendaal, Noordbrabant.......	4E28...	51N32...	-42 08...	- 0 17 52
Rotterdam, Zuidholland	4E30	51N55	-42 00	- 0 18 00
Scheveningen, Zuidholland	4E16	52N06	-42 56	- 0 17 04
Schiedam, Zuidholland	4E24	51N55	-42 24	- 0 17 36
's Gravenhague, Zuidholland	4E19	52N05	-42 44	- 0 17 16
's Hertogenbusch, Noordbrab.....	5E18...	50N42...	-38 48...	- 0 21 12
The Hague see 's Gravenhague.				
Tilburg, Noordbrabant	5E06	51N33	-39 36	- 0 20 24
Utrecht, Utrecht	5E07	52N05	-39 32	- 0 20 28
Valzon, Noordholland	4E39	52N28	-41 24	- 0 18 36
Venloo, Limburg	6E10	51N22	-35 20	- 0 24 40
Vlissingen, Zeeland.............	3E34...	51N26...	-45 44...	- 0 14 16
Zaandam, Noordholland	4E50	52N26	-40 40	- 0 19 20
Zutphen, Gelderland	6E12	52N08	-35 12	- 0 24 48
Zwelle, Overijsel	6E06	52N30	-35 36	- 0 24 24
NETHERLANDS EAST INDIES (now Indonesia) Capital: Djarkata				
(Formerly Batavia). Situated in Southeast Asia.				
Standard Time Meridians 97°30', 105°, 112°30',				
120°, and 127°30' EAST.				
Amboina, Amboina	123E10...	3S42...	+ 2 40...	- 8 32 40
Badjawa, Flores	120E59	8S47	+ 3 56	- 8 03 56
Bandjermasin, Borneo	114E36	3S19	+ 8 24	- 7 38 24
Bandoeng, Java	107E36	6S56	-19 36	- 7 11 24
Banjoemas, Java	109E18	7S31	-12 48	- 7 17 12

			L. M. T. VARIATION FROM S.T.	G. M. T. VARIATION FROM LMT.
NETHERLANDS EAST INDIES (Continued)			m. s.	h. m. s.
Bantaeng see Bonthain.				
Batavia, Java	106E45	6S10	-23 00	- 7 07 00
Benkoelen, Sumatra	102E15	3S47	-11 00	- 6 49 00
Bondowoso, Java...............	113E48...	7S54...	+ 5 12...	- 7 35 12
Bonthain, Celebes	119E57	5S33	- 0 12	- 7 59 48
Buitenzorg, Java	106E48	6S36	-22 48	- 7 07 12
Cheribon, Java	108E33	6S45	-15 48	- 7 14 12
Cupao see Koepang.				
Denpasar, Bali...............	115E13...	8S40...	+10 52...	- 7 40 52
Djailolo, Halmahera	128E27	1N05	+ 3 48	- 8 33 48
Donggala, Celebes	119E41	0S39	- 1 16	- 7 58 44
Djambi, Sumatra	103E37	0S37	- 5 32	- 6 54 28
Ende, Flores	121E38	8S50	+ 6 32	- 8 06 32
Fort de Kock, Sumatra.........	100E22...	0S10...	+11 28...	- 6 41 28
Gorontalo, Celebes	123E03	0N31	+12 12	- 8 12 12
Jogjakarta, Java	110E22	7S48	- 8 32	- 7 21 28
Kediri, Java	112E00	7S50	- 2 00	- 7 28 00
Koepang, Timor	123E35	10S10	+14 20	- 8 14 20
Koeteradja, Sumatra..........	95E20...	5N32...	- 8 40...	- 6 21 20
Madioen, Java	111E32	7S38	- 3 52	- 7 26 08
Magelang, Java	110E14	7S28	- 9 04	- 7 20 58
Makassar (Makasser), Celebes	119E25	5S08	- 2 20	- 7 57 40
Malang, Java	112E38	7S59	+ 0 32	- 7 30 32
Manado see Menado				
Mataram, Lombek	116E07	8S35	+14 28	- 7 44 28
Medan, Sumatra	98E40	3N35	+ 4 40	- 6 34 40
Meester Cornelis, Java	106E51	6S12	-22 36	- 7 07 24
Menado, Celebes	124E50	1N30	+19 20	- 8 19 20
Muntok, Banka...............	105E10...	2S03...	+ 0 40...	- 7 00 40
Padang, Sumatra	100E22	0S58	+11 28	- 6 41 28
Palembang, Sumatra	104E44	3S00	- 1 04	- 6 58 56
Palopo, Celebes	120E12	2S59	+ 0 48	- 8 00 48
Pamekasan, Madoera	113E29	7S10	+ 3 56	- 7 33 56
Pangkalpinang, Banka...........	106E08...	2S08...	+ 4 32...	- 7 04 32
Parepare, Celebes	119E37	4S01	- 1 32	- 7 58 28
Pati, Java	111E02	6S46	- 5 52	- 7 24 08
Pekalongan, Java	109E40	6S53	-11 20	- 7 18 40
Pontianak, Borneo	109E20	0S02	-12 40	- 7 17 20
Posso, Celebes................	120E44...	1S24...	+ 2 56...	- 8 02 56
Samarinda, Borneo	117E10	0S30	+18 40	- 7 48 40
Semarang, Java	110E30	7S00	- 8 00	- 7 22 00
Serang, Java	106E10	6S07	-25 20	- 7 04 40
Sibolga, Sumatra	98E46	1N44	+5 04	- 6 35 04
Singardja, Bali..............	115E06...	8S08...	+10 24...	- 7 40 24
Soembawa, Soembawa	117E25	8S28	-10 20	- 7 49 40
Soerabaja, Java	112E45	7S15	+ 1 00	- 7 31 00
Soerakarta, Java	110E50	7S34	- 6 40	- 7 23 20
Tandjoengpandan, Biliton	107E38	2S44	+10 32	- 7 10 32
Ternate, Ternate............	127E22...	0N47...	- 0 32...	- 8 29 28
Wahai, Ceram	129E29	2S48	+ 7 56	- 8 37 56
Waingapoe, Soemba	120E17	9S38	+ 1 08	- 8 01 08
Watampone, Celebes	120E18	4S33	+ 1 12	- 8 01 12
Weda, Halmahera	127E52	0N20	+ 3 28	- 8 33 28

NETHERLANDS GUIANA, see Surinam

NETHERLANDS NEW GUINEA, Capital: Manokward :

			L. M. T. VARIATION FROM S.T. m. s.	G. M. T. VARIATION FROM LMT. h. m. s.

Colony of the Netherlands situated in :
The East Indies. Standard Time Merid-:
ian 135° EAST.

			L. M. T. VARIATION FROM S.T. m. s.	G. M. T. VARIATION FROM LMT. h. m. s.
Fak Fak	132E17	2S56	-10 52	- 8 49 08
Hollandia	140E43	2S32	+22 52	- 9 22 52
Japero	137E12	4S59	+ 8 44	- 9 08 48
Manokwari	134E05	0S52	- 3 40	- 8 56 20
Merauke	140E22	8S47	+21 28	- 9 21 28
Nime	136E32	4S45	+ 6 08	- 9 06 08
Sorong	131E15	0S54	-15 00	- 8 45 00

NETHERLANDS TIMOR see Netherlands East Indies

NETHERLANDS WEST INDIES (ANTILLES) Capital: Willemstad
Autonomous part of the Kingdom of the Netherlands,
situated in the Lesser Antilles. Composed of Windward
Islands (St. Maarten, Saba and St. Eustatius) Meridian
60°W (A.S.T.); Leeward Islands (Curacuo, Aruba, &
Bonaire) Meridian 67°30' W.

Bottom, Saba	63W14	17N37	-12 56	+ 4 12 56
Kralendijk, Bonaire	68W16	12N10	- 3 04	+ 4 33 04
Oranjestad, Aruba	70W31	12N31	-10 08	+ 4 40 08
Oranjestad, St. Eustatius	62W59	17N29	-11 56	+ 4 11 56
Philipsburg, St. Maarten	63W04	18N01	-12 16	+ 4 12 16
Saint Nicolaas, Aruba	69W54	12N26	- 9 36	+ 4 39 36
Willemstad, Curacao	68W57	12N06	- 5 48	+ 4 35 48

NEU HANNOVER see New Guinea

NEU MECKLENBURG see New Guinea

NEVIS see British West Indies

NEW BRITAIN see New Guinea

NEW BRUNSWICK see Canada

NEW CALEDONIA & DEPENDENCIES. Capital: Noumea.
French Colony in the South Pacific
Standard Time Meridian 165° EAST

Bourake Airport	166E00	21S56	+ 4 00	- 11 04 00
Chepenebe, Loyalty Islands	167E09	20S47	+ 8 36	- 11 08 36
Huailu see Wailu				
Kanala	165E58	21S52	+ 3 52	- 11 03 52
Kuto, Ile des Pins	167E27	22S40	+ 9 48	- 11 09 48
Mus, Wallis Archipelago	176W10	13S21	+1^{h}15 20	+ 11 44 40
Neumea	166E28	22S16	+ 5 52	- 11 05 52
Cuamoea, Loyalty Islands	167E28	22S35	+ 9 52	- 11 09 52
Penela, Loyalty Islands	168E05	21S34	+12 20	- 11 12 20
Sigave, Futuna	178W07	14S16	+1^{h}17 32	+ 11 52 28
Tadinu see Tandine				
Tandine, Loyalty Islands	167E50	21S32	+11 20	- 11 11 20
Tuho (Tuo)	165E14	20S47	+ 0 50	- 11 00 56
Uegoa	164E25	20S20	- 2 20	- 10 57 40
Uves, Loyalty Islands	163E40	19S40	- 5 20	- 10 54 40
Voh	164E43	20S58	- 1 08	- 10 58 52
Wailu	165E38	21S16	+ 2 32	- 11 32 32

NEWFOUNDLAND. Capital: St. Johns, British   L. M. T.   G. M. T.
      Colony, situated in north Atlantic Ocean.   VARIATION   VARIATION
      Standard Time Meridian 52°30' WEST.   FROM S.T.   FROM LMT.

			m. s.	h. m. s.
Bonavista, Bona Vista	53W06	47N38	- 2 24	+ 3 32 24
Burin, Burin, East..............	55W11....	47N03...	-10 44...	+ 3 40 44
Carbonear, Carbonear	53W14	47N44	- 2 56	+ 3 32 56
Channel, Burgeo	59W21	47N34	-27 24	+ 3 57 24
Gander, Fogo	54W34	48N56	- 8 16	+ 3 38 16
Grand Bank, Burin, West	55W47	47N08	-13 08	+ 3 43 08
Grand Falls, Grand Falls........	55W40....	48N56...	-12 40...	+ 3 42 40
Harbour Grace, Harbour Grace	53W15	47N41	- 3 00	+ 3 33 00
St. Johns, St. Johns	52W42	47N34	- 0 48	+ 3 30 48
Torbay, St. Johns	52W45	47N39	- 1 00	+ 3 31 00
Twillingate, Twillingate	54W45	49N39	- 9 00	+ 3 39 00

NEW GEORGIA see British Solomon Islands.
NEW GUINEA. Capital: Rabaul. Mandated Territory,
      administered by the Commonwealth of Australia.
      Formerly Germany Colonies.
        1. N. E. New Guinea, Capital: Nugima.
        2. Bismark Archipelago, Capital: Nugima.
           New Britain, capital: Rabaul.
           New Ireland, Capital: Kawieng.
           Admiralty Islands, Capital: Lorungau.
        3. Solomon Islands, Capital: Kieta.
           Standard Time Meridian 150° EAST, except
           Solomon Islands which is based on 165° EAST.
           (See also Papua and Netherlands New Guinea.)

Alexishafen, Madang	145E48	5S06	-16 48	- 9 43 12
Bonatui, Buka, Solomon Is.	154E34	5S14	-41 44	-10 18 16
Emegan, St. Matthias, Bis. Ar.	149E33	1S17	- 1 48	- 9 58 12
Finschhafen, Morobe.	147E50	6S32	- 8 40	- 9 50 20
Gasmata, New Britain, Bis. Ar.	150E20	6S17	+ 1 20	-10 01 20
Inus, Bougainville, Sol. Is.	155E08	5S42	-39 28	-10 20 32
Kaunun, Bougainville, Sol. Is...	154E44....	5S40...	-41 04...	-10 18 56
Kawieng, New Ireland	150E49	2S34	+ 3 16	+10 03 16
Kelaua Harbor, Admiralty Is.	147E17	2S06	+10 52	- 9 49 08
Kokopo, New Britain	152E19	4S20	+ 9 16	-10 09 16
Kunua see Kaunua.				
Linden Harbor (Lindenhafen),				
New Britain	150E27	6S18	+ 1 48	-10 01 48
Laua, Bougainville	154E55	5S30	-40 20	-10 19 40
Lorungau, Admiralty Islands	147E17	2S01	-10 52	- 9 49 08
Madang, Madang.................	145E48....	5S13...	-16 48...	- 9 43 12
Nomatanai, New Ireland	152E27	3S40	+ 9 48	-10 09 48
Neu Hannover see Nugima.				
Nugima, Lavongai.	150E14	2S27	+ 0 56	-10 00 56
Rabaul, New Britain	152E12	4S12	+ 8 48	-10 08 48
Sag Sag, New Britain...........	148E19.....	5S38..	- 6 44...	- 9 53 16
Salamaoa, Morobe	147E06	7S02	-11 36	- 9 48 24
Talasea, New Britain	150E02	5S17	+ 0 08	-10 00 08
Wau, Morobe	146E44	7S19	-13 04	- 9 46 56
Wewak, Sepik	143E38	3S33	-25 28	- 9 34 32

				: L. M. T. ; VARIATION ; FROM S.T. m. s.	G. M. T. VARIATION FROM LMT. h. m. s.

NEW HANOVER see New Guinea.

NEW HEBRIDES. Capital: Port Villa. British
French Condominium, situated in the South
Pacific. Standard Time Meridian 165° EAST.;

			L.M.T. m. s.	G.M.T. h. m. s.
Dillon Bay, Erromango	168E58	18S46	+15 52	-11 15 52
Fila Harbor see Port Villa.				
Lenakel, Tanna	169E16	19S32	+17 04	-11 17 04
Port Patte(r)son, Banks Is.	167E33	13S49	+10 12	-11 10 12
Port Sandwich, Malecula	167E48	16S25	+11 12	-11 11 12
Port Stanley, Malecula	167E25	16S03	+ 9 40	-11 09 40
Port Villa, Vate	168E18	17S44	+13 12	+11 13 12

NEW IRELAND see New Guinea

NEW NANTUCKET ISLAND see Gilbert & Ellice Islands.

NEW SOUTH WALES see Australia

NEW YORK ISLAND see Gilbert & Ellice Islands

NEW ZEALAND Capital: Wellington. British Dominion,
situated in the South Pacific. Since November
24, 1945, the Standard Time Meridian has been
180° EAST. Prior to that date S. T. Meridian
was 172E30.

Ashburton, Ashburton, S.	171E46	43S54	-32 56	-11 27 04
Auckland, Eden N.	174E45	36S52	-21 00	-11 39 00
Blenheim, Marlborough S	173E59	41S30	-24 04	-11 35 56
Chalmers, Waikouaiti S.	170E38	45S49	-37 28	-11 22 32
Christchurch, Heathcote S.	172E38	43S32	-29 28	-11 30 32
Dargaville, Hobson N.	173E51	35S56	-24 36	-11 35 24
Dunedin, Taieri S.	170E32	45S54	-37 52	-11 22 08
Gisborne, Cook N.	178E04	38S40	- 7 44	-11 52 16
Greymouth, Gray S.	171E12	42S27	-35 12	-11 24 48
Half Moon Bay, Stewart Is.	168E08	46S55	-47 28	-11 12 32
Hamilton, Waipa N.	175E17	37S48	-18 52	-11 41 08
Invercargill, Southland S.	168E22	46S25	-46 32	-11 13 28
Kokitika, Westland S.	171E00	42S18	-36 00	-11 24 00
Masterton, Masterton N.	175E41	40S57	-17 16	-11 42 44
Napier, Hawke+s Bay N.	176E56	39S29	-12 16	-11 47 44
Nelson, Waimea S.	173E19	41S17	-26 44	-11 33 16
New Plymouth, Taranaki N.	174E05	39S03	-23 40	-11 36 20
Palmerston North, Kairanga	175E38	40S21	-17 28	-11 42 32
Queenstown, Lake S.	168E41	45S02	-45 16	-11 14 44
Stratford, Stratford N.	174E18	39S20	-22 48	-11 37 12
Thames, Thames N	175E33	37S08	-17 48	-11 42 12
Wanganui, Wanganui, N.	175E08	39S55	-19 28	-11 40 32
Wellington, Makara N.	174E47	41S18	-20 52	-11 39 08
Westport, Buller, S.	171E38	41S46	-33 28	-11 26 32
Whangarei, Whangarei, N.	174E20	35S43	-22 40	-11 37 20

NICARAGA Capital: Managua. Republic situated in Central America. Standard
Time Meridian 90° WEST

Acopaya, Choutales	85W10	11N53	+19 20	+ 5 40 40
Bluefields, Zelaya	83W46	12N02	+24 56	+ 5 35 04
Cabo Gracias a Dios, C. G. a D.	83W10	15N00	+27 20	+ 5 32 40

			L. M. T. VARIATION FROM S.T.	G. M. T. VARIATION FROM LMT.

NICARAGUA. (Continued)

			m. s.	h. m. s.
Campo Azul see Bluefields				
Chinandega, Chinandega.	87W09	12N37	+11 24	+ 5 48 36
Corinto, Chinandega	87W12	12N29	+11 12	+ 5 48 48
Diriamba, Carazo................	86W15...	11N50...	+15 00...	+ 5 45 00
El Viejo, Chinandega	87W10	12N39	+11 20	+ 5 48 40
Esteli, Esteli	86W22	13N05	+14 32	+ 5 45 28
Granada, Granada	85W58	11N56	+16 08	+ 5 43 52
Greytown see San Juan del Norte.				
Jinotega, Jinotega..............	86W00...	13N06...	+16 00...	+ 5 44 00
Jinotepe, Carazo	86W12	11N50	+15 12	+ 5 44 48
Juigalpa, Chontales	85W24	12N05	+18 24	+ 5 41 36
Leon, Leon	86W54	12N26	+12 24	+ 5 47 36
Managua, Managua	86W18	12N08	+14 48	+ 5 45 12
Masaya, Masaya	86W06...	11N57...	+15 36...	+ 5 44 24
Matagalpa, Matagalpa	85W57	12N53	+16 12	+ 5 43 48
Ocotal, Nueva Segovia	86W30	13N37	+14 00	+ 5 46 00
Puerto Cabezas, Bluefields	83W23	14N02	+26 28	+ 5 33 32
Rema. Siquia	84W15	12N09	+23 00	+ 5 37 00
Rivas, Rivas...................	85W51...	11N26...	+16 36...	+ 5 43 24
San Carlos, Chontales	84W47	11N08	+20 52	+ 5 39 08
San Juan del Norte, Zelaya	83W42	10N56	+25 12	+ 5 34 48
San Juan del Sur, Rivas	85W52	11N15	+16 32	+ 5 43 28

NICOBAR ISLANDS. Capital: Nankauri, The Nicobar
Islands, together with the Andaman Islands
situated in the Indian Ocean, form a province of India. Standard Time Meridian 97°30' EAST.

Arong	92E45	9N10	-19 00	- 6 11 00
Nankauri	93E32	8N02	-15 52	- 6 14 08
Tapong	93E34	8N01	-15 44	- 6 14 16

NIGER see French West Africa. Independent August 3, 1960
Capital: Lagos, formerly British Colony and Pro-
tectorate, situated in West Africa. Independent
October 1, 1960. Standard Time Meridian 16° EAST.

Abakaliki, Eastern Province	8E04	6N20	-27 44	- 0 32 16
Abeokuta, Western Province	3E21	7N09	-46 36	- 0 13 24
Benin City, West. Prov.	5E38	6N20	-37 28	- 0 22 32
Ede, East. Prov................	3E59....	6N35...	-44 04...	- 0 15 56
Ilorin, (Illorin), East. Prov.	4E32	8N30	-41 52	- 0 18 08
Jos, Northern Province	8E53	9N55	-24 28	- 0 35 32
Kano, Northern Province	8E32	12N00	-25 52	- 0 34 08
Lagos, Western Province	3E23	6N27	-46 28	- 0 13 32
Mamfe, Cam.....................	9E18....	5N45...	-38 48...	- 0 21 12
Oshogbo, Western Province	4E40	7N47	-41 20	- 0 18 40
Port Harcourt, East. Prov.	7E00	4N42	-32 00	- 0 28 00
Victoria, Cam.	9E12	4N01	-23 12	- 0 36 48
Zaria, Northern Province	7E42	11N03	-29 12	- 0 30 48

NIPPON see Japan.
NIUE ISLAND see Savage Island.
NON-FEDERATED MALAY STATES see Malaya
NORTH BORNEO see British North Borneo.
NORTH EAST NEW GUINEA see New Guinea.

			L. M. T. VARIATION FROM S.T. m. s.	G. M. T. VARIATION FROM LMT. h. m. s.

NORFOLK ISLAND. Capital: Kingston. Territory of
    the Commonwealth of Australia, situated
    in South Pacific. Standard Time Meridian
    168° EAST.

Kingston	167E58	29S04	- 0 08	-11 11 52

NORTHERN IRELAND see Great Britain.
NORTHERN RHODESIA see Rhodesia.
NORTHERN SHAN TERRITORIES see Burma.
NORTHERN TERRITORIES see 1. Canada.
                           2. Gold Coast
NORTHERN TERRITORY see Australia.

NORWAY. Capital: Oslo. Kingdom situated in
    Northern Europe. Standard Time Meridian 15° EAST

Aalesund, Aalesund	6E09	62N28	-35 24	- 0 24 36
Andalsnes, Andalsnes.............	7E37...	62N34...	-29 32...-	0 30 28
Andesnes, Tromso	16E05	69N20	+ 4 20	- 1 04 20
Arendal, Arendal	8E48	58N27	-24 48	- 0 35 12
Bergen, Bergen	5E21	60N23	-38 36	- 0 21 24
Bodo, Bodo	14E23	67N17	- 2 28	- 0 57 32
Brandvold, Tromso................	18E10...	68N49...	+12 40...-	1 12 40
Drammen, Drammen	10E14	59N44	-19 04	- 0 40 56
Egersund, Rogaland	6E00	58N27	-36 00	- 0 24 00
Grimstad, A.A.	8E36	58N20	-25 36	- 0 34 24
Halden, Halden	11E26	59N08	-14 16	- 0 45 44
Hamar, Hamar.............	11E06...	60N48...	-15 36..	- 0 44 24
Hammerfest, Hammerfest	23E42	70N40	+34 48	- 1 34 48
Haugesund, Haugesund	5E17	59N25	-38 52	- 0 21 08
Kongsberg, Buskerud	9E39	59N39	-21 24	- 0 38 36
Kristiania known as Oslo since January 1, 1925.				
Kristiansand, Kristiansand.......	8E01...	58N09...	-27 56...-	0 32 04
Kristiansund, Kristiansund	7E45	63N07	-29 00	- 0 31 00
.arvik, Larvik	10E00	59N04	-20 00	- 0 40 00
Lillehammer, Opland	10E30	61N08	-18 00	- 0 42 00
Lyngdal, Farsund	7E07	58N09	-31 32	- 0 28 28
Namsos, Namsos....................	11E29...	64N27...	-14 04...-	0 45 56
Narvik, Narvik	17E26	68N26	+ 9 44	- 1 09 44
Oslo, Oslo	10E44	59N55	-17 04	- 0 42 56
Sarpsborg, Sarpsborg	11E08	59N17	-15 28	- 0 44 32
Skien, Skien	9E36	59N12	-21 36	- 0 38 24
Stavanger, Stavanger.............	5E44...	58N58...	-37 04...-	0 22 56
Tonsberg, Tonsberg	10E26	59N16	-18 16	- 0 41 44
Tromso, Tromso	18E58	69N40	+15 52	- 1 15 52
Trondhjam, Trondhjem	10E23	63N26	-18 28	- 0 41 32

NOSSI-BE see Madagascar.
NOUVELLE GALLES DU SUD see New South Wales
NOUVELLE HEBRIDES see New Hebrides.
NOUVELLE ZELANDE see New Zealand.
NOVA SCOTIA see Canada.
NUBIA see 1. Anglo-Egyptian Sudan.
        2. Egypt.

			L. M. T. VARIATION FROM S.T.	G. M. T. VARIATION FROM L.T.

NYASSALAND. Capital: Zomba. British Protectorate in East Africa. Standard Time Meridian 30° EAST.

			m. s.	h. m. s.
Blantyre, Blantyre	35E01	15S48	+20 04	- 2 20 04
Cholo, Cholo...................35E06...	16S06....	+20 24..	- 2 20 24
Fort Johnston, South Nyasa	35E14	14S28	+20 56	- 2 20 56
Port Herald, Lower Shire	35E16	16S54	+21 04	- 2 21 04
Zomba, Zomba	35E18	15S23	+21 12	- 2 21 12

ORANGE FREE STATE see Union of South Africa.

ORANGE RIVER COLONY see Union of South Africa.

OCEAN ISLAND see Gilbert & Ellice Islands

OMAN see Saudi Arabia.

ONTARIO see Canada.

OSTPREUSSEN see Germany.

OTAHEITE see French Establishments in Oceania.

OUBANGI-CHARI see French Equatorial Africa.

OUTER MONGOLIA see China.

PAHANG see Malaya.

PAKISTAN see India. Independent Aug. 15, 1947

PALAOS OR PALAU see South Sea Mandated Territories.

PALESTINE. Capital: Jerusalem. British Mandated Territory. Standard Time Meridian 30° EAST.

Acre (Accra), Acre	35E04	32N56	+20 16	- 2 20 16
Al Bira, Ramallah.............. 35E13...	31N54...	+20 52..	- 2 20 52
Al Yahudiya, Jaffa	34E53	32N02	+19 32	- 2 19 32
Beisan, Beisan	35E30	32N30	+22 00	- 2 22 00
Beer Sheba, Beer Sheba	34E48	31N21	+19 12	- 2 19 12
Beit Jibrin, Hebron	34E54	31N36	+19 36	- 2 19 36
Bethlehem, Bethlehem............ 35E13...	31N42...	+20 52..	- 2 20 52
Bir-es-Saba see Beer Sheba.				
Caesarea see Kaisariye.				
Capernum see Talhum.				
El Faluje, Gaza	34E44	31N37	+18 56	- 2 18 56
El Khabil see Hebron.				
El Majdal, Gaza	34E35	31N45	+18 20	- 2 18 20
Eriha see Jericho.				
Er Ramle, Er Ramle	34E52	31N55	+19 28	- 2 19 28
Falujja see El Faluje.				
Gaza (Ghazza), Gaza............. 34E28...	31N30...	+17 52..	- 2 17 52
Hadera, Haifa	34E55	32N25	+19 40	- 2 19 40
Haifa, Haifa	34E59	32N49	+19 56	- 2 19 56
Hebron, Hebron	35E06	31N01	+20 24	- 2 20 24
Isdud see Sdud.				
Jaffa, Jaffa	34E46	32N04	+19 04	- 2 19 04
Jemmain, Nablus	35E27	32N08	+21 48	- 2 21 48
Jenin, Jenin	35E18	32N28	+21 12	- 2 21 12
Jericho, Jericho	35E28	31N54	+21 52	- 2 21 52
Jerusalem, Jerusalem	35E10	31N47	+20 40	- 2 20 40
Kaisariye, Haifa.................. 34E54...	32N30....	+19 36..	- 2 19 36
Kafr Kama, Nazareth	35E20	32N43	+21 20	- 2 21 20
Khan Yunis, Beer Sheba	34E18	31N25	+17 12	- 2 17 12
Lydda, Er Ramle	34E54	31N57	+19 36	- 2 19 36

			L. M. T. VARIATION FROM S.T.	G. M. T. VARIATION FROM LMT.
			m. s.	h. m. s.
PALESTINE, (Continued)				
Montefiore, Jerusalem	35E11	31N47	+20 44	- 2 20 44
Nablus, Nablus	35E15	32N13	+21 00	- 2 21 00
Nazareth, Nazareth..............	35E14...	32N42...	+20 56...	- 2 20 56
Petah Tiqva, Jaffa	34E53	32N05	+19 32	- 2 19 32
Qalqibiya, Tulkarm	34E58	32N11	+19 52	- 2 19 52
Ramallah, Ramallah	35E12	31N54	+20 49	- 2 20 48
Rehovot, Er Ramleh	34E49	31N54	+19 16	- 2 19 16
Rishon le Zion, Er Ramle........	34E48...	31N58...	+19 12...	- 2 19 12
Safed, Safed	35E29	32N58	+21 56	- 2 21 56
Samaria see Sebustie.				
Sdud, Gaza	34E39	31N45	+18 36	- 2 18 36
Sebustie, Nablus	35E11	32N17	+20 44	- 2 20 44
Sechem see Nablus.				
Seffurie, Nazaereth	35E17	32N45	+21 08	- 2 21 08
Shefa Amr, Haifa	35E10	32N48	+20 40	- 2 20 40
Tabariye, Tabariye	35E33	32N47	+22 12	- 2 22 12
Tantura, Haife	34E55	32N37	+19 40	- 2 19 40
Tarshiha (Tershiha), Acre......	35E16...	33N05...	+21 04...	- 2 21 04
Tel Aviv, Jaffa	34E46	32N04	+19 04	- 2 19 04
Telhum, Tabariye	35E33	32N53	+22 12	- 2 22 12
Tiberas see Tabariye.				
Tubas, Nablus	35E22	32N19	+21 28	- 2 21 28
Tul Karm.....................	35E01...	32N19...	+20 04...	- 2 20 04
Yavneel, Tiberias	34E30	32N42	+18 00	- 2 18 00
Yebnah, Er Ramle	34E45	31N52	+19 00	- 2 19 00
Zikhron Ya'agov, Haifa	34E57	32N35	+19 48	- 2 19 48
PALMOORE ISLAND see Hawaii.				
PALMYRA ISLAND see Hawaii.				
PANAMA. Capital: Panama City. Republic situated in Central America. Standard Time Meridian 75° WEST.				
Aguadulce, Cocle	80W33	8N15	-22 12	+ 5 22 12
Bocas del Toro, Bocas del Toro	82W15	9N20	-29 00	+ 5 29 00
Chitre, Herrera	80W25	7N58	-21 40	+ 5 21 40
Colon, Colon	79W54	9N22	-19 36	+ 5 19 36
David, Chiriqui	82W26	8N26	-29 44	+ 5 29 44
Las Tablas, Los Santos	80W17	7N46	-21 08	+ 5 21 08
Panama City, Panama...........	79W32...	8N57...	-18 08...	+ 5 18 08
Penoneme, Cocle	80W22	8N31	-21 28	+ 5 21 28
Santiago, Veraguas	80W59	8N06	-23 56	+ 5 23 56
PANAMA CANAL ZONE. Capital: Balboa Heights. A possession of the United States, situated in Central America. Standard Time Meridian 75° WEST.				
Allbrook Field	79W34	8N58	-18 16	+ 5 18 16
Ancon	79W33	8N58	-18 12	+ 5 18 12
Balboa	79W34	8N57	-18 16	+ 5 18 16
Balboa Heights..................	79W34...	8N58...	-18 16...	+ 5 18 16
Coco Solo	79W53	9N23	-19 32	+ 5 19 32
Corozal	79W34	8N59	-18 16	+ 5 18 16
Cristobal	79W55	9N21	-19 40	+ 5 19 40

			L. M. T. VARIATION FROM S.T.		G. M. T. VARIATION FROM LMT.		
			m.	s.	h.	m.	s.
PANAMA CANAL ZONE. (Continued)							
Darien	79W46	9N08	-19	04	+ 5	19	04
Fort Amador	79W33...	8N57...	-18	12...	+ 5	18	12
Fort Clayton	79W35	9N00	-18	20	+ 5	18	20
Fort Davis	79W55	9N17	-19	40	+ 5	19	40
Fort Randolph	79W53	9N23	-19	32	+ 5	19	32
Fort Sherman	79W57	9N22	-19	48	+ 5	19	48
France Field	79W53	9N21	-19	32	+ 5	19	32
Frijoles......................	79W48...	9N11 ..	-19	12...	+ 5	19	12
Gamboa	79W42	9N07	-18	48	+ 5	18	48
Gatun	79W56	9N16	-19	44	+ 5	19	44
Mindi	79W55	9N18	-19	40	+ 5	19	40
Mount Hope	79W54	9N20	-19	36	+ 5	19	36
Palo Seco Leper Colony..........	79W34...	8N54...	-18	16...	+ 5	18	16
Pedro Miguel	79W36	9N01	-18	24	+ 5	18	24
Red Tank	79W36	9N01	-18	24	+ 5	18	24
Summit	79W39	9N04	-18	36	+ 5	18	36
PAPUA. Capital: Port Moresby. Territory of the Commonwealth of Australia, situatred in the East Indies. Standard Time Meridian 150° EAST.							
Abau, Eastern	148E42	10S11	- 5	12	- 9	54	48
Aitape, Sepik	142E30	3S08	-30	00	- 9	30	00
Bonagai, Woodlark Island.......	152E42...	9S06...	+10	48...	-10	10	48
Buna Government Sta., North	148E24	8S40	- 6	24	- 9	53	36
Bwagaoia, Louisiade Archi,	152E51	10S41	+11	24	-10	11	24
Daru, Western	143E11	9S04	-27	16	- 9	32	44
Gurewaia, D'Encastreaux Is.	151E03	9S39	+ 4	12	-10	04	12
Ioma, Northern.................	147E49...	8S19...	- 8	44...	- 9	51	16
Kerema, Gulf	145E46	7S59	-16	56	- 9	43	04
Kiroki, Delta	144E15	7S25	-23	00	- 9	37	00
Losuia, Tobriand Islands	151E03	8S33	+ 4	12	-10	04	12
Port Moresby, Central	147E08	9S27	-11	28	- 9	48	32
Samarai, Eastern...............	150E40...	10S37...	+ 2	40...	-10	02	40
Tufi, North-Eastern	149E20	9S02	- 2	40	- 9	57	20
PARAGUAY. Capital: Asuncion. Republic, situated in South America. Standard Time Meridian 60° WEST.							
Asuncion, Asuncion	57W41	25S16	+ 9	16	+ 3	50	44
Caazapa, Caazapa	56W22	26S10	+14	32	+ 3	45	28
Caraguatay, Caraguatay	56W50	25S12	+12	40	+ 3	47	20
Encarnacion, Encarnacion	55W52	27S20	+16	32	+ 3	43	28
Concepcion, Concepcion........	57W28...	23S24...	+10	08	+ 3	49	52
Paraguari, Paraguari	57W08	25S37	+11	28	+ 3	48	32
Pilar, Pilar	58W22	26S50	+ 6	32	+ 3	53	28
Quyyndy, Quyyandy	57W14	25S56	+11	04	+ 3	48	56
San Ignacio, San Ignacio	56W59	26S51	+12	04	+ 3	47	56
San Pedro, San Pedro..........	57W09...	24S05...	+11	24...	+ 3	48	36
Villa Hayes, Chaco	57W36	25S06	+ 9	36	+ 3	50	24
Villerica, Guaira	56W26	25S44	+14	16	+ 3	45	44
Villeta, Villeta	57W35	25S29	+ 9	40	+ 3	50	20
Yhu, Yhu	56W00	25S00	+16	00	+ 3	44	00

100

PATAGONIA see Argentina.
PAYS-BAS see the Netherlands.
PELEW see South Sea Mandated Territories.
PEMBA see Zanzibar.
PENANG see Malaya.
PERIM see Aden.
PERLIS see Malaya.
PERSIA see Iran.
PESCADORES ISLANDS see Japan.

PERU. Capital: Lima. Republic, situated in South America. Standard Time Meridian 75° WEST.

			L. M. T. VARIATION FROM S.T.	G. M. T. VARIATION FROM LMT.
			m. s.	h. m. s.
Abancay, Apurimac	72W55	13S35	+ 8 20	+ 4 51 40
Arequipa, Arequipa	71W33	16S24	+13 48	+ 4 46 12
Ayacucho, Ayacucho	74W13	13S07	+ 3 08	+ 4 56 52
Cajamarca, Cajamarca............	78W31...	7S10...	-14 04...	+ 5 14 04
Callao, Callao	77W09	12S04	- 8 36	+ 5 08 36
Cerro de Pasco, Pasco	76W16	10S41	- 5 04	+ 5 05 04
Chiclayo, Lambayoque	79W51	6S46	- 19 24	+ 5 19 24
Cusco, Cusco	71W59	13S31	+12 04	+ 4 47 56
Huancavelica, Huancavelica......	75W02...	12S46...	- 0 08...	+ 5 00 08
Huanuco, Huanuco	76W14	9S55	- 4 56	+ 5 04 56
Huaras, Ancash	77W32	9S32	-10 08	+ 5 10 08
Ica, Ica	75W42	14S04	- 2 48	+ 5 02 48
Iquitos, Loreto	73W15	3S46	+ 7 00	+ 4 53 00
Junin, Junin..............	76W00...	11S10...	- 4 00...	+ 5 04 00
Lima, Lima	77W03	12S03	- 8 12	+ 5 08 12
Matucana, Lima	76W23	11S53	- 5 32	+ 5 05 32
Mayobamba, San Martin	76W58	6S03	- 7 52	+ 5 07 52
Mollendo, Arequipa	72W01	17S02	+11 56	+ 4 48 04
Moquegua, Moquegua.............	71W01...	17S12...	+15 56...	+ 4 44 04
Piura, Piura	80W38	5S12	-22 32	+ 5 22 32
Puerto Maldonado, Madro de Dios	69W11	12S36	+23 16	+ 4 36 44
Puno, Puno..................	70W02...	15S50...	+19 52...	+ 4 40 08
Tacna, Tacna	70W15	18S01	- 1 00	+ 5 01 00
Trujillo, Libertad	79W02	8S07	-16 08	+ 5 16 08
Tumbes, Tumbes	80W28	3S34	-21 52	+ 5 21 52

PHILIPPINES. Capital: Manila. Commonwealth (Republic since July 4, 1946), situated in Pacific Ocean. Standard Time Meridian 120° EAST.

Abuyog, Leyte	125E00	10N45	+20 00	- 8 20 00
Angeles, Pampanga	120E35	15N08	+ 2 20	- 8 02 20
Aparri, Cayagan................	121E38...	18N21...	+ 6 32...	- 8 06 32
Argao, Cebu	123E36	9N52	+14 24	- 8 14 24
Aroroy, Masbate	123E24	12N30	+13 36	- 8 13 36
Bacolod, Negros Occidental	122E57	10N39	+11 48	- 8 11 48
Bagac, Bataan	120E23	14N36	+ 1 32	- 8 01 32
Bago, Occidental Negros........	122E50...	10N32...	+11 20...	- 8 11 20
Baguio, Mountain Province	120E36	16N25	+ 2 24	- 8 02 24
Bais, Oriental Negros	123E07	9N36	+12 28	- 8 12 28
Balamban, Cebu	123E42	10N30	+14 48	- 8 14 48
Balanga, Bataan	120E32	14N41	+ 2 08	- 8 02 08
Bangued, Abra..................	121E37...	17N36...	+ 6 28...	- 8 06 28
Barilf, Cebu	123E30	10N06	+14 00	- 8 14 00
Bato, Albey	124E18	13N36	+17 12	- 8 17 12

				L. M. T. VARIATION FROM S.T. m. s.	G. M. T. VARIATION FROM LMT. h. m. s.
PHILIPPINES. (Continued)					
Basco, Batanes	121E59	20N23	+ 7 56	- 8 07 56	
Basey, Samar	125E04	11N18	+20 16	- 8 20 16	
Batangas, Batangas	121E03	13N45	+ 4 12	- 8 04 12	
Bauan, Batangas	121E01	13N48	+ 4 04	- 9 04 04	
Bayambang, Pangasinan.........	120E27...	15N49...	+ 1 48...	- 8 01 48	
Baybay, Leyte	124E49	10N41	+19 16	- 8 19 16	
Bayambong, Nueva Vizcaya	121E09	16N29	+ 4 36	- 8 04 36	
Boac, Marinduque	121E50	13N27	+ 7 20	- 8 07 20	
Bontoc, Mountain	120E58	17N05	+ 3 52	- 8 03 52	
Butuan, Agusan.............	125E31...	8N57...	+22 04...	- 8 22 04	
Cabantuan, Nueva Ecija	119E58	15N29	- 0 08	- 7 59 52	
Cagayan, Misamis Oriental	124E38	8N29	+18 32	- 8 18 32	
Calapan, Mindoro	121E11	13N24	+ 4 44	- 8 04 44	
Caloocan, Rizal	120E58	14N39	+ 3 52	- 8 03 52	
Camiling, Tarlac.............	120E25...	15N42...	+ 1 40...	- 8 01 40	
Carcar, Cebu	123E39	10N06	+14 36	- 8 14 36	
Cataingan, Masbata	124E00	12N00	+16 00	- 8 16 00	
Catbalogan, Samar	124E54	11N47	+19 36	- 8 19 36	
Cavite, Cavite	120E55	14N29	+ 3 40	- 8 03 40	
Cebu, Cebu.................	123E53...	10N18...	+15 32...	- 8 15 32	
Concepcion, Tarlac	120E39	15N19	+ 2 36	- 8 02 36	
Corregidor, Cavite	120E35	14N23	+ 2 20	- 8 02 20	
Cotabato, Catabato	124E15	7N14	+17 00	- 8 17 00	
Daet, Camarines Norte	122E57	14N07	+11 48	- 8 11 48	
Dagupan, Pangasinan...........	120E20...	16N03...	+ 1 20...	- 8 01 20	
Dalaguete, Cebu	123E32	9N45	+14 08	- 8 14 08	
Danao, Cebu	124E01	10N31	+16 04	- 8 16 04	
Dansalan, Lanao	124E18	8N00	+17 12	- 8 16 12	
Dapitan, Zamboanga	123E26	8N39	+13 44	- 8 13 44	
Daraga, Albay................	123E43...	13N10...	+14 52...	- 8 14 52	
Davao, Davao	125E37	7N05	+22 28	- 8 22 28	
Dipolog, Zamboanga	123E21	8N35	+13 24	- 8 13 24	
Dulag, Leyte	125E02	10E57	+20 08	- 8 20 08	
Dumaguete, Negros Oriental	123E18	9N16	+13 12	- 8 13 12	
Dumangas, Iloilo..............	122E42...	10N49...	+10 48...	- 8 10 48	
Escalante, Occidental Negros	123E33	10N50	+14 12	- 8 14 12	
Gihulngan, Oriental Negros	123E16	10N07	+13 04	- 8 13 04	
Guimba, Nueva Ecija	120E46	15N40	+ 3 04	- 8 03 04	
Guinobatan, Albay	123E36	13N11	+14 24	- 8 14 24	
Guiunan, Samar................	125E44...	11N02...	+22 56....	- 8 22 56	
Hagonoy, Bulacan	120E44	14N50	+ 2 56	- 8 02 56	
Hilongos, Leyte	124E44	10N23	+18 56	- 8 18 56	
Himamaylan, Occ. Negros	122E52	10N06	+11 28	- 8 11 28	
Hinigaran, Occ. Negros	122E51	10N16	+11 24	- 8 11 24	
Iba, Zambales.................	119E59...	15N19...	- 0 04...	- 7 59 56	
Ilagan, Isabela	121E51	17N09	+ 7 24	- 8 07 24	
Iligan, Lanao	124E14	8N14	+16 56	- 8 16 56	
Iloilo, Iloilo	122E34	10N42	+10 16	- 8 10 16	
Iriga, Camarines Sur	123E24	13N25	+13 36	- 8 13 30	
Janiuay, Iloilo	122E30	10N56	+10 00	- 8 10 00	

			L. M. T. VARIATION FROM S.T.	G. M. T. VARIATION FROM LMT.
			m. s.	h. m. s.

PHILIPPINES. (Continued)

Jaro, Iloilo	122E33	10N43	+11 12	- 8 11 12
Jolo, Sulu	121E00	6N03	+ 4 00	- 8 04 00
Kabankalan, Occ. Negros	122E49	9N59	+11 16	- 8 11 16
Kolambugan, Lanao	123E56	8N08	+15 44	- 8 15 44
La Carleta, Occ. Negros	122E56	10N26	+11 44	- 8 11 44
Laoag, Ilocos Norte............	120E35...	18N12...	+ 2 20...	- 8 02 20
Legaspi, Albay	123E44	13N11	+14 56	- 8 14 56
Ligao, Albay	123E32	13N14	+14 08	+ 8 14 08
Limay, Bataan	120E36	14N34	+ 2 24	- 8 02 24
Lingayen, Pangasinan	120E14	16N03	+ 0 56	- 8 00 56
Lipa, Batangas................	121E10...	13N56...	+ 4 40...	- 8 04 40
Loon, Bohol	123E48	9N48	+15 12	- 8 15 12
Lubao, Pampanga	120E36	14N56	+ 2 24	- 8 02 24
Lucena, Quezon	121E37	13N56	+ 6 28	- 8 06 28
Maasin, Leyte	124E51	10N09	+10 24	- 8 19 24
Malaybalay, Bukidnon..........	125E06...	8N03...	+20 24...	- 8 20 24
Malolos, Bulacan	120E48	14N51	+ 3 12	- 8 03 12
Manila City (Legis. Bldg.)	120E59	14N35	+ 3 56	- 8 03 56
Mariveles, Bataan	120E29	14N26	+ 1 56	- 8 01 56
Masbate, Masbate	123E38	12N22	+14 32	- 8 14 32
Misamis, Misamis Occidental....	123E51...	8N09...	+15 24....	- 8 15 24
Moron, Bataan	120E16	14N41	+ 1 04	- 8 01 04
Nabua, Camarines Sur	123E22	13N26	+13 28	- 8 13 28
Naga, Camarines Sur	123E11	13N37	+12 44	- 8 12 44
Naga, Cebu	123E45	10N13	+15 00	- 8 15 00
Navotas, Rizal................	120E57...	14N40...	+ 3 48...	- 8 03 48
Oas, Albay	123E30	13N16	+14 00	- 8 14 00
Opon, Cebu	123E58	10N19	+15 52	- 8 15 52
Orion, Bataan	120E34	14N37	+ 2 16	- 8 02 16
Ormoc, Leyte	124E36	11N01	+18 24	- 8 18 24
Oroquieta, Misamis Occ.........	123E49...	8N29...	+15 16...	- 8 15 16
Pagadian, Zamboanga	123E27	7N49	+13 48	- 8 13 48
Palo, Leyte	125E00	11N09	+20 00	- 8 20 00
Palompon, Leyta	124E24	11N03	+17 36	- 8 17 36
Paranaque, Rizal	120E59	14N30	+ 3 56	- 8 03 56
Pasay, Rizal..................	121E00...	14N33....	+ 4 00...	- 8 04 00
Pasig, Rizal	121E05	14N34	+ 4 20	- 8 04 20
Passi, Iloilo	122E39	11N06	+10 36	- 8 10 36
Polillo, Quezon	121E56	14N43	+ 7 44	- 8 07 44
Pototan, Iloilo	122E38	10N56	+10 32	- 8 10 32
Puerto Princesa, Palawan......	118E45...	9N44...	- 4 56...	- 7 55 04
Quezon, Quezon	122E11	14N00	+ 8 44	- 8 08 44
Quizon City	121E00	14N58	- 4 00	- 8 40 00
Rizal City see Pasay.				
Romblon, Romblon	122E16	12N35	+ 9 04	- 8 09 04
Rosario, Batangas	121E12	13N51	+ 4 48	- 8 04 48
Sagay, Occidental Negros.......	123E26...	10N56...	+13 44...	- 8 13 44
San Carlos, Occidental Neg.	123E25	10N29	+13 40	- 8 13 40
San Fernando La Union	120E19	16N36	+ 1 16	- 8 01 16
San Fernando, Pampanga	120E42	15N02	+ 2 48	- 8 02 48
San Isidro, Leyte	124E21	11N24	+17 24	- 8 17 24

			L. M. T. VARIATION FROM S.T. m. s.	G. M. T. VARIATION FROM LMT. h. m. s.
PHILIPPINES. (Continued)				
San Jose, Nueva Ecija	121E00	15N48	+ 4 00	- 8 04 00
San Jose Buenavista, Antiq.....	121E57...	10N44...	+ 7 48...	- 8 07 48
San Pablo City, Laguna	121E19	14N04	+ 5 16	- 8 05 16
Santa Barbara, Iloilo	122E31	10N50	+10 04	- 8 10 04
Santa Cruz, Laguna	121E25	14N17	+ 5 40	- 8 05 40
Santiago, Isabela	121E33	16N42	+ 6 20	- 8 06 20
Sariaya, Quezon...............	121E32...	13N58...	+ 6 08...	- 8 06 08
Silay, Occidental Negros	122E58	10N48	+11 52	- 8 11 52
Sindangan, Zamboanga	123E00	8N14	+12 00	- 8 12 00
Sorsogon, Sorsogon	124E00	13N00	+16 00	- 8 16 00
Surigao, Surigao	125E29	9N46	+21 56	- 8 21 56
Tabaco, Albay.................	123E44...	13N19...	+14 56...	- 8 14 56
Tacloban, Leyte	125E00	11N14	+20 00	- 8 20 00
Tagbilaran, Bohol	123E52	9N39	+15 28	- 8 15 28
Talibon, Bohol	124E19	10N09	+17 16	- 8 17 16
Tanauan, Batangas	121E09	14N05	+ 4 36	- 8 04 36
Tanjay, Oriental Negros........	123E10...	9N31...	+12 40...	- 8 12 40
Tarlac, Tarlac	120E35	15N29	+ 2 20	- 8 02 20
Tiaong, Quozon	121E19	13N57	+ 5 56	- 8 05 56
Toledo, Cebu	123E38	10N22	+14 32	- 8 14 32
Tuburan, Cebu	123E49	10N43	+15 16	- 8 15 16
Tuguegarao, Cagayan...........	121E43...	17N37...	+ 6 52...	- 8 06 52
Urdaneta, Panganisan	120E34	15N59	+ 2 16	- 8 02 16
Vigan, Ilocos Sur	120E23	17N34	+ 1 32	- 8 01 32
Zamboanga, Zamboanga	122E04	6N55	+ 8 16	- 8 08 16

PHOEBE ISLAND see Gilbert & Ellice Islands.

PHOENIX GROUP see Gilbert & Ellice Islands.

PINS, ILES DES see New Caledonia.

PITCAIRN ISLAND. Capital: Adamstown, British Colony,
    situated in South Pacific. Standard Time
    Meridian 150° WEST.

| Adamstown | 130W05 | 25S00 | +1h19 40 | + 8 40 20 |

PODKARPATSKA see Czechoslovakia.

POLAND. Capital: Warszawa (Warsaw). Republic
    situated in Europe. Standard Time Meridian
    15° EAST. Eastern parts of Poland ceded
    to U.S.S.R. in 1945 and clocks have been
    advanced 1 hour in those places.

Augustow, Bial	22E59	53N51	+31 56	- 1 31 56
Auschwitz see Oswiecim.				
Baranowicze, Nowogrodek.........	26E00...	53N08...	+44 00...	- 1 44 00
Bialystok, Bialystok	23E10	53N08	+32 40	- 1 32 40
Bielsko (Bielitz), Slask	19E01	49N49	+16 04	- 1 16 04
Bromberg see Bygdoszcz.				
Brzesc n.B. (Breast-Litovsk), Polesie....................	23E41...	52N06...	+34 44...	- 1 34 44
Bygdoszcz, Pom.	18E00	53N07	+12 00	- 1 12 00
Chorczow, Slask	18E47	50N19	+15 08	- 1 15 08
Cieszyn	18E38	49N50	+14 32	- 1 14 32
Czestochowa, Kielce	19E07	50N49	+16 28	- 1 16 28

			L. M. T. VARIATION FROM S.T.	G. M. T. VARIATION FROM LMT.
			m. s.	h. m. s.
POLAND (Continued)				
Gdynia, Pom.	18 E34	54N30	+14 16	- 1 14 16
Gdansk see Danzig, Free City of.				
Gorlice, Krakow...................	21E10...	49N39...	+24 40...	- 1 24 40
Graudenz see Grudziadz.				
Grodek Jagiel, Lwow	23E39	49N46	+34 36	- 1 34 36
Grodno, Bial	23E50	54N41	+35 20	- 1 35 20
Grudziadz, Pom.	18E47	53N30	+15 08	- 1 15 08
Gotenhafen see Gdynia.				
Hindenburg see Chorczow.				
Hohensalza see Inowroclaw.				
Inowroclaw, Pom.	18E16	52N48	+13 04	- 1 13 04
Jaroslaw (Jaroslau), Lwow	22E41	50N01	+30 44	- 1 30 44
Kalisz, Poznan....................	18E06...	51N46...	+12 24...	- 1 12 24
Katowice (Kattowitz), Slask	19E02	50N16	+16 08	- 1 16 08
Kielce, Kielce	20E37	50N52	+22 28	- 1 22 28
Kolomya (Kolomea), Stan.	25E03	48N32	+40 12	- 1 40 12
Kowel, Wolyn	24E43	51N13	+38 52	- 1 38 52
Krakow (Krakau), Krakow..........	19E58...	50N04...	+19 52...	- 1 19 52
Lemberg see Lwow.				
Leslau see Wloclawek.				
Lida, Nowogrodek	25E19	53N53	+41 16	- 1 41 16
Litzmannstadt see Lodz.				
Lodz, Lodz........................	19E27...	51N46...	+17 48...	- 1 17 48
Lublin, Lublin	22E33	51N14	+30 12	- 1 30 12
Lwow, Lwow	24E00	49N50	+36 00	- 1 36 00
Luck, Wolyn	25E20	50N44	+41 20	- 1 41 20
Neusandetz see Nowy Sacz.				
Nowogrodek, Nowogrodek...........	25E51...	53N35...	+43 24...	- 1 43 24
Nowy Sacz, Krakow	20E43	49N38	+22 52	- 1 22 52
Oswiecim, Krakow	19E14	50N02	+16 56	- 1 16 56
Petrikau see Piotrkow.				
Piotrkow, Lodz	19E42	51N25	+18 48	- 1 18 48
Poznan (Posen), Poznan...........	16E55...	52N25...	+ 7 40...	- 1 07 40
Praga, Warszawa	21E02	52N16	+24 08	- 1 24 08
Przemysl, Lwow	22E46	49N46	+31 04	- 1 31 04
Radom, Kielce	21E09	51N24	+24 36	- 1 24 36
Rawa Ruska, Lwow	23E34	50N14	+34 16	- 1 34 16
Sambor, Lwow.....................	23E12...	49N31...	+32 48...	- 1 32 48
Sanok, Lwow	22E14	49N35	+28 56	- 1 28 56
Siedlce, Lublin	22E17	52N10	+29 08	- 1 29 08
Stanislawow(Stanislau). Stan....	24E42	48N56	+38 48	- 1 38 48
Stryj, Stan.	23E52	49N15	+35 28	- 1 35 28
Suwalki, Bial....................	22E56...	54N06...	+31 44...	- 1 31 44
Tarnopol, Tarnopol	25E38	49N33	+42 32	- 1 42 32
Tarnow, Krakow	21E00	50N02	+24 00	- 1 24 00
Toschen see Cieszyn.				
Torun, Pom.	18E36	53N01	+14 24	- 1 14 24
Tschenstochau see Czestochowa.				
Vilnius see Wilno.				
Warszawa (Warsaw), Warszawa	21E00	52N14	+24 00	- 1 24 00
Wilno, Wilno	25E17	54N41	+41 08	- 1 41 08
Wloclawek, Pom.	19E05	52N39	+16 20	- 1 16 20

POLOGNE see Poland.

PONDOLAND   see Union of South Africa.

PORTO RICO   see Puerto Rico.

PORTUGAL.   Capital: Lisboa (Lisbon). Republic,
   situated in Western Europe. Standard Time
   Meridian 0°

			L. M. T. VARIATION FROM S.T.	G. M. T. VARIATION FROM LMT.
			m. s.	h. m. s.
Abrantes, Santarem	8W13	39N28	-32 52	+ 0 32 52
Almada, Setubal	9W10	38N40	-36 40	+ 0 36 40
Aveiro, Aveiro	8W39	40N39	-34 36	+ 0 34 36
Braganca, Braganca	6W45	41N49	-27 00	+ 0 27 00
Beja, Beja.....................	7W52...	38N01...	-31 28...	+ 0 31 28
Braga, Braga	8W25	41N33	-33 40	+ 0 33 40
Caldas da Rainha, Leiria	9W09	39N24	-36 36	+ 0 36 36
Campo Maior, Portalegre	7W05	39N01	-28 20	+ 0 28 20
Castelo-Branco, C.-B.	7W30	39N50	-30 00	+ 0 30 00
Coimbra, Coimbra................	8W26...	40N12...	-33 44...	+ 0 33 44
Elvas, Portalegre	7W11	38N53	-28 44	+ 0 28 44
Estromez, Evora	7W38	38N50	-30 32	+ 0 30 32
Evora, Evora	7W56	38N34	-31 44	+ 0 31 44
Faro, Faro	7W56	37N01	-31 44	+ 0 31 44
Figuera da Foz, Coimbra.........	8W51...	40N09...	-35 24...	+ 0 35 24
Guarda, Guarda	7W16	40N32	-29 04	+ 0 29 04
Lagos, Faro	8W41	37N06	-34 44	+ 0 34 44
Leiria, Leiria	8W48	39N44	-35 12	+ 0 35 12
Lisboa, Lisboa	9W10	38N43	-36 40	+ 0 36 40
Lissabon see Lisboa.				
Oporto see Porto.				
Pombal, Leiria	8W38	39N55	-34 32	+ 0 34 32
Portalegre, Portalegre	7W27	39N18	-30 28	+ 0 30 28
Porto, Porto	8W36	41N09	-34 24	+ 0 34 24
Penafiel, Porto.,...............	8W17...	41N12...	-33 08...	+ 0 33 08
Santarem, Santarem	8W42	39N14	-34 48	+ 0 34 48
Setubel, Lisboa	8W54	38N32	-35 36	+ 0 35 36
Tavira, Faro	7W30	37N08	-30 36	+ 0 30 36
Viana de Castelo, V. do C.	8W49	41N42	-35 16	+ 0 35 16
Vila Real, Vila Real...........	7W45	41N18	-31 00	+ 0 31 00

PORTUGUESE EAST AFRICA (MOCAMBIQUE)
   Capital: Lourenco-Marques. Portuguese
   Colony, situated in East Africa. Standard
   Time Meridian 30° EAST.

Angoche see Antonio Enes.				
Antonio Enes Nam.	39E55	16S12	39 40	- 2 39 40
Beira, Beira	34E53	19S51	+19 32	- 2 19 32
Bela Vista, L.M.	32E40	26S21	+10 40	- 2 10 40
Inhambane, Inhambane............	35E26...	23S48...	+21 44...	- 2 21 44
Lourence-Marques, L.M.	32E35	25S58	+10 20	- 2 10 20
Memba, Nam.	40E28	14S10	+41 52	- 2 41 52
Mocambique, Nam.	40E40	15S01	+42 40	- 2 42 40
Nampula, Nampula	39E20	15S10	+37 20	- 2 37 20
Porto Amelia, Porto Amelia.....	40E31	12S57	+42 04	- 2 42 04
Quelimane, Quelimane	36E50	17S52	+27 20	- 2 27 20

PORTUGUESE GUINEA see Portuguese West Africa.

PORTUGESE INDIA. Capital: Nova Goa. Portuguse Colony, situated in the Indian sub-continent. Standard Time Meridians, 82°30' and 120° EAST			: L. M. T. VARIATION FROM S.T. m. s.	G. M. T. VARIATION FROM LMT. h. m. s.
Damao Grande, Damao	72E50	20N26	-38 40	- 4 51 20
Goa...........................	73E55...	15N30...	-34 20...	- 4 55 40
Nova Goa	73E+9	15N30	-34 44	- 4 55 16
Macca (Macau)	113E34	22N11	-25 44	- 7 34 16
Pangim see Nova Goa.				
PORTUGUESE TIMOR. Capital: Dilli. Portuguese Colony situated in the East Indies. Standard Time Meridian 120° EAST.				
Botana	125E42	9S10	+22 48	- 8 22 48
Dilli	125E35	8S34	+22 20	- 8 22 20
Lautem see Vila Nova Malaca				
Vila Nova Malaca	126E55	8S22	+27 40	- 8 27 40
PORTUGUESE WEST AFRICA. Portuguese Colony, situated in Africa.				
ANGOLA. Capital: Loanda. S.T. Meridian 15° EAST.				
Benguela, Benguela	13E24	12S35	- 6 24	- 0 53 36
Cabinda, Luanda	12E11	5S34	-11 16	- 0 48 44
Dalatando, Salazar	14E55	9S18	- 0 20	- 0 59 40
Huambo see Nova Lisboa.				
Loanda, Loanda	13E14	8S49	- 7 04	- 0 52 56
Lobito, Benguela..............	13E24...	12S22...	- 6 24...	- 0 53 36
Malange, Malange	16E22	9S32	+ 5 28	- 1 05 28
Mossamedes, Huila	12E09	15S11	-11 24	- 0 48 36
Nova Lusboa, Benguela	15E46	12S44	+ 3 04	- 1 03 04
Nova Redondo. Benguela	13E52	11S11	- 4 32	- 0 55 28
Sa da Bandeira, Huila............13E29		14S41	- 6 04	- 0 53 56
S. Paulo de Loanda see Loanda.				
Vila Luso, Bie	19E52	11S48	+19 28	- 1 19 28
PORTUGUESE GUINEA. Capital: Bissau. Standard Time Meridian 15° WEST				
Bissau	15W32	11N51	- 2 08	+ 1 02 08
Bolama	15W26	11N34	- 1 44	+ 1 01 44
Farim	15W11	12N29	- 0 44	+ 1 00 44
PRINCIPE ISLAND S.T. Meridian 0°.				
S. Antonio	7E25	1N39	+29 40	- 0 29 40
SAO TOME ISLAND. S.T. MERidian 0°.				
Sao Tome	6E43	0N20	+26 52	- 0 26 52

PRADES THAI see Siam.

PRINCE EDWARD ISLAND see Canada.

PRINCE'S ISLAND see Portuguese West Africa.

PRINCIPE ISLAND see Portuguese West Africa.

PROVINCE WELLESLEY see Malaya.

QATAR see Saudi Arabia.

QUEBEC see Canada.

QUEENSLAND see Australia.

RAPA ISLAND. see French Establishments in Oceania.

RAPA NUI ISLAND see Easter Island.

RAOUL ISLAND see Kermadec Islands.

RARATONGA ISLAND see Cook Islands.

REDONDA ISLAND see British West Indies.

REPUBLIQUE DOMINICAINE see Dominican Republic.

REPUBLIQUE FEDERATIVE POPULAIRE DE L'ALBANIE see Albania.
REPUBLIQUE FEDERATIVE POPULAIRE DE BULGARIE see Bulgaria.

			L. M. T.	G. M. T.
REPUBLIQUE ORIENTALE DE L'URUGUAY see Uruguay			VARIATION	VARIATION
REUNION. Capital: St. Pierre. French Colony,			FROM S.T.	FROM LMT.
situated in the Indian Ocean.				
Standard Time Meridian 60° EAST.			m. s.	h. m. s.
Pointe-des Galets	55E18	20S55	-18 48	- 3 41 12
St. Denis	55E33	20S52	-17 48	- 3 42 12
St. Paul	55E17	21S00	-18 52	- 3 41 08
St. Pierre	55E31	21S19	-17 56	- 3 42 04

RHODESIA. 1. Northern Rhodesia. British Protector-
 ate. Capital: Livingstone.
    2. Southern Rhodesia. British Colony
 Capital: Salisbury.
 Standard Time Meridian 30° EAST.

Abercorn, Abercorn	31E22	8S50	+ 5 28	- 2 05 28
Broken Hill, Broken Hill	28E27	14S27	- 6 12	- 1 53 48
Bulawayo, Bulawayo	28E35	20S10	- 5 40	- 1 54 20
Fort Jameson, Fort Jameson	32E41	13S38	+10 44	- 2 10 44
Fort Victoria, Victoria	30E50	20S04	+ 3 20	- 2 03 20
Gwelo, Gwelo....................	30E01..	19S24...	+ 0 04...	- 2 00 04
Hartley, Hartley	30E08	18S08	+ 0 32	- 2 00 32
Kasama, Kasama	31E12	10S12	+ 4 48	- 2 04 48
Livingstone, Livingstone	25E52	17S51	-16 32	- 1 43 28
Lusaka, Lusaka	28E18	15S25	- 6 48	- 1 53 12
Melsetter, Melsetter............	32E44..	20S01...	+10 56...	- 2 10 56
Ndola, Ndola	28E39	12S59	- 5 24	- 1 54 36
Salisbury, Salisbury	31E03	17S50	+ 4 12	- 2 04 12
Umtali, Umtali	32E41	18S58	+10 44	- 2 10 44
Victoria Falls, Matabeleland	25E56	17S52	-16 16	- 1 43 44
Wankie,Wankie..................	26E48..	18S02...	-12 48...	- 1 47 12

RHODESIA DU NORD see Rhodesia.
RHODESIA DU SUD see Rhodesia.
RIO DE ORO. Capital: Villa Cisneros. Spanish
 Colony, situated in West Africa. Standard
 Time Meridian 15° WEST

Mesied	13W00	26N36	+ 8 00	+ 0 52 00
Villa Cisneros	15W55	23N40	- 3 40	+ 1 03 40

RODRIQUEZ ISLAND. Capital: Port Mathuria.
 Dependency of Mauritius, situated in the
 Indian Ocean. Standard Time Mer. 60° EAST.

Port Mathurin	63E26	19S40	+13 44	- 4 13 44

ROMANIA see Rumania.
ROTUNDA ISLAND see Fiji.
ROUMANIE see Rumania.
ROYAUME HACHEMITE DE TRANSJORDANIE see Transjordan.
RUANDA AND URANDI see Belgian Congo.
RUHR TERRITORY see Germany
RUMANIA. Capital: Bucuresti. Kingdom, situated
 in Eastern Europe. Standard Time Meridian
 30° EAST.

Alba-Julia. Alba	23E35	46N06	-25 40	- 1 34 20
Arad, Arad	21E19	46N10	-34 44	- 1 25 16
Baia-Mare, Satu-Mare............	23E35..	47N40...	-25 40...	- 1 34 20
Balti, Balti	27E55	47N46	- 8 20	- 1 51 40

			L. M. T. VARIATION FROM S.T.	G. M. T. VARIATION FROM LMT.
			m. s.	h. m. s.
RUMANIA (Continued)				
Botosani, Botosani	26E40	47N45	-13 20	- 1 46 40
Braila, Braila	28E57	45N17	- 4 12	- 1 55 48
Brasov (Brasso), Brasov	25E35	45N39	-17 40	- 1 42 20
Bucuresti (Bucharest), Ilfov....	26E06...	44N26...	-15 36...	- 1 44 24
Buzau, Buzau	26E50	45N09	-12 40	- 1 47 20
Caransebes, Severin	22E13	45N25	-31 08	- 1 28 52
Cernauti, Cernauti	25E56	48N18	-16 16	- 1 43 44
Chisinau, Chisinau	28E50	47N02	- 4 40	- 1 55 20
Cluj, Cluj.....~..............	23E35...	46N47...	-25 40...	- 1 34 20
Constanta, Constanta	28E41	44N11	- 5 16	- 1 54 44
Craiova, Dolj	23E48	44N19	-24 48	- 1 35 12
Czernowitz see Cornauti.				
Deva, Hunedoara	22E55	45N53	-28 20	- 1 31 40
Galati, Cevurlui..............	28E03...	45N26...	- 7 48...	- 1 52 12
Grosswardein see Oradea.				
Gyulafehervar see Alba-Julia.				
Hermannstadt see Sibiu.				
Iasi, Iasi	27E35	47N10	- 9 40	- 1 50 20
Ismail, Ismail...............	28E49...	45N21...	- 4 44...	- 1 55 16
Jassy see Iasi.				
Karansebes see Caransebes.				
Kishenev see Chisinau.				
Klasenburg see Cluj.				
Kolozsvar see Cluj.				
Kronstandt see Brasov.				
Lugoj (Lugos), Severin	21E54	45N41	-32 24	- 1 27 36
Maramarossziget see Sighet.				
Marosvasarhelv see Targu-Muros.				
Nagybanya see Baia-Mare.				
Nagyszalonta see Salonta.				
Nagyszeben see Sibiu.				
Nagyvarad see Oradea.				
Oradea, Bihor	21E55	47N03	-32 20	- 1 27 40
Orsova, Severin................	22E23...	44N43...	-30 28...	- 1 29 32
Ploiesti, Prahova	26E02	44N57	-15 52	- 1 44 08
Roman, Roman	26E54	46N57	-12 24	- 1 47 36
Salonta, Bihor	21E39	46N48	-33 24	- 1 26 36
Satu-Mare, Satu-Mare	22E52	47N48	-28 32	- 1 31 28
Sibiu. Sibiu................	24E09...	45N48...	-23 24...	- 1 36 36
Sighet, Maramures	23E54	47N56	-24 24	- 1 35 36
Sinaia, Prahova	25E33	45N21	-17 48	- 1 42 12
Szatmarnemeti see Satu-Mare.				
Targu-Muros, Mures	24E35	46N32	-21 40	- 1 38 20
Temesvar see Timisoara.				
Tighina, Tighina..............	29E29...	46N49...	- 2 04...	- 1 57 56
Timisoara, T.T.	21E14	45N46	-35 04	- 1 24 56
Turda (Torda), Turda	23E47	46N35	-24 52	- 1 35 08
Turnu Severin, Mehedinti	22E40	44N38	-29 20	- 1 30 40
Zalau, Salaj	23E04	47N11	-27 44	- 1 32 16
Zilah see Zalau.				

RUPERT'S LAND see Northwest Territories, Canada.
RUSSIA see U. S. S. R.
RUS-KARPATSKA see Czechoslovakia.
RUTHENIA   see Czechoslovakia.
SAAR BASIN see Germany.
SABA see Netherlands West Indies.
SACHSEN see Germanh.
SAHARA see 1. Algeria.
              2. French West Africa.
              3. Rio de Oro.
SAINT BARTHELEMY see Guadeloupe.
SAINT CHRISTOPHER see British West Indies.

			: L. M. T.	G. M. T.
SAINT EUSTACHIUS see Netherlands West Indies.			: VARIATION	VARIATION
SAINT HELENA. Capital: Saint Helena. British			: FROM S.T.	FROM LMT.
Colony, situated in the South Atlantic			:	
Standard Time Meridian 5°45' WEST			: m. s.	h. m. s.
Jamestown	5W42	15S55	+ 0 12	+ 0 22 48
Longwood	5W40	15S57	+ 0 20	+ 0 22 40

SAINT KITTS see British West Indies.
SAINT LUCIA see British West Indies.
SAINT MARIN see San Marino.
SAINT MARTIN see Guadeloupe.
ST. PIERRE & MIQUELON. Capital: St Pierre.
      French Colony situated in North Atlantic
      Southwest of Newfoundland. Standard
      Time Meridian 60° WEST.

St. Pierre	56W10	46N46	+15 20	+ 3 44 40

SAINT THOMAS see Portuguese West Africa.
SAINT VINCENT see British West Indies.
SAKHALIN, JAPANESE see Japan.
     "   , RUSSIAN see U. S. S. R.
SALOMON, ILES DE see 1. British Solonom Islands.
                      2. New Guinea.
SAMARANG ISLAND see Hawaii.
SAMOA see 1. American Samoa.
           2. Western Samoa.
SAN FRANCISCO ISLAND see Wake Island.
SAN MARINO. Capital: San Marino. Republic, sit-
      uated in the area of Italy. Standard Time
      Meridian 15° EAST.

San Marino	12E27	43N56	-10 12	- 0 49 48

SAO THOME see Portuguese West Africa.
SARAWAK Capital: Kuching. British Protectorate
      situated in the East Indies. Standard Time
      Meridian 112°30' EAST. In 1948 meridian 120°
      was being used for S.T.

Bintulu, 4th Div.	113E02	3N10	+ 2 08	- 7 32 08
Kuching, 1st. Div.	110E21	1N33	- 8 36	- 7 21 24
Limbang, 5th Div.	115E01	4N45	+10 04	- 7 40 04
Sibu, 3d Div.	111E49	2N18	- 2 44	- 7 27 16
Simanggand, 2d Div.	111E28	1N13	- 4 08	- 7 25 52

SARDEGNE see Italy
SARDINIA see Italy
SASKATCHEWAN see Canada.

SAUDI ARABIA   (Including all Independent States on
      the Arabian Peninsula.) Kingdom since January
      1, 1927, situated on Arabian Peninsula. Cap-
      itals: Mecca and Riyadh. No Standard Time
      used in 1939. In some parts 60° EAST is used
      as Standard Time Meridian since 1947, as
      indicated.

			L. M. T. VARIATION FROM S.T. m. s.	G. M. T. VARIATION FROM LMT. h. m. s.
Al Qunfidha, Hejaz	41E04	19N08		- 2 44 16
Al Manomah, Bahrain.............	50E36	26N14	(-37 36)	- 3 22 24
Anaiza, Nejd	44E08	26N05		- 2 56 32
Bida see Doha.				
Buraida, Nejd	44E07	26N19		- 2 56 28
Doha, Qatar	51E32	25N17		- 3 26 08
El Jauf, Djebel Shammar........	39E34.,.	29N58.............		- 2 38 16
Hael see Hail.				
Hail, Nejd	42E02	27N30		- 2 48 08
Hodeida, Yemen	42E56	14N48		- 2 51 44
Hofuf (Hufuf), Hasa	49E34	25N23		- 3 18 16
Jauf-al-Amir see El Jauf.				
Jeddah, Hejaz	39E11	21N29		- 2 36 44
Jidda see Jeddah.				
Kamaran Island see Aden.				
Kuwait, Kuwait	47E59	29N23		- 3 11 56
Loheya, Yemen...................	42E40...	15N42.............		- 2 50 40
Manana, Behrain	50E35	26N14	(-37 40)	- 3 22 20
Maskat, Maskat & Oman	58E37	23N37	(- 5 32)	- 3 54 28
Mecca, Hejaz	39E49	21N26		- 2 39 16
Medina, Hejaz	39E53	24N35		- 2 39 32
Mocha, Yemen....................	43E15...	13N20.............		- 2 53 00
Muharrak, Bahrain	50E37	26N15	(-37 32)	- 3 22 28
Muskat see Maskat.				
Ras al Khaina, Trucial Oman	55E56	25N48		- 3 43 44
Riyadh, Nejd	46E42	24N39		- 3 06 48
Sana, Yemen.....................44E13...		15N23.............		- 2 56 52
Shaqra, Nejd	45E19	25N14		- 3 05 16
Sharja, Trucial Oman	55E23	25N21		- 3 41 32
Zilfi, Nejd	44E51	26N13		- 2 59 24

SAVAGE ISLAND. Capital: Alofi. Dependency of
      New Zealand, situated in the South Pacific.
      Standard Time Meridian 170° WEST.

Alofi	169W55	19S02	+ 0 20	+11 19 40

SAVOY see France.

SAXONY see Germany.

SCHLESIEN see Germany.

SCHWABEN see Germany.

SCHWEIZ see Switzerland.

SENEGAL see French West Africa. Independent June 20, 1960

SEYCHELLES. Capital: Victoria. British Colony
      situated in the Indian Ocean. Standard Time
      Meridian 60° EAST.

Victoria (Maho), Mahe	55E28	4S36	-18 08	- 3 41 52

SHAN STATES see Burma.

SHETLAND ISLANDS see Great Britain.

SIAM. Capital: Bangkok. Kingdom, situated in
Southeastern Asia. Name of country changed
to Thailand on October 3, 1939 and changed
back to Siam on September 7, 1945.
Standard Time Meridian 105° EAST.

			L. M. T. VARIATION FROM S.T.	G. M. T. VARIATION FROM LMT.
			m. s.	h. m. s.
Ang Dhong	99E35	11N25	-21 40	- 6 38 26
Ayuthia	100E40	14N20	-17 20	- 6 42 40
Bangkok	100E31	13N45	-17 56	- 6 42 04
Bhisanulok	100E20	16N50	-18 40	- 6 41 20
Buriram........................	103E10...	15N00...	- 7 20...	- 6 52 40
Chandaburi	102E10	12N35	-11 20	- 6 48 40
Chiengmai	99E00	18N45	-24 00	- 6 36 00
Chiengrai	99E50	19N55	-20 40	- 6 39 20
Chumphon see Jumbhoni.				
Jumbhoni........................	99E10...	10N30...	-23 20...	- 6 36 40
Kamphaeng Phet	99E30	16N28	-22 00	- 6 38 00
Korat	102E10	15N00	-11 20	- 6 48 40
Krung Thep see Bangkok.				
Lampang	99E30	18N20	-22 00	- 6 38 00
Prachin Buri..................101E25...		14N05...	-14 20...	- 6 45 40
Prachuab Girikhan	99E50	11N50	-20 40	- 6 39 20
Rajburi	99E50	13N30	-20 40	- 6 39 20
Rayohng	101E15	12N40	-15 00	- 6 45 00
Songkhala	100E40	7N10	-17 20	- 6 42 40
Ubon........................	104E55...	15N15...	- 0 20...	- 6 59 40
Uttradit	100E05	17N40	-19 40	- 6 40 20
Yala	101E20	6N30	-14 40	- 6 45 20

SICILY see Italy.

SIEBENBUERGEM see Rumania.

SIERRA LEONE. Capital: Freetown. Formerly British Colony
and Protectorate, situated in West Africa.
Independent April 27, 1961.
Standard Time Meridian 15° WEST.

Bo, Southern Province	11W45	7N58	+13 00	+ 0 47 00
Bonthe, Sherbro Island	12W30	7N32	+10 00	+ 0 50 00
Freetown, Southern Prov.	13W12	8N29	+ 7 12	+ 0 52 48
Kambia, Northern Province	12W55	9N07	+ 8 20	+ 0 51 40
Moyamba, Southern Prov.	12W26	8N09	+10 16	+ 0 49 44
Port Loko, Northern Prov.	12W47	8N47	+ 8 52	+ 0 51 08
Waterloo, Southern Prov.	13W04	8N21	+ 7 44	+ 0 52 16

SILESIA see Germany.

SINGAPORE see Malaya.

SINT MARTIN see Netherlands West Indies.

SLAVONIA see Yugoslavia.

SLOVAKIA see Czechoslovakia.

SLOVENIA see Yugoslavic

SLOVENSKO see Czechoslovakia.

SOCIETE, ILES DE see French Establishments in Oceania.

SOCIETY ISLANDS see French Establishments in Oceania.

SOCOTRA ISLAND see Aden.

SOLOMON ISLANDS see 1. British Solomon Islands
                  2. New Guinea.

SOMALIA, formerly BRITISH SOMALILAND. Independent July 1, 1960.

SOMALILAND see British, French or Italian Somaliland.

112

| | L. M. T. VARIATION FROM S.T. | G. M.T. VARIATION FROM LMT. |
| | m. s. | h. m. s. |

SOMBRERO see British West Indies.
SOQOTRA ISLAND see Aden.
SOUDAN ANGLO-EGYPTIAN see Anglo-Egyptian Sudan.
SOUTH AFRICAN REPUBLIC SEE Union of South Africa.
SOUTH AUSTRALIA see Australia.
SOUTHERN RHODESIA see Rhodesia.
SOUTHERN SHAN STATES see Burma.
SOUTH GEORGIA. Capital: Grytviken. Dependency
 of Falkland Islands, situated in the South
 Atlantic. Standard Time Meridian
 31°45' WEST.

			L.M.T.	G.M.T.
Grytviken	36W32	54S16	-19 08	+ 2 26 08
Husvik Harbor	36W45	54S10	-20 00	+ 2 27 00
Prince Olaf Harbor	37W09	54S03	-21 36	+ 2 28 36

SOUTH SEA MANDATED TERRITORIES. Japanese mandated
 Territories (former German Possession),
 situated in the North Pacific. (Taken from
 Japan in World War II.)1.Marianne or Iadrone
 Islands, Capital: Tanapag. S.T. Mer. 135° EAST.
 2. (a) Eastern Carolines, Capital: Truk.
 S.T. Mer. 150° EAST. (b) Western Carolines.
 Capital: Yap. S.T. Mer.135° EAST. 3.
 Marshall Islands; Capital: Jaluit. S.T.
 Meridian 150° EAST.

Alamagan, Mariannes	145E45	17N36	+43 00	- 9 43 00
Arecifes see Ujelong.				
Asuncion Island; Mariannes	145E20	19N45	+41 20	- 9 41 20
Babelthuap, Palau Is.	134E35	7N30	- 1 40	- 8 58 20
Bikini Atoll, Marshall Is.	165E25	11N35	+1^{h}01 40	-11 01 40
Brown Island see Eniwetok Island.				
Chittoin, Ebon Island	168E42	4N35	+1^{h}14 48	-11 14 48
Dalap Island, Control Tower,				
Marshall Islands	171E23	7N05	+1^{h}25 32	-11 25 32
Engebi Island, Airfield, M. is	162E15	11N40	+49 00	-10 49 00
Eniwetok Island, Astro Pier	162E21	11N33	+49 24	-10 49 24
Eten Anchorage, East. Caro.	151E54	7N22	+ 7 36	-10 07 36
Gaferut Island, West. Caro.....	145E23...	9N14..	+41 32...	- 9 41 32
Jaluit, Marshall Is.	169E38	5N55	+1^{h}18 32	-11 18 32
Kwajalein Island, Astrol.				
position, Marshall Is.	167E29	8N44	+1^{h}09 56	-11 09 56
Lib Island, Marshall Is.	167E24	8N19	+1^{h}09 38	-11 09 38
Malakal Harbor, Palau Is.	134E28	7N19	- 2 08	- 8 57 52
Menschikoo Island see Kwajalein Island				
Mille or Mile Island Airfield				
Marshall Islands	171E44	6N05	+1^{h}26 56	-11 26 56

SOUTH SEA MANDATED TERRITORIES. (Continued)

Ponape Harbor, Ponape Is.	158E12	7N00	+32 48	-10 32 48
Providence see Ujelang.				
Rongelap (Rongorappu) Is.				
Obs. Sta. Marshall Is.	166E54	11N09	+1^{h}07 36	-11 07 36
Ronkiti Harbor, East. Car.	158E10	6N48	+32 10	-10 32 10
Roto Island, Mariannes	145E12	14N10	+40 48	- 9 40 48
Saipan (Sipan) see Tanapag Harbor.				

SOUTH SEA MANDATED TERRITORIES. (Continued)			L. M. T. VARIATION FROM S.T. m. s.	G. M. T. VARIATION FROM LMT. h. m. s.
Senyavin Island, see Ponape				
Sonsoral Island, West. Car.	132E13	5N19	-11 08	- 8 49 52
Sunharon Roads Harbor,				
Tinian Island, Mariannes	145E36	14N57	+42 24	- 9 42 24
Tanapag Harbor, Mariannes	145E41	15N14	+42 44	- 9 42 44
Taongi Atoll, Marshall Is......	168E58...	14N37	..+1^{h}15 52...	-11 15 52
Taroa Island Airfield,				
Marshall Islands	171E14	8N43	+1^{h}24 56	-11 24 56
Tinian Harbor see Sunharon Roads Harbor.				
Tobi Island, West. Caro.	131E11	3N01	-15 16	- 8 44 44
Truk Harbor see Eten Anchorage.				
Ujelang Island Obs. Mars. Is.	160E58	9N46	+43 52	-10 43 52
Ululi Island, East. Caro.	149E40	8N36	- 1 20	- 9 58 40
Yap, Western Carolines	138E08	9N31	+12 32	- 9 12 32
Wotje Island, Marshall Is.	170E15	9N28	+1^{h}21 00	-11 21 00
SOUTHWEST AFRICA see Union of South Africa.				
SPAIN. Capital: Madrid. Kingdom (now a Dictatorship), situated in Southern Europe. Standard Time Meridian 0°.				
Albacete, Albacete	1W52	39N00	- 7 28	+ 0 07 28
Alcala de Henares, Madrid........	3W22...	40N29...	-13 28...	+ 0 13 28
Alcoy, Alicante	0W30	38N21	- 2 00	+ 0 02 00
Algeciras, Cadiz	5W26	36N08	-21 44	+ 0 21 44
Alicante, Alicante	0W30	38N21	- 2 00	+ 0 02 00
Almeria, Almeria	2W27	36N51	- 9 48	+ 0 09 48
Aranda de Duero, Burgos..........	3W41...	41N40...	-14 44...	+ 0 14 44
Aranjuez, Madrid	3W37	40N02	-14 28	+ 0 14 28
Avila, Avila	4W42	40N39	-18 48	+ 0 18 48
Badajoz, Badajoz	6W58	38N52	-27 52	+ 0 27 52
Barcelona, Barcelona	2E09	41N23	+ 8 36	- 0 08 36
Bilboa, Vizcaya.................	2W56	43N15	-11 44	+ 0 11 44
Burgos, Burgos	3W42	42N21	-14 48	+ 0 14 48
Caceres, Caceres	6W23	39N28	-25 28	+ 0 25 28
Cadiz, Cadiz	6W17	36N32	-25 08	+ 0 25 08
Cartegena, Murcia	0W59	37N37	- 3 56	+ 0 03 56
Castellon de la Plana,				
Castellon	0W03	39N59	- 0 12	+ 0 00 12
Ciudad Real, Ciudad Real	3W56	38N59	-15 44	+ 0 15 44
Cordoba, Cordoba	4W47	37N53	-19 08	+ 0 19 08
Escorial see San Lorenzo de el Escorial.				
Gerona, Gerona.................	2E50	41N59	+11 20	- 0 11 20
Gijon, Oviedo	5W39	43N32	-22 36	+ 0 22 36
Gondomar, Pontevedra	8W45	42N07	-35 00	+ 0 35 00
Granada, Granada	3W35	37N10	-14 20	+ 0 14 20
Guadalajara, Guadalajara	3W10	40N38	-12 40	+ 0 12 40
Huelva, Huelva	6W57	37N15	-27 48	+ 0 27 48
Huesca, Huesca.................	0W25...	42N08...	- 1 40...	+ 0 01 40
Jaen, Jaen	3W47	37N46	-15 08	+ 0 15 08
Jerez de la Frontera, Cadiz	6W08	36N41	-24 32	+ 0 24 32
La Coruna, Coruna	8W24	43N22	-33 36	+ 0 33 36
Leon, Leon	5W35	42N36	-22 20	+ 0 22 20

			L. M. T. VARIATION FROM S.T.	G. M. T. VARIATION FROM LMT.
			m. s.	h. m. s.
SPAIN (Continued)				
Lerida, Lerida	0E38	41N37	+ 2 32	- 0 02 32
Linares, Jaen	3W37	38N06	-14 28	+ 0 14 28
Llanes, Oviedo	4W46	43N25	-19 04	+ 0 19 04
Logrono, Logrono	2W26	42N28	- 9 44	+ 0 09 44
Lugo, Lugo	7W34	43N01	-30 16	+ 0 30 16
Madrid, Madrid...................	3W41...40N25...		-14 44...	+ 0 14 44
Mahon, Manorca	4E15	39N54	+21 00	- 0 21 00
Malaga, Malaga	4W24	36N43	-17 36	+ 0 17 36
Manacor, Mallorca	3E13	39N34	+12 52	- 0 12 52
Manresa, Barcelona	1E50	41N43	+ 7 20	- 0 07 20
Murcia, Murcia...................	1W09.. 37N59...		- 4 36...	+ 0 04 36
Orense, Orense	7W52	42N20	-31 28	+ 0 31 28
Oviedo, Oviedo	5W50	43N21	-23 20	- 0 23 20
Palencia, Palencia	4W32	42N00	-18 08	+ 0 18 08
Palma, Mallorca	2E39	39N34	+10 36	- 0 10 36
Pamplona, Pamplona...............	1W38.. 42N48...		- 6 32...	+ 0 06 32
Pontevedra, Pontevedra	8W38	42N26	-36 32	+ 0 36 32
Reus, Tarragona	1E06	41N09	+ 4 24	- 0 04 24
Sabadell, Barcelona	2E06	41N33	+ 8 24	- 0 08 24
Salamanca, Salamanca	5W40	40N58	-22 40	+ 0 22 40
San Lorenzo de El Escorial, Madrid	4W09	40N36	-16 36	+ 0 16 36
San Sebastian, Guipuzcoa	1W59	43N19	- 7 56	+ 0 07 56
Santander, Santander	3W48	43N28	-15 12	+ 0 15 12
Santiago, Coruna	8W33	42N54	-34 12	+ 0 34 12
Saragossa see Zaragoza.				
Segovia, Segovia	4W07	40N57	-16 28	+ 0 16 28
Sevilla, Sevilla	6W00	37N23	-24 00	+ 0 24 00
Soria, Soria	2W28	41N46	- 9 32	+ 0 09 32
Tarragona, Tarragona	1E15	41N07	+ 5 00	- 0 05 00
Tarrasa, Barcelona...............	2E01.. 41N34...		+ 8 04...	- 0 08 04
Teruel, Nueva Castilla	1W06	40N21	- 4 24	+ 0 04 24
Toledo, Toledo	4W02	39N52	-16 08	+ 0 16 08
Tordesillas, Valladolid	5W00	41N30	-20 00	+ 0 20 00
Tortosa, Tarragona	0E32	40N49	+ 2 08	- 0 02 08
Valdepenas, Ciudad Real..........	3W23.. 38N46...		-13 32...	+ 0 13 32
Valencia, Valencia	0W22	39N29	- 1 28	+ 0 01 28
Valladolid, Valladolid	4W44	41N39	-10 56	+ 0 10 56
Vigo, Pontevedra	8W43	42N14	-34 52	+ 0 34 52
Victoria, Alava	2W40	42N51	-10 40	+ 0 10 40
Zamora, Zamora..................	5W46	41N30	-23 04	+ 0 23 04
Zaragoza, Zaragoza	0W54	41N39	- 3 36	+ 0 03 36
SPANISH GUINEA, Capital: Santa Isabel				
Spanish Colony, situated in West Africa.				
Standard Time Meridian 0°.				
Bata	9W45	1N51	+39 00	- 0 39 00
Ipeia, Corisco	9E20	0N54	+37 20	- 0 37 20
La Concepcion, Fernande Po	8E46	3N21	+35 04	- 0 35 04
Santa Isabel, Fernando Po	8E48	3N45	+35 12	- 0 35 12
SPANISH MOROCCO See Morocco.				
SPANISH SAHARA See Rio de Oro				

ET. see under SAINT.

STRAITS SETTLEMENTS see Malaya

SUDAN. See Anglo Egyptian Sudan. Independent
January 1, 1956.

SUEDE see Sweden.

SUISSE see Switzerland

SUMATRA see Indonesia

SUNDAY ISLAND see Karmadec Islands.

SUOMI see Finland.

SURINAM. Capital: Paramaribo. Aotonomous
part of the kingdom of the Netherlands
situated in South America. Time Meridian
52°30', WEST, since October 1, 1945.
Prior to that date S.T. Meridian was
55°08'35" WEST.

			L. M. T. VARIATION FROM S.T.	G. M. T. VARIATION FROM LMT.
			m. s.	h. m. s.
Albina	54W05	5N50	- 6 20	+ 3 36 20
Charlottenburg	54W49	5N52	- 9 16	+ 3 39 16
Coronie	56W23	5N52	-15 32	+ 3 45 32
Niew Amsterdam	55W08	5N54	-10 32	+ 3 40 32
Niew Nickerie	57W02	5N57	-18 08	+ 3 48 08
Paramaribo	55W13	5N50	-10 52	+ 3 40 52
Republiek	55W15	5N30	-11 00	+ 3 41 00

SWABIA see Germany

SWAZILAND see Union of South Africa.

SWEDEN. Capital: Stockholm. Kingdom, situated
in Northern Europe, Standard Time Meridian
15° EAST.

Boras, Alvsborg	12E55	57N43	- 8 20	- 0 51 40
Borgholm, Kalmar	16E39	56N53	+ 6 36	- 1 06 36
Djursholm, Stockholm	18E05	59N24	+12 20	- 1 12 20
Eskiltuna, Sodermanland	16E30	59N22	+ 6 00	- 1 06 00
Falkoping, Skaraborg	13E31	58N10	- 5 56	- 0 54 04
Falun, Kopparberg	15E38	60N36	+ 2 32	- 1 02 32
Gavle, Gavleborg	17E10	60N40	+ 8 40	- 1 08 40
Goteborg, G. och Bohus	11E58	57N43	-12 08	- 0 47 52
Gothenburg, see Goteborg				
Halmstad, Halland	12E50	56N39	- 8 10	- 0 51 20
Halsingborg, Malmohus	12E42	56N03	- 9 12	- 0 50 48
Haparanda, Norrbotten	24E10	65N50	+36 40	- 1 36 40
Harnosand, Vasternorrland	17E56	62N38	+11 44	- 1 11 44
Jonkoping, Jonkoping	14E11	57N47	- 3 16	- 0 56 44
Kalmar, Kalmar	16E22	56N40	+ 5 28	- 1 05 28
Karlskrona, Blekinge	15E35	56N10	+ 2 20	- 1 02 20
Karlstad, Varmland	13E30	59N22	+-6 00	- 0 54 00
Kristianstad, Kristianstad	14E08	56N02	- 3 28	- 0 56 32
Kristienhamn, Varmland	14E07	59N20	- 3 32	- 0 56 28
Landskrona, Malmohus	12E50	55N52	- 8 40	- 0 51 20
Lidingo, Stockholm	18E08	59N22	+12 32	- 1 12 32
Linkoping, Ostergotland	15E37	58N25	+ 2 28	- 1 02 28
Lulea, Norrbotten	22E10	65N34	+28 40	- 1 28 40
Lund, Malmohus	13E11	55N42	- 7 16	- 0 52 44
Malmo, Malmohus	13E00	55N36	- 8 00	- 0 52 00
Norrkoping, Ostergotland	16E11	58N36	+ 4 44	- 1 04 44
Orebro, Orebro	15E13	59N17	+ 0 52	- 1 00 52

			L. M. T. VARIATION FROM S.T.	G. M. T. VARIATION FROM LMT.
SWEDEN (Continued)			m. s.	h. m. s.
Oskarahamn, Kalmar	16E36	57N16	+ 6 24	- 1 06 24
Ostersund, Jamtland	14E39	63N11	- 1 24	- 0 58 36
Skovde, Skarsborg	12E50	58N24	+ 8 40	- 0 51 20
Soderhamn, Gavleborg	17E03	61N18	+ 8 12	- 5 08 12
Sodertalge, Stockholm...........	17E38...	59N12...	+10 32...	- 1 10 32
Stockholm, Stockholm	18E03	59N20	+12 12	- 1 12 12
Sundsvall, Vasternorrland	17E18	62N23	+ 9 12	- 1 09 12
Tralleborg, Malmohus	13E10	55N22	- 7 20	- 0 52 40
Trollhattan, Alvsborg	12E18	58N17	-10 48	- 0 49 12
Uddevalla, G. & B..............	11E55...	58N21...	-12 20...	- 0 47 40
Umea, Vaterbotten	20E15	63N50	+21 00	- 1 21 00
Uppsala, Uppsala	17E38	59N52	+10 32	- 1 10 32
Vasteras, Vastmauland	16E33	59N37	+ 6 12	- 1 06 12
Vastervik, Kalmar	16E39	47N45	+ 6 36	- 1 06 38
Vaxholm, Stockholm.............	18E21...	59N25...	+13 24...	- 1 13 24
Visby, Gotland	18E18	57N38	+13 12	- 1 13 12
Ystad, Malmohus	13E49	55N25	- 4 44	- 0 04 44

SWITZERLAND. Capital: Berne. Confederation
    of Republican form, situated in Central
    Europe. Standard Time Meridian 15° EAST.

Aarau, Aargau	8E03	47N23	-27 48	- 0 32 12
Altdorf, Uri	8E39	46N53	-25 24	- 0 34 36
Appenzell, Appenzell	9E24	47N19	-22 24	- 0 37 36
Bale, Bale	7E36	47N33	-29 36	- 0 30 24
Bellinzona, Ticino..............	9E02...	46N12...	-23 52...	- 0 36 08
Bern (Berne), Bern	7E28	46N57	-30 08	- 0 29 52
Biel, Bern	7E14	47N09	-31 04	- 0 28 56
Bienne see Biel.				
Buchs, St. Gallen	9E28	47N10	-22 08	- 0 37 52
Chiasso, Ticino.................	8E59...	45N52...	-24 04...	- 0 35 56
Chur, Graubunden	9E32	46N51	-21 52	- 0 38 08
Coire see Chur.				
Davos, Graubunden	9E49	46N43	-20 44	- 0 39 16
Frauenfeld, Thurgau	8E54	47N34	-24 24	- 0 35 36
Freiburg see Fribourg.				
Fribourg, Frobourg	7E10	46N49	-31 20	- 0 28 40
Geneve (Geneva), Geneve	6E09	46N12	-35 24	- 0 24 36
Genf see Geneve.				
Glarus (Glaris), Glarus	9E04	47N03	-23 44	- 0 36 16
Iferten see Yverdon.				
Interlaken, Bern	7E52	46N41	-28 32	- 0 31 28
La Chaux-de-Fonds, Neuchatel	6E50	47N06	-32 40	- 0 27 20
Lausanne, Vaud	6E39	46N31	-33 24	- 0 26 36
Locarno, Ticino	8E48	46N10	-24 28	- 0 35 12
Lugano, Ticino	8E57	46N00	-24 12	- 0 35 48
Luzern (Lucerne), Luzern........	8E18...	47N03...	-26 48...	- 0 33 12
Montreux, Vaud	6E56	46N26	-32 16	- 0 27 44
Neuchatel (Neuenberg), Necha.	6E55	47N00	-32 20	- 0 27 40
Olten, Solothurn	7E54	47N22	-28 24	- 0 31 36
Porrentruy, Bern	7E04	47N25	-31 44	- 0 28 16

			L. M. T. VARIATION FROM S.T.	G. M. T. VARIATION FROM LMT.
			m. s.	h. m. s.
SWITZERLAND (Continued)				
Romanshorn, Thurgau..............	9E23...	47N34...	-22 28...	- 0 37 32
Rorschach, St. Gallen	9E29	47N28	-22 04	- 0 37 56
Sarren, Obwalden	8E14	46N54	-27 04	- 0 32 56
Schaffhausen (Schaffhouse), Schaffhausen	8E38	47N41	-25 28	- 0 34 32
Schwyz, Schwyz..................	8E39...	47N01...	-25 24...	- 0 34 36
Soleure, see Solothurn.				
Solothurn, Solothurn	7E32	47N12	-29 52	- 0 30 08
St. Gallen (St. Gall), St. G.	9E23	47N25	-22 28	- 0 37 32
St. Moritz, Graubunden	9E52	46N30	-20 32	- 0 39 28
Thun, Bern.....................	7E38...	46N46...	-29 28...	- 0 30 32
Vevey, Vaud	6E51	46N28	-32 36	- 0 27 24
Winterthur, Zurich	8E44	47N30	-25 04	- 0 34 56
Yverdon, Vaud	6E39	46N47	-33 24	- 0 26 36
Zofingen, Aargau	7E57	47N17	-28 12	- 0 31 48
Zug (Zoug), Zug.................	8E31...	47N10...	-25 56...	- 0 34 04
Zurich, Zurich	8E32	47N22	-25 52	- 0 34 08

SYRIA see Levant States.

TADJIK S. S. R. see U. S. S. R.

TAHITI see French Establishments in Oceania.

TAI-HAN see Korea.

TAIWAN. Capital: Taihoku. Japanese possession situated in the Chinese Sea, returned to China in 1945. Standard Time Meridian 120° EAST.

Kagi, Taiwan	120E27	23N27	-58 12	- 8 01 48
Karenko, Taiwan	121E36	23N58	-53 36	- 8 06 24
Kurun, Taiwan	121E44	25N08	-53 04	- 8 06 56
Kwarenko see Krenko.				
Shinshiku, Taiwan..............	121E00...	24N48...	-56 00...	- 8 04 00
Taichu, Taiwan	120E42	24N08	-57 12	- 8 02 48
Taihoku, Taiwan	121E31	25N02	-53 56	- 8 06 04
Tainan, Taiwan	120E11	23N00	-59 16	- 8 00 44
Takao, Taiwan	120E16	22N38	-58 56	- 8 01 04

TANGANYIKA. Capital: Dar-es-Salam. British Formerly Mandated territory (Formerly German East Africa), situated in East Africa. Independent December 28, 1961. Standard Time Meridian 41°15' EAST.

Arusha, Northern Province	36E42	3S22	-18 12	- 2 26 48
Bagamoyo, Eastern Province......	38E54...	6S26...	- 9 24...	- 2 35 36
Bismarckburg see Kasanga.				
Dar-es-Salem, Eastern Prov.	39E17	6S50	- 7 52	- 2 37 08
Dodoma, Central Province	35E47	6S10	-21 52	- 2 23 08
Iringa, Iringa	35E37	7S47	-22 32	- 2 22 28
Kasanga, Ufipa	31E08	8S28	-40 28	- 2 04 32
Kigoma, Western Province	29E38	4S52	-46 28	- 1 58 32
Kilwa Kivinga, Lindi Prov.......	39E25...	8S45...	- 7 20...	- 2 37 40
Lindi, Lindi Province	39E43	10S00	- 6 08	- 2 38 52
Lushoto, Tanga Province	38E17	4S43	-11 52	- 2 33 08

			L. M. T. VARIATION FROM S. T.	G. M. T. VARIATION FROM LMT.
			m. s.	h. m. s.

TANGANYIKA   (Continued).

Moshi (Moschi), Northern P.	37E21	3S21	-15 36	- 2 29 24
Mwansa, Lake Province	32E54	2S32	-33 24	- 2 11 36
Neu Laugenburg, see Nkutuyu.				
Nkutuyu, Iringa Province	33E38	9S16	-30 28	- 2 14 32
Tabora, Western Province	32E49	5S01	-33 44	- 2 11 16
Tanga, Tanga	39E06	5S06	- 8 36	- 2 36 24
Ujiji (Ugoi), Western Prov.	29E41	4S56	-46 16	- 1 58 44
Wiedhaven, Iringa Province......	34E34...	10S28...	-26 44...	- 2 18 16
Wilhelmstal see Lushoto.				

TANGER (Tangier) see Morocco.

TANNU-TUVA see U. S. S. R.

TASMANIA see Australia.

TCHAD see French Equatorial Africa.

TCHECOSLOVAQUIE see Czechoslovakia.

TERNATE see Netherlands East Indies.

TERRE NEUVE see New Foundland.

THAILAND see Siam.

THURINGIA see Germany.

TIMOR see 1. Netherlands Timor.
          2. Portuguese Timor.

TOBAGO see British West Indies.

TOGOLAND see 1. French West Africa.) New Ghana, Independent Mar. 6, 1957
             2. Gold Coast.   ) and Togo Independent April 27, 1960

TONGA ISLANDS. Capital: Nukualofa. Native Kingdom
      under British Protectorate, situated in the
      South Pacific. Standard Time Mer. 175° WEST.

Houma, Tonga Island	175W18	21S10	- 1 12	+ 11 41 12
Mua, Tonga Island	175W07	21S11	- 0 28	+ 11 40 28
Nukualofa, Tonga Island	175W12	21S08	- 0 48	+11 40 48
Ohonua, Eua	174W57	21S21	+ 0 12	+11 39 48

TONKIN see French Indo-China.

TORRES ISLAND see New Hebrides.

TOSCANA see Italy.

TRANS-JORDAN. Capital: Amman. Kingdom, situated
      in Western Asia. Standard Time Meridian
      45° EAST.

Amman	35E56	31N57	-36 16	- 2 23 44
Aqaba (Akabah)	35E00	29N32	-40 00	- 2 20 00
Bayir	36E41	30N45	-33 16	- 2 26 44
Es Salt	35E43	32N03	-37 08	- 2 22 52
Jerash	35E54	32N17	-36 24	- 2 23 36
Ma!an	34E43	30N12	-41 08	- 2 18 52
Turf-ed-Darawish	35E52	30N42	-36 32	- 2 23 28

TRANSJUBALAND see Italian East Africa.

TRANSVAAL see Union of South Africa.

TRANSYLVANIA see Rumania.

TRENGGANU see Malaya.

TRINIDAD see British West Indies.

TRINITE see British West Indies.

TRIPOLIS see Libya.

TRIPOLITANA see Libya.

			L. M. T. VARIATION FROM S.T. m. s.	G. M. T. VARIATION FROM LMT. h. m. s.
TRISTAN DA CUNHA. Dependency of Saint Helena, situated in the South Atlantic. Standard Time Meridian 15° WEST.				
Tristan da Cunha Island	12W19	37S03	+10 44	+ 0 49 16

TRUCIAL COAST see Saudi Arabia.

TUBUAI ISLANDS see French Establishments in Oceania.

TUNISIA. Capital: Tunis. Formerly Regency under French Administration, situated in North Africa. Independent March 20, 1956. Standard Time Meridian 15° EAST.

Beja	9E11	36N43	-23 16	- 0 36 44
Bizerta..........................	9E52...	37N17...	-20 32...	- 0 39 28
Carthage	10E20	36N51	-18 40	- 0 41 20
Djerba	10E52	32N53	-16 32	- 0 43 28
Ferryville	9E48	37N09	-20 48	- 0 39 12
Gabes	10E07	33N54	-19 32	- 0 40 28
Gafsa........................	8E48...	34N25..	-24 48...	- 0 35 12
Kairouan	10E06	35N40	-19 36	- 0 40 24
La Goulette	10E18	36N49	-18 48	- 0 41 12
Mateur	9E40	37N03	-21 20	- 0 38 40
Sfax	10E46	34N43	-16 56	- 0 43 04
Souk-el-Arba..................	8E46	36N30	-24 56	- 0 35 04
Sousse	10E40	35N50	-17 20	- 0 42 40
Tabarka	8E45	36N57	-25 00	- 0 35 00
Tunis	10E10	36N48	-19 20	- 0 40 40
Zaghouan	10E09	36N23	-19 24	- 0 40 36

TUNIVIAN PEOPLE'S REPUBLIC see U. S. S. R. (Tannu-Tuva).

TURKESTAN see U. S. S. R.

TURKEY. Capital: Ankara. Republic, situated in Europe and Asia. Standard Time Meridian 30° EAST.

Ada-Bazar see Adapazari.				
Adalia see Antalya.				
Adana, Seyhan	35E18	36N59	+21 12	- 2 21 12
Adapazari, Kocaeli	30E23	40N46	+ 1 32	- 2 01 32
Adje-Abad see Eceabat.				
Adrianople see Edirno.				
Afyonkarahisar, Afyon	30E32	38N46	+ 2 08	- 2 02 08
Aintap see Gazi-Antep.				
Alexandrette see Iskendrun.				
Angora see Ankara.				
Ankara, Ankara	32E50	39N57	+11 20	- 2 11 20
Antakya (Antioch), Hatay	36E06	36N13	+24 24	- 2 24 24
Antalya, Antalya	30E42	36N54	+ 2 48	- 2 02 48
Balikesir, Balikesir	27E52	39N38	- 8 32	- 1 51 28
Beyoglu (pera) see Istanbul.				
Bolu, Bolu	31E35	40N44	+ 6 20	- 2 06 20
Bronsse (Brussa) see Bursa.				
Bursa, Bursa	29E05	40N11	- 3 40	- 1 56 20
Canakkale, Canakkale	26E23	40N09	-14 28	- 1 45 32
Caesarea see Kayseri.				

120

			L. M. T. VARIATION FROM S. T. m. s.	G. M. T. VARIATION FROM LMT. h. m. s.
TURKEY (Continued)				
Castamoni see Kastamonu.				
Cesaree see Kayseri.				
Catalca, Istanbul	28E28	41N09	- 6 08	- 1 53 52
Constantinople see Istanbul.				
Corum, Corum	34E57	40N34	+19 48	- 2 19 48
Diyarbekir, Diyarbekir..........	40E13...	37N55..	+40 52	- 2 40 52
Eceabat, Canakkale	26E20	40N11	-14 40	- 1 45 20
Edesa see Urfa.				
Edirne, Edirne	26E33	41N40	-13 48	- 1 46 12
Erzurum (Erzerum), Erzurum	41E18	39N55	+45 12	- 2 45 12
Gallipoli see Galibolu.				
Gazi-Antep, Gazi-Antep	37E21	37N05	+29 24	- 2 29 24
Golibolu, Canakkale	26E39	40N25	-13 24	- 1 46 36
Germanicia see Maras.				
Ghazi-Aintep see Gazi-Antep				
Giresun, Giresun..............	38E23...	40N55..	+33 22...	- 2 33 32
Inebolu, Kastamonu	33E45	41N59	+15 00	- 2 15 00
Iskenderun, Turkey	36E10	36N35	+24 40	- 2 24 40
Ismid see Koeseli.				
Istanbul, Istanbul	28E58	41N01	- 4 08	- 1 55 52
Izmir, Izmir..................	27E08...	38N26..	-11 28...	- 1 48 32
Karassi see Balikosir.				
Kastamonu, Kastamonu	33E45	41N23	+15 00	- 2 15 00
Kayseri, Kayseri	35E29	38N47	+21 56	- 2 21 56
Kerassound see Giresun.				
Kersond see Giresun.				
Kirklarali (Kirklisse) Kirk.	27E12	41N44	-11 12	- 1 48 48
Kocaeli, Locaeli	29E54	40N46	- 0 24	- 1 59 36
Konya, Konya	32E35	37N48	+10 20	- 2 10 20
Magnesia see Manisa.				
Maidos see Eceabat.				
Malatya, Malatya	38E18	38N22	+33 12	- 2 33 12
Manisa, Manisa	27E26	38N37	-10 16	- 1 49 44
Maras, Maras	36E53	37N37	+27 32	- 2 27 32
Mersin(a), Icel	34E36	36N48	+18 24	- 2 18 24
Ouchak see Usak.				
Ordu, Ordu	37E52...	41N00..	+31 28...	- 2 31 28
Pora see Istanbul.				
Rodosta see Tekirdag.				
Samaun, Samaun	36E21	41N17	+25 24	- 2 25 24
Sarouhan see Manisa.				
Scutari see Uskudar.				
Sebaste (Sebastia) see Sivas.				
Sivas, Sivas	37E00	39N45	+28 00	- 2 28 00
Smyrna see Izmir.				
Tarsus, Icel...................	34E52...	36N55...	+19 28...	- 2 19 28
Tekfour-Dagh see Tekirdag.				
Tekirdag, Tekirdag, E.	27E30	40N59	-10 00	- 1 50 00
Trabzon, Trabzon	39E43	41N00	+38 52	- 2 38 52
Trapezunt see Trabzon				
Trebizond see Trabzon.				

			L. M. T. VARIATION FROM S.T.	G. M. T. VARIATION FROM LMT.
			m. s.	h. m. s.
TURKEY (Continued)				
Urfa, Urfa	38E48	37N09	+35 12	- 2 35 12
Usak, Kutahya	29E24	38N41	- 2 24	- 1 57 36
Uskudar, Istanbul.............	29E01...	41N00...	- 3 56...	- 1 56 04
Van, Van	43E22	38N29	+53 28	- 2 53 28
Zonguldak, Zonguldak	31E47	41N27	+ 7 08	- 2 07 08

TURKMAN, S. S. R. See U. S. S. R.

TURKS ISLANDS   see British West Indies.

TURQUES, ILES see British West Indies.

TURQUIE see Turkey.

TUSCANY see Italy.

TYOSEN see Korea.

UBANGI SHARI see French Equatorial Africa.

UEA ISLANDS see Wallis Islands.

UGANDA. Capital: Entebbe, British Protectorate
situated in East Africa. Standard Time
Meridian 41°15' EAST.

Arua	30E55	3N01	-37 20	- 2 07 40
Entebbe	32E28	0N03	-35 08	- 2 09 52
Jinja	33E12	0N26	-32 12	- 2 12 48
Kampala	32E34	0N19	-34 44	- 2 10 16
Masaka	31E44	0S20	-38 04	- 2 06 56
Port Bell	32E39	0N18	-34 24	- 2 10 36
Soroti	33E37	1N43	-30 32	- 2 14 28

UKRANIAN S. S. R. see U. S. S. R.

UNFEDERATED MALAY STATES see Malaya.

UNION DE L'AFRIQUE DU SUD see Union of South Africa.

UNION DES REPUBLIQUES SOVIETIQUES SOCIALIESTES see U. S. S. R.

UNION OF SOUTH AFRICA. Capital: Pretoria.
Legislative Union of self-governing
British Colonies, situated in South
Africa. Standard Time Meridian 30°
EAST.

Angra Pequena see Luderitz(bucht).

Aus, South West Africa	16E16	26S40	-54 56	- 1 05 04
Benoni, Transvaal	28E19	26S11	- 6 44	- 1 53 16
Bethlehem, Orange Free State	28E18	28S14	- 6 48	- 1 53 12
Bethulie, Orange Free State.....	25E56...	30S29...	-16 08...	- 1 43 52
Bloemfontein, Orange F.S.	26E13	29S08	-15 08	- 1 44 52
Bloemhof, Transvaal	25E35	27S58	-17 40	- 1 42 20
Boksburg, Transvaal	28E15	26S13	- 7 00	- 1 53 00
Brakpan, Transvaal	28E22	26S14	- 6 32	- 1 53 28
Bredasdrop, Cape Colony........	20E03...	34S32...	-39 48...	- 1 20 12
Bremersdorp, Swaziland	32E22	26S29	+ 9 28	- 2 09 28
Bulwer, Natal	29E47	29S48	- 0 52	- 1 59 08
Capetown, Cape Colony	18E25	33S55	-46 20	- 1 13 40
Carnarvon, Cape Colony	22E08	30S57	-31 28	- 1 28 32
Durban, Natal................	31E01...	29S50...	+ 4 04...	- 2 04 04
East London, Cape Colony	27E54	33S01	- 8 24	- 1 51 36
Francistown, Bechuanaland	27E31	21S13	- 9·56	- 1 50 04
Germiston, Transvaal	28E11	26S13	- 7 16	- 1 52 44

			L. M. T. VARIATION FROM S.T. m. s.	G. M. T. VARIATION FROM LMT. h. m. s.

UNION OF SOUTH AFRICA   (continued)

Location	Long.	Lat.	L.M.T. Var. from S.T.	G.M.T. Var. from LMT
Graaff Reinet, Cape Colony	24E32	32S14	-21 52	- 1 38 08
Grahamstown, Cape Colony	26E31	33S18	-13 56	- 1 46 04
Harrismith, Orange F. S.........	29E07...	28S16...	- 3 32...	- 1 56 28
Heilbron, Orange Free State	27E58	27S17	- 8 08	- 1 51 52
Hoopstad, Orange Free State	25E55	27S50	-16 20	- 1 43 40
Johannesburg, Transvaal	28E02	26S12	- 7 52	- 1 52 08
Kaapstad see Capetown.				
Kenhardt, Cape Colony...........	21E09...	29S21...	-35 24...	- 1 24 36
Ketmanshoop, Southwest A.	18E08	26S35	-47 28	- 1 12 32
Kimberley, Cape Colony	24E46	28S44	-20 56	- 1 39 04
Kroonstad, Orange Free St.	27E14	27S40	-11 04	- 1 48 56
Krugersdorp, Transvaal	27E46	26S06	- 8 56	- 1 51 04
Ladysmith, Natal...............	29E47...	28S33...	- 0 52...	- 1 59 08
Laingsburg, Cape Colony	20E52	33S12	-36 32	- 1 23 28
Lobatsi, Bechuanaland	25E40	25S13	-17 20	- 1 42 40
Luderitz(bucht), S. W.A.	15E09	26S39	-59 24	- 1 00 36
Lydenburg, Transvaal	30E27	25S06	+ 1 48	- 2 01 48
Maclear, Cape Colony...........	28E21...	31S03...	- 6 36...	- 1 53 24
Mafeking, Cape Colony	24E39	25S52	-21 24	- 1 38 36
Maseru, Basutoland	27E30	29S18	-10 00	- 1 50 00
Mbanane, Swaziland	31E08	26S19	+ 4 32	- 2 04 32
Middelburg, Cape Colony	25E01	31S27	-19 56	- 1 40 04
Middelburg, Transvaal..........	29E29...	25S46...	- 2 04...	- 1 57 56
Molepolole, Bochuanaland	25E32	24S25	-17 52	- 1 42 08
Newcastle, Natal	29E55	27S44	- 0 20	- 1 59 40
Palapye, Bechuanaland	27E08	22S34	-11 28	- 1 48 32
Paulpietersburg, Natal	30E49	27S25	+ 3 16	- 2 03 16
Pietermaritzburg, Natal........	30E23...	29S35...	+ 1 32...	- 2 01 32
Pietersburg, Transvaal	29E27	23S54	- 2 12	- 1 57 48
Piet Retief, Transvaal	30E48	27S00	+ 3 12	- 2 03 12
Port Elizabeth, Cape Colony	25E37	33S58	-17 32	- 1 42 28
Potchefstroom, Transvaal	27E05	27S42	-11 40	- 1 48 20
Preteria, Transvaal............	28E11...	25S45...	- 7 16...	- 1 52 44
Roodepoort, Transvaal	27E52	26S10	- 8 32	- 1 51 28
Serowe, Bechuanaland	26E58	22S19	-12 08	- 1 47 52
Simons Town, Cape Colony	18E26	34S12	-46 16	- 1 13 44
Springs, Transvaal	28E28	26S15	- 6 08	- 1 53 52
Standerton, Transvaal..........	29E15...	26S57...	- 3 00...	- 1 57 00
Swakopmund, Southwest Af.	14E32	22S40	-1h01 52	- 0 58 08
Victoria West, Cape Colony	23E06	31S23	-27 36	- 1 32 24
Vryburg, Cape Colony	24E40	26S57	-21 20	- 1 38 40
Walvis Bay, Southwest Af.	14E31	22S57	-1h01 56	- 0 58 04
Windhook, Southwest Africa......	17E04...	22S33...	-51 44...	- 1 08 16
Zeerust, Transvaal	26E05	25S42	-15 40	- 1 44 20

UNION OF SOVIET SOCIALIST REPUBLICS.

Capital: Moskva (Moscow). Soviet Socialist Republics situated in Europe and Asia. The U. S. S. R. consisted of the following eleven Constituent Republics in 1939:

1. Russian Soviet Federated Republic, Capital: Moskva.
2. Ukranian Soviet Socialist Republic, Capital: Kiyev,
3. White Russian Soviet Socialist Republic, Capital: Minsk.
4. Azerbaidjan Soviet Socialist Republic, Capital: Baku.
5. Georgian Soviet Socialist Republic, Capital: Thilisi.
6. Armenian Soviet Socialist Republic, Capital: Yerevan.
7. Turkman Soviet Socialist Republic, Capital: Ashkhabad.
8. Uzbek Soviet Socialist Republic, Capital: Taskkent.
9. Tadjik Soviet Socialist Republic, Capital: Stalinabad.
10. Kazakh Soviet Socialist Republic, Capital: Alma-Ata.
11. Kirghiz Soviet Socialist Republic, Capital: Frunze.

The number (1 to 11) following the name of a city indicates in which Constituent Republic that city is situated. In addition, administrative subdivisions have been given in the cases of cities located in the first three, i. e. 1 Russian Soviet Federated Republic, 2 Ukranian Soviet Socialist Republic, and 3 White Russian Soviet Socialist Republic.

ABBREVIATIONS USED:

A. R......Autonomous Republic
A. Reg....Autonomous Region.
Arkh......Arkhangelsk.
Chel.......Chelyabinsk.
Dnepr......Dnepropetrovsk.
Kaz........Kazakstan.
Khab.......Dhabarovsk.

Krd.......Krasnodar.
Kry.......Krasnovarsk.
Nakh......Nakhichevan.
Nik.......Nikolayev.
N. R......Northern Region.
Sverdl....Sverdlovsk.

Daylight Saving Time (Summer Time) has been used throughout the entire territory of the U. S. S. R. since 1937.

The country has been divided into the following eleven zones:

	FROM	TO	G. M. T. VARIATION - MINUS
Zone 1	20°30' E.	37°30' E.	- 2
2	37°30' E.	52°30' E.	- 3
3	52°30' E.	67°30' E.	- 4
4	67°30' E.	82°30' E.	- 5
5	82°30' E.	97°30' E.	- 6
6	97°30' E.	112°30' E.	- 7
7	112°30' E.	127°30' E.	- 8
8	127°30' E.	142°30' E.	- 9
9	142°30' E.	157°30' E.	- 10
10	157°30' E.	172°30' E.	- 11
11	172°30' E.	and Eastward.	- 12

* after city name indicates it is situated in Asia.

			L. M. T. VARIATION FROM S.T.	G. M. T. VARIATION FROM LMT.
			m. s.	h. m. s.
U. S. S. R. (Continued)				
Abakan, 1, Kry. *	91E30	53N45	- 54 00	- 6 06 00
Abdalliar see Lachin.				
Akkermanovka, 1, Orenburg	58E15	51N14	- 07 00	- 3 53 00
Ak-Mechet see Kzyl-Orda				
Akmolinsk, 10, *	71E30	51N10	- 14 00	- 4 46 00
Aktyubinsk, 10, *	57E10	50N17	- 11 20	- 3 48 40
Alexandrovsk see Zaporozhye.				
Alexandrovsk-Sakhalinskiy, 1, Khab. *.................142N54...		50N54...	- 31 20...	- 9 28 40
Alma-Ata, 10*	76E57	43N12	+ 7 48	- 5 07 48
Anadyr, 1, Khab. *	177E35	64N 45	- 09 40	-11 50 20
Andizhan, 8 *	72E22	40N45	- 10 32	- 4 29 28
Arkhangelsk, 1, N. R.	40E32	64N34	+ 42 08	- 2 42 08
Artemovsk, 1, Kry. *...........93E26...		54N24...	+ 18 49...	- 6 13 44
Ashkabad, 7 *	58E23	37N57	- 06 28	- 3 53 32
Astrakhan, 1, Stalingrad	48E03	46N21	+ 12 12	- 3 12 12
Bakhmut see Artemovsk				
Baku, 4	49E50	40N25	+ 19 20	- 3 19 20
Balaklava, 1, Crimea........... 33E35...		44N30...	+ 14 20...	- 2 14 20
Banki see Krasnogorsk.				
Barnaul, 1, Altai *	83E48	53N20	- 24 48	- 5 35 12
Batumi (Batum), 5, A. R. of Adjaristan	41E40	41N36	- 13 20	- 2 46 40
Bek Budi, 8..................... 65E48...		38N50...	+ 23 12...	- 4 23 12
Belgorod, 1, Kurak	36E34	50N36	+ 26 16	- 2 26 16
Belomorsk, 1, A. R. of Karelia	34E48	64N32	+ 19 12	- 2 19 12
Berdichev	28E35	49N55	- 05 40	- 1 54 20
Birobidjan, 1, Khab (autonomous Jewish Region) *	132E57	48N48	- 08 12	- 8 51 48
Blagovaschensk, 1, Khab. *	127E30	50N25	+ 30 00	- 8 30 00
Bobriki see Stalinogorsk.				
Bobruysk, 3, Bobruysk	29E14	43N09	- 03 04	- 1 56 56
Borizov, 3, Borizov............. 28E31...		54N15	...- 05 56...	- 1 54 04
Borodino, 1, Kalinin	35E50	55N29	- 36 40	- 2 23 20
Borogontsy, 1, A.R. of Yakutsk,*131E06		62N35	- 15 36	- 8 44 24
Bryansk, 1, Western Region	34E20	53N15	+ 17 20	- 2 17 20
Bukhara, 8 *	64E25	39N48	+ 17 40	- 4 17 40
Chardju (Chardzhou), 7 *	63E36	39N08	+ 14 24	- 4 14 24
Cheboksary, 1, A.R. of Chuvash	47E15	56N09	+ 9 00	- 3 09 00
Chelyabinsk, 1, Chelyabinsk *	61E24	55N10	+ 05 36	- 4 05 36
Cherepovets, 1, Vologda......... 37E54...		59N08...	+ 31 36...	- 2 31 36
Cherkessk, 1, Stavropol	42E03	44N14	+ 11 48	- 2 48 12
Chernigov, 2, Chernigov	31E16	51N30	+ 05 04	- 2 05 04
Chernoye, 1, Gorki	43E24	56N15	- 06 24	- 2 53 36
Chimkent, 10, *	69E36	42N18	- 21 36	- 4 38 24
Chita, 1, E. Sib. *.............113E30...		52N03...	- 26 00..	- 7 34 00
Chkalov, 1, Chkalov	55E06	51N45	- 19 36	- 3 40 24
Detskoye Selo, 1, Leningrad	30E25	59N42	+ ol 40	- 2 01 40
Djalal-Abad, 11 *	73E00	40N56	- 08 00	- 4 52 00

			L. M. T. VARIATION FROM S.T.	G. M. T. VARIATION FROM LMT.
			m. s.	h. m. s.
U. S. S. R. (Continued)				
Djambul, 10 *	71E23	42N55	− 14 28	− 4 45 32
Dnepropetrovsk, 2, Dnepr.	35E01	48N27	+ 20 04	− 2 20 04
Dudinka, 1, Krd. *..............	86E10...	69N25...	− 15 20..	− 5 44 40
Dushamb see Stalinabad.				
Dzaudjikau, 1. A.R. of Ossetia.*	44E40	43N00	− 01 20	− 2 58 40
Ekaterinburg see Sverdlovsk.				
Eksterinodar see Krasnodar.				
Ekaterinoslav see Dnepropetrovsk.				
Elista see Stepnoy				
Elizavetgrad see Kirovograd.				
Engels, 1, A.R. of Germans of the Volga................	..46E05...	51N30...	+ 04 20...	− 3 04 20
Erevan (Erivan) see Yerevan				
Feddosyia, 1, Crimea	35E24	45N02	− 38 24	− 2 21 36
Fergana, 8 *	71E44	40N23	− 13 04	− 4 46 56
Frunze, 11 *	74E36	42N54	− 01 36	− 4 58 24
Garm, 9 *	70E25...	39N00...	− 18 20...	− 4 41 40
Gomel, 3, Gomel	31E00	52N27	+ 04 00	− 2 04 00
Gorki, 1, Gorki	44E00	56N20	− 04 00	− 2 56 00
Grozny, (Groznyy),1, Northern Caucasus	45E42	43N20	+ 02 48	− 3 02 48
Guryev (Guriev), 10 *..........	51E53...	47N07...	+ 27 32...	− 3 27 32
Igarka, 1, Krd. *	86E35	57N30	− 13 40	− 5 46 20
Irkutsk, 1, E. Sib. *	104E20	52N16	− 02 40	− 6 57 20
Ivanovo, 1, Kirov	41E00	57N00	+ 44 00	− 2 44 00
Ivanova-Voznessensk see Ivanovo.				
Izhevsk, 1, A.R. of Udmar........	53E14...	56N51...	+ 32 56...	− 3 32 56
Kalinin, 1, Kalinin	35E55	56N50	+ 23 40	− 2 23 40
Kaluga, 1, Moskva	36E18	54N30	− 34 48	− 2 25 12
Kamenets-Podolskiy, 2, Vinnitsa	26E34	48N40	− 13 44	− 1 46 16
Kamenskoye, 1, Khab. *.........	165E08,..	62N30...	+ 00 32...	−11 00 32
Karaganda, 10*	73E10	49N50	− 07 20	− 4 52 40
Karaklis see Kirovakan.				
Karski see Bed Budi.				
Kazan, 1, A.R. of Tatars	49E08	55N45	+ 16 32	− 3 16 32
Kemerove, 1, West Sib...........	86E05...	55N20...	− 15 40...	− 5 44 20
Kenimekh, 8 *	65E05	40N15	+ 20 20	− 4 20 20
Kerch, 1, Crimea	36E26	45N24	+ 25 44	− 2 25 44
Kerki, 7 *	65E12	37N52	+ 20 48	− 4 20 48
Keshishkend see Mikoyan.				
Khabarovsk, 1, Khab. *.........135E06...	135E06...	48N30...	+ 00 24...	− 9 00 24
Khankendy see Stepanekert.				
Khanty-Mansiysk, 1, Omsk *	69E00	61N00	− 24 00	− 4 36 00
Kharkov, 2, Kharkov	36E15	50N00	+ 24 00	− 2 25 00
Kherson, 2, Odessa	32E35	46N40	+ 10 20	− 2 10 20
Khibinogorsk see Kirovsk.				
Khiva, 8 *	60E22	41N24	+ 01 28	− 4 01 28
Khorog, 9 *	71E36	37N30	− 13 36	− 4 46 24
Kiev (Kiyev), 2, Kiev	30E32	50N27	+ 02 23	− 2 02 08

			L. M. T. VARIATION FROM S. T.			G. M. T. VARIATION FROM LMT.		
				m.	s.	h.	m.	s.
U. S. S. R. (continued)								
Kirensk, 1, E. Siberia *	108E06	57N47	+12	24		- 7	12	24
Kirov, 1, Krrov	49E42	58N33	-41	12		- 3	18	48
Kirovakan, 6..................	44E30...	40N48...	-02	00...		- 2	58	00
Kirovo see Kirovograd.								
Kirovograd, 2, Nik.	32E18	48N30	+09	12		- 2	09	12
Kirovsk, 1, Leningrad								
(Artic Circle)	33E39	67N34	+14	36		- 2	14	36
Klintsy, 1, Orel................	32E16...	52N45...	+09	04	...- 2		09	04
Klukhori, 1, Stavropol	41E54	43N47	-12	24		- 2	47	36
Kokand, S. *	70E59	40N30	-16	04		- 4	43	56
Kokohetav, 10 *	69E25	53N15	-22	20		- 4	37	40
Kola, 1, Leningrad	33E00	68N52	+12	00		- 2	12	00
Komsomolsk-na-Amure, 1,								
Far East *	137E02	50N35	+08	08		- 9	08	08
Korosten, 2, Zhitomir	28E36	50N57	-05	36		- 1	54	24
Kostroma, 1, Ivanovo	40E52	57N40	-16	32		- 2	43	28
Krasnodar, 1, Black Sea & Azov *.	39E00...	45N02...	-24	00...		- 2	36	00
Krasnogorsk, 1, Moskva	37E19	55N50	+29	16		- 2	29	16
Krasnokokchaisk see Yoshkar-Ola.								
Krasnouralsk, 1, Sverdl.	60E05	58N21	+00	20		- 4	00	20
Krasnovodsk, 7 *	52E58	40N01	-28	08		- 3	31	52
Krasnoyarsk, 1, Kry. *.........	92E48...	56N02...	+11	12...		- 6	11	12
Kremenchug, 2, Poltava	33E28	49N03	+13	52		- 2	13	52
Krivoi Rog, 2, Dnepr.	33E21	47N54	+13	24		- 2	13	24
Kronstadt, 1, Leningrad	29E45	59N59	-01	00		- 1	59	00
Krosnokokshaisk see Yoshkar-Ola.								
Kuliab see Kulyab.								
Kulyab, 9 *	69E48	37N57	-20	48		- 4	39	12
Kurgan, 1, Chel. *	65E18	55N26	+21	12		4	21	12
Kurgan-Tyube, 9 *	68E48	37N49	-24	48		- 4	35	12
Kursk, 1, Kursk	36E12	51N42	+24	48		- 2	24	48
Kustanai, 10 *...............	63E35...	53N10...	+14	20...		- 4	14	20
Kutais, 5, Kutais	42E40	42N15	-09	20		- 2	50	40
Kuybyshev, 1, Kuybyshev	50E09	53N12	+20	36		- 3	20	36
Kuznetsk-Sibirski see Staliank.								
Kyzyl, 1, A. Reg. of Tannu Tuba..	94E04...	51N40...	+16	16...		- 6	16	16
Kzyl-Orda, 10 *	65E31	44N48	+22	04		- 4	22	04
Lachia, 4, Tbilisi	46E32	39N38	+06	08		- 3	06	08
Leninabad, 9 *	69E37	40N17	+21	32		- 4	38	28
Leningrad, 1, Leningrad	30E15	59N55	+01	00		- 2	01	00
Lenkoran, 4....................	48E50	38N46	+15	20		- 3	15	20
Lepel, 3, Vitebsk	28E41	54N52	-05	16		- 1	54	44
Lugansk see Voroshilovgrad.								
Magnitogorsk, 1, Chel., *	59E00	53N28	-04	00		- 3	56	00
Maikop see Maykop.								
Makhachkala, 1, A.R. of								
Daghestan	47E27	42N58	+ 9	48		- 3	09	48
Mardakert, 4	46E48	40N12	+07	12		- 3	07	12
Mariinsk, 1, W. Siberia	87E45	56N11	-09	00		- 5	51	00
Mariupol, 2, Donetz	37E36	47N05	+30	24		- 2	30	24

			L. M. T. VARIATION FROM S. T.	G. M. T. VARIATION FROM LMT.
			m. s.	h. m. s.
U. S. S. R. (Continued)				
Mary, 7 *	61E50	37N36	+ 06 20	- 4 06 20
Matochin Shar, 1, Nov. Zenlya	56E27	73N16	- 14 12	- 3 45 48
Maykop, 1, Krd..................	40E10...	44N35...	- 19 20,...	- 2 40 40
Melitopol, 2, Dnepr.	30E22	46N50	+ 21 28	- 2 21 28
Mikoyan, 6	45E20	39N45	+ 1 20	- 3 01 20
Mikoyan-Chakhar see Klukhori.				
Minsk, 3, Minsk	27E35	53N50	- 09 40	- 1 50 20
Mogilev, 2, Knepr.............	30E21...	53N54...	+ 01 28...	- 2 01 24
Mogilev-Podolskiy, 2 Vinnitsa	27E49	48N26	- 08 44	- 1 51 16
Molotov, 1, Sverdl.	56E15	58N00	- 15 00	- 3 45 00
Moscow see Moskva.				
Moskva, 1, Moskva	37E35	55N45	+ 30 20	- 2 30 20
Mosovsk, 1, Muryat-Mong. *....	105E53...	51N44...	+ 03 32...	- 7 03 32
Mozyr, 3, Mozyr	29E16	52N03	- 02 56	- 1 57 04
Mukhor-Shibir, 1, Buryat-Mongolia *	107E49	51N03	+ 11 16	- 7 11 16
Murmansk, 1, Leningrad	33E05	68N58	+ 12 20	- 2 12 20
Nakhichevan, 4, A.R. of Nakh....	45E24...	39N12...	+ 01 36...	- 3 01 36
Nalchik, 1, A.R. of Kabarda	43E37	43N30	- 05 32	- 2 54 28
Namangan, 8 *	71E38	41N00	- 13 28	- 4 46 32
Naryn, 11 *	76E00	41N28	+ 04 00	- 5 04 00
Nerchinsk, 1, E. Siberia *	116E33	51N58	- 13 48	- 7 46 12
Nikolayev, 2, Odessa..........	32E00...	46N58...	+ 08 00...	- 2 08 00
Nikolayevak na Amure, 1 Khab.	*140E42	53N10	+ 22 48	- 9 22 48
Nikolsk Ussuriisky see Voroshilov.				
Nikopol, 2, Donetz	34E24	47N32	+ 17 36	- 2 17 36
Nizhni Novgorod see Gorki.				
Novaya Ladoga, 1, Leningrad	32E19	60N07	+ 09 16	- 2 09 16
Novgorod, 1, Leningrad	31E16	58N33	+ 05 04	- 2 05 04
Novocherkassk, 1, Rostav	40E06	47N24	- 19 36	- 2 40 24
Novograd-Volynskiy, 2, Zhitomir..	27E37....	50N36...	- 09 32...	- 1 50 28
Novo-Kuzetsk see Stalinsk.				
Novo Mariinsk see Anadyr.				
Novonikolayevsk see Novosibrisk.				
Novorossiyak, 1, Rostav	37E50	44N44	- 28 40	- 2 31 20
Novosibirsk, 1, W. Siberia *	82E53	55N02	- 28 28	- 5 31 32
Novy Margelan see Fergana.				
Nukus, 9, A.R. of Kara-Kalpak *	59E38	42N29	-1^{h}01 28	- 3 58 32
Odessa, 2, Odessa..............	30E44...	46N29...	+ 02 56...	- 2 02 56
Oirot-Tura see Cyrot-Tura.				
Okhotsk, 1, Far East *	143E18	59N23	- 26 48	- 9 33 12
Cmsk, 1, Omsk *	73E24	55N00	- 06 24	- 4 53 36
Onega, 1, Arkh.	38E08	63N54	+ 32 32	- 2 32 32
Ordzhonikidze see Dzaudjikau.				
Orel, 1, Orel...................	36E00	52N55	+ 24 00	- 2 24 00
Orenburg see Chkalov.				
Osh. 11 *	72E48	40N32	- 08 48	- 4 51 12
Ostyako-Vogulsk see Khanty-Mansiyk				

			L. M. T. VARIATION FROM S. T.		G. M. T. VARIATION FROM LMT.		
			m.	s.	h.	m.	s.
U. S. S. R. (Continued)							
Oyrot-Tura, 1, Altai *	85E57	51N58	-16	12	- 5	43	48
Palana, 1, Khab. *	100E01	59N09	-19	56	- 6	40	04
Pavlodar, 10 *	77E00...	52N18...	+08	00...	- 5	08	00
Penza, 1, Kyub.	45E03	53N12	+00	12	- 3	00	12
Pereslavil-Zalesskiy, 1,Vladimir	38E52	56N44	+35	28	- 2	35	28
Perm see Molotov.							
Permskoye see Komsomolsk-na-Amure.							
Peterhof see Petrodvorets.							
Petroalexandrovsk see Turtkul.							
Petrodvorets, 1, Leningrad	29E54	59N53	-00	24	- 1	59	36
Petrokrepost, 1, Leningrad	31E03	59N57	+04	12	- 2	04	12
Petropavlovsk, 10 *	69E06	54N55	-23	36	- 4	36	24
Petropavlovsk-Kamchatskiy, 1, Khab. *	158E39	53N01	-25	24	-10	34	36
Petrovsk, 1, Ivanova *	108E50	51N17	+15	20	- 7	15	20
Petrovsk-Port see Makhachkala.							
Petrozavodsk, 1, A.R. of Karelia......................	34E20...	61N49...	+17	20...	- 2	17	20
Piatigorsk see Pyatigorsk.							
Pinsk, 3, Pinsk	26E07	52N09	-15	32	- 1	44	28
Pishpek see Frunze.							
Pokrevsk see Engels.							
Polotsk, 3, Polotsk............	28E47	55N30	-04	52	- 1	55	08
Poltava, 2, Kharbov	34E36	49N35	+18	24	- 2	18	24
Poltoratsk see Ashkabab.							
Prokopievak, 1, W. Siberia *	86E49	53N50	-12	44	- 5	47	16
Proskurov, 2, Vinnitsa	27E00	49N25	-12	00	- 1	48	00
Przevalsk, 11 *...............	78E24...	42N30...	+13	36...	- 5	13	36
Pskov, 1, Leningrad	28E20	57N50	-06	40	- 1	53	20
Pushkino, 1, Moskva	37E51	56N01	+31	24	- 2	31	24
Pyatigorsk, 1, Stavropol	43E05	44N01	-07	40	- 2	52	20
Ramenskoye, 1, Moskva	38E13	55N34	+32	52	- 2	32	52
Riazan see Tyazan.							
Rostav-na-Donu, 1, Rostav	39E53	47N15	-20	28	- 2	39	32
Rostov see Rostav-na-Donu.							
Rovno, 2, Vinnitsa	26E09	50N35	-15	24	- 1	44	36
Rukhlovo see Skovorodino.							
Ryazen, 1, Moskva..............	39E40	54N40	-21	20	- 2	38	40
Rhev 1, Kalinin	34E20	56N15	+17	20	- 2	17	20
Sad-Gorod see Stalinsk.							
Saint Petersburg see Leningrad.							
Samara see Kuybyshev.							
Samarkand, 8 *	66E58...	39N40...	+27	52...	- 4	27	52
Saransk, 1, A.R. of Mordovia	45E12	54N11	+00	48	- 3	03	12
Saratov, 1, Saratov	46E02	51N34	+04	08	- 3	04	08
Schluesselburg see Petrokrepost.							
Sebastopol see Sevastopol.							
Semipalatinsk, 10 *............	80E13...	50N28...	+20	52...	- 5	20	52
Sevastopol, 1, Crimea	33E34	44N35	+14	16	- 2	14	16
Shepetcvka, 2, Vinnitsa	27E04	50N12	-11	44	- 1	48	16
Shtcheglovsk see Kemerovo.							

			L.M.T. VARIATION FROM S.T. m. s.	G.M.T. VARIATION FROM LMT. h. m. s.
U. S. S. R. (Continued)				
Simbirsk see Ulyanovsk.				
Simferopol, 1, Crimea	34E05	44N58	+16 20	- 2 16 20
Skovorodino, 1, Khab. *.........	123E55	53N59	+15 40	- 8 15 40
Sliudynka, 1, E. Siberia *	103E44	51N39	-05 04	- 6 54 56
Slutsk, 3, Minsk	27E33	53N02	-09 48	- 1 50 12
Smolensk, 1, W. Region	32E03	54N46	+08 12	- 2 08 12
Smolyensk see Smolensk.				
Soroka see Belomorsk.				
Sosnovo-Ozerskoye, 1,				
Buryat-Mongolia	111E33	52N32	+26 12	- 7 26 12
Sretensk, 1, E. Siberia *	117E41	52N15	-09 16	- 7 50 44
Stalinabad, 9 *	68E48	38N34	-24 48	- 4 35 12
Stalingrad, Stalingrad..........	44E25...	48N45...	-02 20...	- 2 57 40
Stalinir, 1, A. Reg. of				
South Ossetia	43E58	42N14	-04 08	- 2 55 52
Stalino, 2, Donets	37E48	48N00	+31 12	- 2 31 12
Stalinogorsk, 1, Moskva	38E15	54N04	+33 00	- 2 33 00
Stalinsk, 1, W. Siberia *......	131E36...	47N41...	-13 36...	- 8 46 24
Stamina Bukhara see Bukhara.				
Staraya Russa, 1, Leningrad	31E23	58N00	+05 32	- 2 05 32
Stavropol see Voroshilovsk.				
Stepanakert, 4, A.Reg. of				
Karabakh.....................	46E46...	39N50...	+ 07 04...	- 3 07 04
Stepnoy, 1, A.R. of Kalmuks	44E16	46N19	-02 56	- 2 57 04
Sukhumi, 5, A. Reg. of Abkhazia	41E02	43N01	-15 52	- 2 44 08
Sumy, 2, Kharkov	34E46	50N54	+19 04	- 2 19 04
Sverdlovsk, 1, Sverdlovsk	60E38	56N50	+02 32	- 4 02 32
Syktyvkar, 1, A.R. of Komi	50E51	61N40	+23 24	- 3 23 24
Taganrog, 1, Rastov	38E57	47N14	+35 48	- 2 35 48
Talas, 11	72E13	42N32	-11 08	- 4 48 52
Taldy-Kurgan, 10 *	78E24	45N00	+13 36	- 5 13 36
Tambov, 1, Voronej..............	41E29...	52N43...	-14 04...	- 2 45 56
Tara, 1, Omsk	74E22	56N53	-02 32	- 4 57 28
Tashauz, 7 *	59E58	41N50	-00 08	- 3 59 52
Tashkent, 8 *	69E18	41N20	-22 48	- 4 37 12
Tbilisi, 5	44E55	41N45	-00 20	- 2 59 40
Termez, 8 *...................	67E13...	37N11...	-13 08...	- 4 28 52
Theodosia see Feodosiya.				
Tiflis see Tbilisi.				
Tikhonkaya see Biribidjan.				
Tiraspol, 2 A.R. of Moldavia	29E36	46N50	-01 36	- 1 58 24
Tobolsk, 1, Omsk, *...........	68E20...	58N10...	+33 20...	- 4 33 20
Tomsk, 1, W. Siberia *	84E58	56N30	-20 08	- 5 39 52
Troitskoye, 1, Khab. *	136E31	49N28	+05 04	- 9 05 04
Tsaritsyn see Stalingrad.				
Tsarskoye Selo see Detskoye Selo.				
Tula, 1, Moskva............	37E36...	54N12...	-29 36...	- 1 30 24
Tumen see Tyumen.				
Tura, 1, Kry. *	99E58	64N10	-20 08	- 6 39 52
Turkestan, 10 *	68E15	43N20	-27 00	- 4 33 00

			L. M. T. VARIATION FROM S. T.	G. M. T. VARIATION FROM LMT.
			m. s.	h. m. s.
U. S. S. R. (Continued)				
Turtkul, 8, A.R. of Kara-Kalpak	61E03	41N28	+04 12	- 4 04 12
Tver see Kalinin.				
Tyrtkul see Turtkul.				
Tyumen, 1, Tyumen	65E30	57N11	+22 00	- 4 22 00
Ufa, 1, A.R. of the Bashkirs	55E55	54N43	-16 20	- 3 43 40
Ulala see Oyrot-Tura.				
Ulan-Ude, 1 A.R. of Buryat-Mongolia *	107E37	51N50	+10 28	- 7 10 28
Uliyanovsk see Ulyanovsk.				
Ulyanovsk, 1, Kuybyshev	48E24	54N20	+13 36	- 3 13 36
Uralmedstroi see Krasnouralsk.				
Uralsk, 10 *.....................	51E22...	51N14...	+25 28...	- 3 25 28
Ura-Tyube, 9 *	69E00	39N55	-24 00	- 4 36 00
Urgench, 8 *	60E36	41N32	+02 24	- 4 02 24
Urluk, 1, Buryat-Mongolia *	107E54	50N05	+11 36	- 7 11 36
Ust-Abanskoye see Abakan.				
Ust-Kamenogorsk, 10 *	82E40	49N58	-29 20	- 5 30 40
Ustmaya, 1, Yakutsk *	134E31	60N25	-01 56	- 8 58 04
Ust-Sysolsk see Syktyvkar.				
Velikiye Luki, 1, Kalinin	30E32	56N20	+02 08	- 2 02 08
Verkhne-Udinsk see Ulan-Ude.				
Vernoleninsk see Nikolayev.				
Verney see Alma-Ata.				
Viazma see Vyazma				
Vinnitsa, 2, Vinnitsa	28E29	49N13	-06 04	- 1 53 56
Vitebsk, 3	30E12	55N12	+00 48	- 2 00 48
Vladikavkaz see Dzaudjikan.				
Vladimir, 1, Ivanono	40E25	56N10	-18 20	- 2 41 40
Vladivostok, 1, Prim. *	131E50	43N05	-12 40	- 8 47 20
Vologda, 1, N.R.	39E40	59N20	-21 20	- 2 38 40
Voronezh, 1, Voronezh	39E10	51N40	-23 20	- 2 36 40
Voroshilov, 1, Khab............131E55...		43N47...	-13 20...	- 8 47 40
Voroshilovgrad, 2, Donetz	39E20	48N34	-22 40	- 2 37 20
Voroshilovsk, 1, Stavropol	41E58	45N03	-12 08	- 2 47 52
Vyatka see Kirov.				
Vyazma, 1, Western Region	34E18	55N14	+17 12	- 2 17 12
Yakutsk, 1, A.R. of Yakutsk *..129E40...		62N00...	-21 20...	- 8 38 40
Yalta, 1, Crimea	34E10	44N18	+16 40	- 2 16 40
Yaroslavl, 1, Ivanovo	39E50	57N35	-20 40	- 2 39 20
Yekaterinburg see Sverdlovsk.				
Yelizavetgrad see Kirivograd.				
Yerevan, 6.....................44E30		40N11	-02 00	- 2 58 00
Yezhovo-Cherkessk see Cherkessk				
Yoshkar-Ola, 1, A.R. of the Mari	47E55	56N40	+11 40	- 3 11 40
Yuzovka see Stalino.				
Zaporozhya, 2, Dnepr..........35E10		47N48	+20 40	- 2 20 40
Zhitomir, 2, Zhitomir	28E40	50N19	-05 20	- 1 54 40
Zinovievsk see Kirovograd.				
Zmerinka, 2, Vinnitsa	28E08	49N02	-07 28	- 1 52 32

UPPER SENEGAL, see French West Africa.
UPPER VOLTA see French West Africa. Independent
August 5, 1960.

URUGUAY. Capital: Montevideo. Republic, situated in South America. Standard Time Meridian 52°30' WEST.

			L. M. T. VARIATION FROM S.T.	G. M. T. VARIATION FROM LMT.
			m. s.	h. m. s.
Artigas, Artigas	56W28	30S24	-15 52	+ 3 45 52
Canelones, Canelones	56W16	34S32	-15 04	+ 3 45 04
Colonia del Sacramento, Colonia	57W51	34S28	-21 24	+ 3 51 24
Durazno, Durazno	56W31	33S20	-16 04	+ 3 46 04
Florida, Florida............	56W13...	34S06...	-14 52...	+ 3 44 52
Fray Bentos, Rio Negro	58W19	33S07	-23 16	+ 3 53 16
Guadalupe see Canelones.				
Melo, Cerro-Largo	54W10	32S22	- 6 40	+ 3 36 40
Mercedes, Soriano	58W03	33S15	-22 12	+ 3 52 12
Minas, Lavalleja.............	55W16...	34S24...	-11 04...	+ 3 41 04
Montevideo, Montevideo	56W10	34S53	-14 40	+ 3 44 40
Paysandu, Paysandu	58W05	32S19	-22 20	+ 3 52 20
Rivera, Rivera	55W33	30S55	-12 12	+ 3 42 12
Rocha, Rocha	54W22	34S30	- 7 28	+ 3 37 28
Salto, Salto...............	57W58...	31S23...	-21 52...	+ 3 51 52
San Jose Mayo, San Jose	56W42	34S20	-16 48	+ 3 46 48
Tacuarembo, Tacuarembo	56W03	31S40	-14 12	+ 3 44 12
Treinta y Tres, Treinta y Tres	54W20	33S14	- 7 20	+ 3 37 20
Trinidad, Flores...............	56W55...	33S29...	-17 40...	+ 3 47 40

URUNDI see Belgian Congo.
UVEA ISLAND see New Caledonia.
UZBEK S. S. R. see U. S. S. R.
VATICAN CITE, ETAT DU see Vatican City State.
VATICAN CITY STATE. Situated in Italy, within the City of Rome. Standard Time Meridian 15° EAST.

Vatican Observatory	12E27	41N54	-10 12	- 0 49 48

VENEZUELA. Capital: Caracas. Republic situated in South America. Standard Time Meridian 67°30' WEST.

Acarigua, Port.	69W12	9N33	- 6 48	+ 4 36 48
Barcelona, Anz.	64W41	10N08	+11 16	+ 4 18 44
Barinas, Zamora	70W13	8N37	-10 52	+ 4 40 52
Barquisimeto, Lara.............	69W19	10N03	- 7 16	+ 4 37 16
Caracas, D.F.	66W55	10N30	+ 2 20	+ 4 27 40
Carupaño, Sucre	63W15	10N40	+17 00	+ 4 13 00
Ciudad Bolivar, Bolivar	63W32	8N09	+15 52	+ 4 14 08
Coro, Falcon	69W41	11N26	- 8 44	+ 4 38 44
Cumana, Sucre.............	64W10...	10N28...	+13 20...	+ 4 16 40
El Tigre, Anz.	64W15	8N54	+13 00	+ 4 17 00
Guatire see La Guaira, D.F.				
La Asuncion, Nueva Esparta	63W52	11N03	+14 32	+ 4 15 28
La Guaira, D. F.	66W56	10N36	+ 2 16	+ 4 27 44
Los Teques, Miranda	67W03	10N21	+ 1 48	+ 4 28 12
Maracaibo, Zulia.............	71W37...	10N38...	-16 28...	+ 4 46 28
Maracay, Aragua	67W36	10N15	- 0 24	+ 4 30 24
Maturin, Monagas	63W10	9N44	+17 20	+ 4 12 40
Merida, Merida	71W10	8N36	-14 40	+ 4 44 40

			L. M. T. VARIATION FROM S.T.	G. M. T. VARIATION FROM LMT.
			m. s.	h. m. s.
VENEZUELA (Continued)				
Porlamar, N. E.	63W51	10N57	+14 36	- 4 15 24
Puerto Cabello, Carabobo	68W01	10N32	- 2 04	+ 4 32 04
San Carlos, Cojedes.............	68W36...	9N40...	- 4 24...	+ 4 34 24
San Felipe, Yaracuy	68W44	10N21	- 4 56	+ 4 34 56
San Cristobal, Tachira	72W14	7N43	-18 56	+ 4 48 56
San Fernando de Apure, Apure	67W28	7N54	+ 0 08	+ 4 29 52
Trujillo, Trujillo	70W27	9N23	-11 48	+ 4 41 48
Tucupita, Delta Amecuro........	62W03...	9N04...	+21 48...	+ 4 08 12
Valencia, Carabobo	68W00	10N11	- 2 00	+ 4 32 00
Valle de la Pascua, Guarico	66W00	9N13	+ 6 00	+ 4 24 00

VICTORIA see 1. Australia.
         2. Nigeria.

VIERGES, ILES DES see 1. British West Indies.
         2. Virgin Islands.

VIET NAM, REPUBLIC OF AND Democratic Republic of.
    Formerly French Indo-China. Independent
    December 29, 1954.

VIRGIN ISLANDS. Capital: Charlotte Amalie.
    Possession of the United States situated in
    the Lesser Antilles. Standard Time Meridian
    60° WEST. See also British Virgin Islands
    under heading British West Indies.

Cruz Bay, Saint John	64W48	18N20	-19 12	+ 4 19 12
Kingshill, Saint Croix	64W48	17N44	-19 12	+ 4 19 12
Frederksted, Saint Croix	64W53	17N43	-19 32	+ 4 19 32
Christiansted, Saint Croix......	64W42...	17N45...	-18 48...	+ 4 18 48
Charlotte Amalie, Saint Thomas	64W56	18N21	-19 44	+ 4 19 44

WAKE ISLAND. Possession of the United States of
    America, situated in the North Pacific.
    Standard Time Meridian 180° EAST.

Wake Island, Administration Bldg.	166E35	19N19	-53 40	-11 06 20

WALES see Great Britain.

WALLACHIA see Rumania.

WALLIS ISLANDS. Capital: Mata-Utu. French Protec-
    torate, situated in the South Pacific.
    Standard Time Meridian 180° WEST

Mata Uta	176W08	13S17	+15 28	+11 44 32
Mua	176W10	18S21	+15 20	+11 44 40

WALVIS BAY see Union of South Africa.

WASHINGTON ISLAND see Gilbert & Ellice Islands.

WELLESLEY PROVINCE see Malaya.

WESTERN AUSTRALIA see Australia.

WESTERN SAMOA. Capital: Apia. British Mandate
    under the Administration of New Zealand,
    situated in the South Pacific. Standard
    Time Meridian 165° WEST.

Apia, Upolu	171W46	13S49	-27 00	+11 27 00
Falealili, Upolu	171W41	14S01	-26 44	+11 26 44
Safetu, Savaii	172W24	13S26	-29 36	+11 29 36
Safutolafai, Savali	172W08	13S40	-28 32	+11 28 32
Saluafata, Upolu	171W35	13S51	-26 20	+11 26 20

WHARE-KAURI see Chatham Island.
WHITE RUSSIA see U. S. S. R.
WINDWARD ISLANDS see British West Indies
WURTTEMBERG see Germany.
YEMEN see Saudi Arabia.
YOUGOSLAVIE see Yugoslavia.

YUGOSLAVIA. Capital: Beograd. Kingdom of Serbs, Croates and Slovenes from 1918 October 3, 1929. Standard Time to Meridian 15° EAST.

			L. M. T. VARIATION FROM S. T.	G. M. T. VARIATION FROM LMT.
			m. s.	h. m. s.
Agram see Zagreb.				
Apatin, Dun.	18E59	45N41	+15 56	- 1 15 56
Benja Luka, Vrbaska	17E11	44N46	+ 8 44	- 1 08 44
Bela Crkva, Dun.	21E25	44N54	+25 40	- 1 25 40
Belgrad see Beograd.				
Beograd, Beograd District	20E27	44N49	+21 48	- 1 21 48
Bitolj, Vard.	21E19	41N03	+25 16	- 1 25 16
Cattaro see Kotor.				
Cetinje, Zetska	18E56	42N24	+15 44	- 1 15 44
Dubrovnik, Zetska	18E07	42N40	+12 28	- 1 12 28
Esseg see Osijek.				
Eszek see Osijek.				
Fehertemplom see Bela Crkva.				
Kotor, Zetska	18E47	42N25	+15 08	+ 1 15 08
Kreguljevac, Dun.	20E54	44N01	+23 36	- 1 23 36
Kraljevo, Mor.	20E40	43N42	+22 40	- 1 22 40
Kumanova, Vard.	21E43	42N08	+26 52	- 1 26 52
Laibach see Ljubljana.				
Ljubljana, Drav.	14E31	46N03	- 1 56	- 0 58 04
Marburg see Maribor.				
Maribor, Drav.	15E39	46N34	+ 2 36	- 1 02 36
Monastir see Bitolj.				
Mostar, Prim.	17E50	43N20	+11 20	- 1 11 20
Nagybecskerek see Petrovgrad.				
Neusatz see Novi Sad.				
Nish, Mor.	21E54	43N18	+27 36	- 1 27 36
Novi Pazar, Zetska	20E31	43N08	+22 04	- 1 22 04
Novi Sad, Dun.	19E52	45N15	+19 28	- 1 19 28
Ohrid, Vard.	20E48	42N08	+23 12	- 1 23 12
Osijek, Sav.	18E42	45N33	+14 48	- 1 14 48
Pancevo, Beograd District	20E40	44N52	+22 40	- 1 22 40
Petrovgrad, Dun.	20E22	45N23	+21 28	- 1 21 28
Pragersko (Pragerhof), Sav.	15E39	46N25	+ 2 36	- 1 02 36
Prizeren, Vard.	20E43	42N14	+22 52	- 1 22 52
Ragusa see Dubrovnik.				
Sabac, Sav.	19E44	44N45	+18 56	- 1 18 56
Sarajevo, Vrbaska	18E27	43N37	+13 48	- 1 13 48
Sebenico see Sibenik.				
Semendria see Smederovo.				
Semun see Zemun.				
Senta, Dun.	20E06	45N57	+20 24	- 1 20 24
Sibenik, Prim.	15E56	43N45	+ 3 44	- 1 03 44
Skoplje, Vard.	21E25	42N00	+25 40	- 1 25 40
Smederovo, Dun.	20E57	44N40	+23 48	- 1 23 48

			L. M. T. VARIATION FROM S. T.	G. M. T. VARIATION FROM LMT.
			m. s.	h. m. s.

YUGOSLAVIA.   (Continued)

Sombor, Dun.	19E08	45N47	+16 32	- 1 16 32
Spalato see Split.				
Split, Prim.	16E26	43N31	+ 5 44	- 1 05 44
Strumica, Vard.................22E37,...		41N27...	+30 28...	- 1 30 28
Subotica, Dun.	19E40	46N06	+18 40	- 1 18 40
Szabadka see Subotica.				
Ujvidek see Novi Sad.				
Uskub see Skoplje.				
Veliki Beckerek see Petrovgrad.				
Versec see Vrsac.				
Vrsac, Dun.	21E18	45N06	+25 12	- 1 25 12
Weisskirchen see Bela Crkva.				
Werschetz see Vrsac.				
Zagreb, Sav................... 15E59		45N50	+ 3 56	- 1 03 56
Zemun, Dun.	20E25	44N51	+21 40	- 1 21 40
Zenta see Senta.				
Zimony see Zemun.				
Zombor see Sombor.				

YUKON see Canada.

ZANZIBAR. Capital: Zanzibar. British Protec-
    torate, situated in the Indian Ocean.
      Standard Time Meridian 41°15' EAST.

Chake Chake, Pemba	39E47	5S14	- 5 52	- 2 39 08
Chwaka	39E26	6S10	- 7 16	- 2 37 44
Weti, Pemba	39E43	5S03	- 6 08	- 2 38 52
Zanzibar	39E11	6S10	- 8 16	- 2 36 44

ZULULAND see Union of South Africa.

F I N I S .

FOR INFORMATION ON:

Astrological Books

Astrological Computers and Software

Membership

Examinations

Biennial Conventions

Referrals to Teaching and Practicing Professional Astrologers

contact:

American Federation of Astrologers, Inc.
P.O. Box 22040 Tempe, AZ 85282 602/838-1751